HOW TO SURVIVE IN TEACHING:

The Legal Dimension

by M. CHESTER NOLTE

How to anticipate
and avoid action
that can get you
in trouble

teach'em Inc.
CHICAGO
1978

Library of Congress Catalog Card Number:
78-57206

International Standard Book Number:
0-931028-06-X

Second printing 1980
Third printing 1983

Cover Design by Richard Seeger

Typesetting and Assembly by Accent Graphics, Chicago, Ill.

Printed in the United States of America

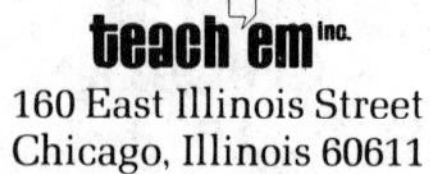

160 East Illinois Street
Chicago, Illinois 60611

To

Margaret Anne Wolford
Who Teaches by Example
This Book is Respectfully Dedicated

Preface

The printing press is a useful, if awesome, invention. You may now buy books on making love, books on how to raise parakeets or alfalfa, books on every conceivable subject. This is a book — the first of its kind, incidentally — to help individuals find their way through the trackless, confusing, shifting sands of classroom teaching.

As the title suggests, the volume is aimed at helping you survive as a teacher. As the title further suggests, this has been done through the medium of the law — your own legal rights and liabilities, if you will — that comes with the territory.

Why study law? If you had needed to know the law, you would have been so instructed by your college. Unfortunately, only recently have schools of education awakened to the need for a working knowledge for all teachers of the law as it affects their work. We hope this volume will help you, the classroom teacher, fill gaps in your knowledge in an area which has grown increasingly more complex and more confusing with each passing year.

It all started with the civil rights movement — every minority was out to gain for itself those constitutional rights to which it had aspired but which it had been denied. Since the avenue being used to assert such rights was through the courts, teachers took up the fight through litigation. There is a growing volume of such cases, and there is no end in sight.

The odds that you will be involved during your teaching career not once but multiple times are quite high — perhaps three out of four. To say that a single book will reduce those odds or eliminate them entirely would be foolish. But in a limited way, that's one of the purposes of the volume.

To recognize when and where possible suits may arise is the first sign of legal awareness on your part, and may help you to avoid needless ligitation when to sue may be self-defeating. You should know only enough law to know what to do till the lawyer comes.

That's the major purpose of the book. In it, you'll find that teachers face five legal hurdles every teaching day of their lives. First, and perhaps most important, is the question of how to conduct yourself to obtain pupil discipline and control. Without that, you're never going to survive in teaching. Once over that hurdle, however, there are others: your legal liability when a student is injured, your right to expect re-employment with each concluded contract, your right to introduce controversial materials into your classroom, the right to join organizations of your choice and to be active in them, and to collectively bargain on wages, hours and conditions of employment. Each of these categories is a chapter in this book. Finally, there's the concluding chapter on how to pick a good lawyer and place your future in his or her hands.

All this won't add up to total escape from litigation, but it will help you to understand what is needed in times where litigation is forced upon you, either as a defendant or as plaintiff. You'll learn that teaching, like the other professions, is having its share of civil rights action, and that what was taken for granted for so many years has now become an open question. You'll find that more often than you think, the only way to achieve your full rights as teacher and as citizen is to sue.

Truly, the printing press is a useful, if awesome, invention.

M. CHESTER NOLTE

DENVER, COLORADO
February 1978

School law books tend to become outdated unless stringent effort is made to revise, correct and add to them on a periodic basis. That would be ample justification for this third printing. Even more important, however, are the invaluable suggestions we have received from those who found the earlier printings useful in their daily lives in the classroom. For these reasons, you will find this printing up to date as well as still so unchanged as to make it possible to use it alongside the others without loss of continuity.

DENVER, COLORADO — M. CHESTER NOLTE
AUGUST 1983

Table of Contents

Preface v

I. **From Classroom to Courtroom** 3
- This Volume 5
- Cases Illustrating the Need 7
- The Teacher and the Law 9
- The State and Education 14
- The Courts and Education 18
- The Federal Government and Education 21
- Answers to Cases Illustrating the Need 23

II. **Your Employment Security** 26
- Cases in Point 27
- Certification 28
- Contracting and Tenure 32
- Sex Discrimination in Education 45
- Resolution of Cases in Point 51

III. **Student Discipline and Control** 53
- Cases in Point 55
- The *In Loco Parentis* Doctrine 57
- Student Discipline and Control 64
- Due Process and Equal Protection 72
- Sex Education 86
- Sex Discrimination in Education 88
- Resolution of Cases in Point 91

IV. **Teacher Liability for Pupil Injury** 93
Cases in Point 95
Negligence. 97
Defenses Against Charges of Negligence 109
Assault and Battery 114
Defamation 118
Field Trips, Errands and Similar Hazards 120
Constitutional Torts 126
Resolution of the Cases in Point 130

V. **You and Academic Freedom** 133
Cases in Point 135
Academic Freedom in General 136
Symbolic Speech 142
Utterances Outside the Classroom 145
Assignments in the Classroom 147
Freedom of the Press 156
Loyalty Oaths. 160
Resolution of the Cases in Point 164

VI. **The Teacher and Collective Bargaining** 166
Cases in Point 168
Collective Bargaining as a Game 170
How the Rules are Enforced 176
Dealing With the Strike 181
Other Considerations 185
Resolution of the Cases in Point 188

VII. **What To Do Until The Lawyer Comes** 190
Cases in Point 193
Resolution of the Cases in Point 198

Amendments to the United States Constitution 201

Table of Cases 212

How Much Do You Know About the Gay Rights Issue? 219

A Test on Supreme Court Decisions Affecting Education 221

Index 224

HOW TO SURVIVE IN TEACHING:

The Legal Dimension

Chapter One

From Classroom to Courtroom

The resolution of the Board of Education was brief:

> *Resolved: that Named Teacher be dismissed and the contract terminated as a teacher in the district because of her immorality of being a practicing homosexual. Motion carried unanimously.*

Charging that her dismissal was a violation of her constitutional rights, the teacher sought damages and reinstatement to her position. The U.S. District Court awarded her damages and attorney fees but denied her request for reinstatement. She appealed. The U.S. Court of Appeals upheld the District Court, affirming the award of damages and denying her request for reinstatement.

The facts were not in dispute. The teacher had been successful in her first year of teaching and had been reemployed the following year. One day her principal confronted her with being a homosexual. At a conference with the principal, the teacher acknowledged that she was a "practicing homosexual." A meeting with the board followed, and the resolution passed.

The District Court was faced first with defining "immorality," which was recognized by the state legislature as one of the proper causes for dismissal of a teacher. There was no allegation that she was derelict in her teaching duties — in fact, one of the board members was heard to say, "But she's one of our *best* teachers!"

Said the District Court judge:

> *Immorality means different things to different people, and its definition depends on the idiosyncrasies of the individual board members. It may be applied so broadly that every teacher in the state could be subject to discipline. . . . A statute so broad makes those charged with its enforcement the arbiters of morality for the entire community. . . . The statute is vague because it fails to give fair warning of what conduct is prohibited and because it permits erratic and prejudiced exercises of authority.*

Because she had been unfairly dismissed, the teacher was entitled to back pay and court costs, but what about reinstatement? The teacher was not under tenure; however, in cases where teachers have been illegally dismissed, non-tenured teachers have sometimes been ordered reinstated, although not in every case.

Federal courts have ordered reinstatement of teachers who were the target of racial discrimination, or where dismissal was in reprisal for the legal exercise of free expression in a manner critical of the public employer. But even in these cases, the courts have intimated that there must be a careful weighing of all facts and circumstances, and then only after a full and impartial hearing. When the teacher appeared before the board she had freely admitted her homosexuality thus eliminating the basis for any possible stigma in the future.

Because the District Court had awarded the teacher an additional half-year's salary beyond the back pay called for in her original contract, the Appeals Court felt that the court below had been "generous" and would not overturn that court's findings.

Today, teachers are an endangered species. The perils you face from day to day are limitless. Every case in this book will attest to the fact that teaching has become one of the most dangerous of the professions, if not physically, at least legally, speaking. (There are some positions which in fact *are* physically dangerous to the teacher!)

You cannot learn to avoid lawsuits or handle your job with coolness until you understand the nature and scope of the problem you face. That is the simple purpose of this volume — to provide you with sample cases (and all of them are true!) so that you can defend yourself against needless litigation, loss of your good name, or your own personal fortune.

For example, the case you just read about happened in Oregon in 1973. It is "cited" in legal literature as *Peggy Burton v. Cascade School District Union High School No. 5,* 353 F.Supp. 254, 1973; affirmed, 512 F.2d 850 9CA March 28, 1975.

The numbers in the citation have special significance. The one before the publication is the *volume;* the one following, the *page.* If you visit your law library, ask the librarian how to find Volume 353 of the *Federal Supplement* (F.Supp.), which contains all United States District Court decisions. The number following the name of the publication (254) tells you on which page the case begins.

The same applies to the appellate court's decision. It will be found in Volume 512 of *Federal Reporter, Second Series* (F.2d) beginning on page 850. There you will find the reasoning of the United States Court of Appeals for the Ninth Circuit (9CA) and the date the case was decided (March 28, 1975).

This Volume

Q. WHY A BOOK ON THE LEGAL ASPECTS OF TEACHING?

A. There are three reasons why this book is important to you as a classroom teacher. First, lawsuits in which teachers are either defendants or plaintiffs are proliferating at an alarming rate. Second, your preparation for teaching, if you are typical, did not include information about your legal rights and liabilities. Third, your job as a teacher has been changed considerably by what the Supreme Court and lesser courts have ruled regarding students' rights. This book is designed to help you, the teacher, become aware of your legal rights and responsibilities, so that you may avoid needless litigation and operate within your constitutional rights in your daily work in the classroom.

Q. WILL THIS VOLUME ALLEVIATE THE NEED FOR AN ATTORNEY?

A. No, of course not. This book is designed to give you a general knowledge of the law as it applies to the classroom teacher. It is meant to make you aware of your legal rights and liabilities just as any other citizen is assumed to know the law. While this volume will give you much information on your legal relationships with students, administrators and the board of education, it cannot replace the need for a competent attorney when potential litigation arises.

Q. HOW IS THE BOOK ORGANIZED?

A. There are five legal "hurdles" that teachers must clear in order to survive in the classroom. Each of these hurdles makes up a chapter in this book.

Your Right to Employment Security	Chapter 2
Your Right to Discipline and Control Pupils	Chapter 3
Your Liability for Pupil Injury	Chapter 4
Your Right to Academic Freedom	Chapter 5
Your Right to Bargain Collectively	Chapter 6

In addition to these legal hurdles, the final chapter will deal with what you should do "till the lawyer comes." There is also a comprehensive index to your legal questions, so that you may easily look up answers to your legal problems as they arise.

Q. HOW CAN I AS A TEACHER BECOME MORE AWARE OF THE NEW RULES UNDER WHICH THE SCHOOLS ARE NOW OPERATING?

A. An obvious way is to complete reading this volume. Another is to check those articles in current periodicals which cover educational litigation (see the sub-title "Actions and Defenses" in the *Education Index*). The daily newspapers carry stories related to the emerging body of the law, particularly decisions of the Supreme Court and lesser courts in your jurisdiction. There may be publicity on legislative actions (usually called statutes) related to teachers, students or boards of education. A favorite convention topic is how these legal changes affect your work in the classroom. Or you may wish to visit a law school or county bar association library for first hand information on the cases cited herein. Attendance at a college or university for a course in school law would be most helpful. Whatever is done should be planned well and carried out according to plan.

Before we get into particulars, here are five cases which illustrate what can happen to the classroom teacher. These are like the rest — actual cases from the files. You may wish to read the entire case. The verdict in each case is not given so that you may discuss it before looking up the answer. The outcomes of the cases are given at the end of this chapter.

Case No. 1 deals with Employment Security (as do the cases in Chapter 2);
Case No. 2 deals with Academic Freedom (Chapter 5);
Case No. 3 deals with Teacher Liability for Pupil Injury (Chapter 4);
Case No. 4 deals with Teacher Negotiations (Chapter 6);
Case No. 5 deals with Student Discipline and Control (Chapter 3).

Cases Illustrating the Need

Case No. 1 — BIRDS OF A FEATHER

A non-tenured teacher's contract was not renewed and she brought suit in federal district court claiming denial of her civil rights. The board gave as its reasons for not renewing her contract that she lacked discipline in the classroom, that she was untidy, and that her teaching methods were inadequate. The teacher said that in reality the board was acting in bad faith — that she was really being nonrenewed because of lack of church attendance, her physical size, the location of her trailer, and the conduct of her personal life. She sought back pay, punitive damages, and attorney's fees. Her case was tried to a jury. Do you feel that the teacher was unconstitutionally dismissed?

Case No. 2 — THOSE DIR-R-R-TY BOOKS

The board of education approved a list of 1,275 textbooks for use in the high schools but disapproved ten books. Plaintiffs, senior high school English teachers, challenged the board's action, claiming denial of academic freedom in the classroom. The negotiated agreement between the board and the organization representing all teachers in the district contained a clause providing that "the board shall have the right to determine the processes, techniques, methods and means of teaching any and all subjects." The board claimed this clause gave it final control of which textbooks could or could not be used. Did the teachers bargain away their rights to choose which textbooks they could use in the classroom?

Case No. 3 — PRACTICE MAKES PERFECT

In Michigan, two boys were overcome by heat prostration during summer football practice. One of them died; the other received a permanent injury. Parents of the boys brought suit for damages against the district, the superintendent, the principal, and the teacher-coaches in charge of the practice session. The board argued that those who go out for a team sport assume a risk, which makes the district and its employees immune from liability. Should the district have to pay, or are the individual teacher-coaches liable for wrongful death and permanent injury?

Case No. 4 — YOU'RE IN GOOD HANDS...

After negotiations for renewal of an agreement failed, teachers went on strike in violation of a state law. Letters were sent by the board to striking teachers, inviting them to return to work or be discharged. While a few returned to work, some eighty-eight teachers refused and were called before the board and dismissed at twenty-minute intervals. Claiming the board was not an impartial tribunal and that it had denied them due process of law, the eighty-eight brought an action in federal court to have their jobs restored. The case finally reached the U.S. Supreme Court. Do you think the teachers received due process of law? Was the board biased because it had been on the case from the beginning? Should the Supreme Court allow the firings to stand on the grounds that the teachers had violated the law?

Case No. 5 — KER-R-R CHOOOO!

Maude Casey, sixty-nine, had taught school for forty-eight years. She was on an annual contract in a junior high in the inner city. Discipline was a problem, although teachers used detention, corporal punishment, suspension, and expulsion. Afraid for her own safety, Maude secretly bought and carried with her at all times a small, pencil-like device called a "sneeze gun," which discharged a substance causing temporary eye irritation and sneezing to the person affected.

One day a large, fifteen-year-old girl would not allow Miss Casey to leave her classroom. Feeling threatened, she shot the girl in the face with the "sneeze gun." Although she suffered no permanent injury, the girl brought suit for $50,000 damages against Miss Casey for assault and battery. Should the court allow her to recover damages under these circumstances?

The Teacher and the Law

Q. WHAT IS MEANT BY "THE LAW" IN THE UNITED STATES?

A. The term is generic and applies to the body *(corpus juris)* of the general rules which govern our society. The law may be either written or unwritten. Written law includes those Congressional Acts, state statutory enactments, city council ordinances, and board of education policies which result from actions of the legislative branch of government. The unwritten law (sometimes called the *common law*), on the other hand, is made up of court decisions, customs, opinions of attorneys general, and similar rulings emanating from either the judicial or executive branches of government. Taken together, these are what is generally referred to as "the law."

Q. WHAT HAS BEEN THE TREND IN SCHOOL LAW?

A. Since *Brown v. Board of Education* in 1954, much of what is considered "school law" is of the judge-made variety. Between 1953 and 1969, the Warren Court decided some three dozen cases dealing with schools, and the Burger Court has not been far behind.

Q. WHY ARE LAWSUITS INVOLVING TEACHERS ON THE INCREASE?

A. In a very real sense the problems of the teacher are the problems of society at large. As society changes, so must laws change to accommodate newer values and protect the rights of individuals. The civil rights movement triggered hundreds of court cases on the rights of individuals. What was taken for granted for many years was no longer acceptable. Instead of expecting legislative bodies to implement change, the people turned to the courts — partly because it was quicker, and partly because the model by which social change was to be handled was radically revised.

Q. IS TEACHER "MALPRACTICE" ON THE INCREASE?

A. The accountability movement has led in some cases to so-called "malpractice" suits against teachers. This may follow a trend in other professions, particularly medicine and law. Malpractice is defined in the law as "any professional misconduct, unreasonable lack of skill or fidelity in professional duties, or (performance) related to evil practices, and/or illegal or immoral conduct." When applied to teaching, malpractice has come to mean either a breach of professional ethics on the part of the practitioner or failure to impart knowledge to pupils. A person bringing a malpractice suit against a teacher has a heavy burden of proof, however.

Q. WHAT IS NECESSARY IN ORDER FOR SOMEONE TO WIN A MALPRACTICE SUIT AGAINST A TEACHER?

A. Malpractice suits in other professions normally call for expert testimony from those who should be able to judge whether the person acted in bad faith or fell short of expected performance of duty. Such expert testimony usually must come from someone inside the profession itself. Since you as the defendant in a malpractice suit could call your own expert witnesses, their testimony would conflict with plaintiff's witnesses' testimony. It would then be a matter for the court to decide which of the witnesses to believe.

Q. WHAT IS THE RELIEF SOUGHT IN TEACHER MALPRACTICE SUITS?

A. Parents who bring malpractice suits against teachers ordinarily do not seek monetary damages but rather a declaration by the board of education that the teacher is incompetent, immoral, or otherwise unable to perform duties assigned in the classroom. The result would be removal from the position of teacher.

There is, therefore, a great deal at stake — freedom of the teacher to go elsewhere to seek other employment, or in the case of the tenured teacher, to property (both liberty and property interests are protected under the due process clause of the Fourteenth Amendment).

Additional aspects of teacher malpractice are discussed in Chapter 2.

Q. ARE TEACHERS EXPECTED TO KNOW THE LAW?

A. Yes. Teachers, like other American citizens, are expected to know and abide by the law. Nor will the courts accept ignorance of the law as a defense. This is not because all citizens know the law, but because there is no way to refute such a claim. If courts allowed citizens to plead ignorance of the law, everybody would use this defense, and there would be no legal accountability. In short, the price we must pay for our freedom is eternal vigilance against breaking the law.

Said another way, "The first duty of every citizen is to obey the law." Considering the tremendous influence teachers have over their charges, and the malleability of the material entrusted to their care, teachers have a double duty not only to know the law but also to abide by it at all times.

Q. WHAT ARE THE ODDS THAT A CLASSROOM TEACHER WILL BE INVOLVED IN A LEGAL ISSUE DURING HIS/HER CAREER?

A. Throughout most of our nation's history, the odds that a classroom teacher would be in a legal battle were very long indeed — perhaps one in 10,000. Now, however, it is almost a certainty that anyone who teaches for fifteen years or more will become involved in at least one legal case. One out of every five teachers during the 1970's will be either the plaintiff, defendant, or a grievant in an action that is job-related. As a matter of fact, you may have already been involved without your knowledge. In class actions, such as those on problems of sick leave for pregnancy-related absences, you may have been included in the class without service of notice nor opportunity given to appear in court. Yet what was decided by the courts in those class actions controls your legal situation just as if you had been one of the parties involved in the suit.

Q. SHOULD TEACHERS BECOME LAWYERS?

A. No. Such a level of expertise is neither possible nor necessary. You need to know enough law, however, to spot potentially dangerous legal situations and to avoid needless litigation. The purpose of the book, therefore, is not to make lawyers out of teachers, but to assist you in meeting your legal obligations by providing you with some guidelines for day-to-day management of the classroom. You will still need to rely on a lawyer knowledgeable in school law and keep his/her telephone number handy for an emergency. (More will be said in Chapter 7 on what to do till the lawyer comes).

Q. WHY CAN'T I ACT AS MY OWN ATTORNEY WHEN A LEGAL PROBLEM ARISES?

A. While you have the legal right to plead your own case in court, your potential loss is generally so substantial as to warrant hiring an attorney familiar with school law to represent you. There is an old saying that "one who acts as his own attorney has a fool for a client." You should keep handy the telephone number of an attorney or firm which specializes in school cases. The complexity of the law involved in teacher-rights cases is so great that even lawyers have difficulty keeping abreast of on-going changes. A courtroom is no place to air your own ignorance of the law. In a later chapter of this volume are some further suggestions on what to do till the lawyer comes.

Q. IS GOING TO COURT THE BEST WAY TO SOLVE LEGAL HASSLES?

A. Ordinarily, no. A lengthy court battle can be very costly, sometimes running to six figures. Some issues take up to six years for final determination, and it is not uncommon for cases in which desegregation is involved to run twenty years and still be unresolved. In a court battle, too, the loser pays court costs and attorneys' fees. Of course, if you can get an organization to back you, such as the DuShane Fund or the American Civil Liberties Union, your costs will be such as to insure you won't be bankrupted. But despite these disadvantages of litigation, you should not knuckle under where you feel that your cause is just and that a constitutional issue is involved.

Q. WHAT ARE THE ALTERNATIVES TO GOING TO COURT?

A. Negotiations, for one. Collective bargaining agreements almost universally contain grievance procedures for resolving questions which could end up in court. Of course, one can always appeal such awards to a court of competent jurisdiction, after the administrative procedure has been exhausted.

In New York and New Jersey, issues in education are submitted to a hearing examiner who then turns over his findings to the commissioner of education. In other states, conflicts may be submitted to the county superintendent or to the state board of education. Some school districts have policies for fact-finding and arbitration of disputes between personnel and the board of education.

Q. WHAT ADVANTAGES MIGHT IN-HOUSE RESOLUTION OF A GRIEVANCE HAVE OVER TAKING THE MATTER TO COURT?

A. There are three reasons why resolving personnel problems in-house are better than going to court. First, *time:* there are usually deadlines to be met in grievance resolution which are not present in court-sponsored litigation. Second, the *cost:* labor relations practices call for halving the costs between the parties. Third, *publicity:* in-house resolution is much more likely to keep the matter confidential whereas taking the matter to court would put the matter on the record for the world to see. In addition, one can always appeal an award to a court if the parties have not agreed in advance to binding arbitration. Of course, if there is a constitutional issue involved, a federal court might accept jurisdiction despite a binding arbitration award.

Q. IN WHAT AREA OF THE TEACHER'S WORK DO THE MOST LEGAL CASES ARISE?

A. Cases related to teacher employment, dismissal and non-renewal equal all other cases combined. Despite contracts between school boards and teachers' associations or unions, issues related to probationary-tenure status, contract-constitutional jurisdiction, reduction in force, assignment-reassignment, and the First Amendment rights of freedom of expression and right to privacy seem to be matters which boards are asking the courts to decide. Many of these have wound up in the Supreme Court of the United States (see Chapter 2 for more details).

Q. IS HOMOSEXUALITY GROUNDS FOR REVOCATION OF THE TEACHING CERTIFICATE?

A. No, unless the employer can show that the lifestyle and sexual preference is detrimental to the teacher's effectiveness in the classroom. In California, a certificated teacher was convicted in municipal court on a charge of committing homosexual acts on a public beach. The State Board of Education revoked his certificate on the grounds of "evident unfitness for service." Claiming double jeopardy, the teacher appealed to the courts for relief. The court held that in view of the teacher's duty as a teacher to "endeavor to impress upon the minds of his pupils the principles of morality" the court found no abuse of the State Board's discretionary power (*Sarac v. St.Bd. of Educ.*, 249 Cal.App.2d 58, 1967). However, in *Morrison v. St.Bd. of Educ.* (82 Cal.Rptr. 175, 1969), the court held that the board must show detrimental effects of homosexual acts in private on teaching.

Q. DOES HOLDING A TEACHING CERTIFICATE IMPLY COMPETENCY TO TEACH?

A. Yes. The courts have consistently ruled that the certificate is *prima facie* (on its face) evidence of the competency of the teacher, at least at the time the certificate was issued. The board which charges the teacher with incompetency must first overcome, therefore, the prior assumption that the teacher is competent, or was at the time of issuance. Thus, the burden of proof of a teacher's *in*competency is upon the employer, and the evidence must be presented factually rather than in the form of an opinion (i.e., "This teacher is not up to our high standards in Pumpkinville").

The State and Education

Q. WHAT IS THE LEGAL STATUS OF THE PUBLIC SCHOOLS?

A. Education is considered to be a state, as contrasted with a federal, governmental function. Thus, in each of the fifty states, the constitution provides for a system of publicly-supported, universal common-school education and specifies the ages for school attendance.

Q. WHAT IS THE LEGAL NATURE OF A LOCAL SCHOOL DISTRICT?

A. School districts are *quasi*-corporations (like a corporation). As agencies of the state, they have the purpose of carrying into effect educational policies of state-wide concern. On the other hand, municipal corporations, such as cities and towns, are not primarily instruments of state policy, but are created to help local groups of people to regulate and administer their own peculiar local concerns.

Q. HOW DID EDUCATION BECOME A STATE RATHER THAN A FEDERAL FUNCTION?

A. The Constitution is silent on how education is to be provided. The Tenth Amendment, however, does say that "the powers not delegated to the United States by the Constitution, nor prohibited by it to the States, are reserved to the States respectively, or to the people." Thus, in each of the states, education is a matter for the people of that state to determine through their elected officials in the legislative branch of the government.

Q. WHAT IS MEANT BY "THE AMERICAN SCHOOL SYSTEM"?

A. Actually, instead of a unified educational "system," Americans have fifty separate and distinct school systems. However, there is an amazing similarity between these disparate systems for the following reasons: 1) all are under the direct authority of the legislative branch of state government; 2) both students and teachers are quite mobile and carry ideas (education is a transportable commodity); and 3) the decisions of the United States Supreme Court are equally applicable to schools in all the various states. While there may be slight differences from state to state, there is more similarity than difference among the fifty state systems of education.

Q. WHAT LIMITS ON STATE POWER ARE IMPOSED BY THE U.S. CONSTITUTION?

A. The Supreme Court has held that school board members, who are considered under law to be state officials, have important and necessary powers and duties, but none which they cannot perform within the limits of the Constitution. One limitation prohibits a state from passing legislation impairing the obligation of contracts. No state may deprive a person of equal protection of the laws, nor deny to any person within its boundaries due process of law. No state may deprive any person of life, liberty or property without due process of law. The Supreme Court of the United States is the final arbiter of whether or not a state has acted within its powers in denying an individual a right, privilege, or immunity guaranteed under the Constitution.

Q. HOW MUCH POWER DOES THE LEGISLATURE EXERCISE OVER EDUCATION IN EACH OF THE STATES?

A. Legislatures are said to have *plenary* (complete) power over education within a state so long as they are acting within the limits of their own state and the federal constitutions. For example, a legislature may, if it chooses, eliminate school districts and operate the schools directly. While the legislature has plenary power, it goes without saying that this power must be exercised in a legal fashion. And all acts of the legislature are subject to review by the courts.

Q. HOW MUCH POWER DOES THE LOCAL SCHOOL BOARD EXERCISE IN RUNNING THE SCHOOLS?

A. Local boards derive their powers from the legislature and are limited also by the state constitution, Acts of Congress, and decisions of the Supreme Court. In general, local boards have three kinds of powers: 1) enumerated, or listed powers; 2) implied, meaning they are assumed although not written down; and 3) necessary, such as the power to close the schools during an epidemic and require vaccination as a condition of re-entry.

Q. ARE LOCAL SCHOOL BOARDS AS POWERFUL AS THEY ONCE WERE?

A. No. During most of our nation's history, local boards were quite powerful bodies having legislative, executive, and judicial powers which they were allowed to exercise almost without limitation. However, over the years, their area of discretion has been limited by court action, through mutual agreement with local teachers' unions, membership in voluntary associations, such as the state's student activities association, and through statutes which have tended to deprive local boards of their decision-making powers. In some respects, local boards have much more responsibility for solving social issues (busing, financing, employment security) than they have power or authority to deal realistically with these issues.

Q. WHAT DO MOST STATE CONSTITUTIONS SAY ABOUT FREE PUBLIC EDUCATION?

A. State constitutions use general wording in assigning to their legislative bodies responsibility for educating their citizens. For example, the Colorado Constitution (Art. IX, Sec. 2) provides only for "a thorough and uniform" system of education. These words are so vague that the courts are often called on to determine what they mean.

Q. DOES THE RIGHT TO AN EDUCATION FOR ALL CITIZENS REQUIRE A STATE TO PROVIDE A COLLEGE EDUCATION FOR ALL?

A. Apparently not, although the question is still being litigated. If the state provides minimal schooling to enable its citizens to function as citizens, then it is not obligated to provide further educational opportunities. Once it elects to provide such additional opportunities, however, it may not discriminate — that is, it must provide equal treatment to all in the distribution of the benefits of education.

Q. WHAT ARE THE MINIMAL COMPETENCIES WHICH THE STATE MUST LEGALLY PROVIDE TO MEET ITS OBLIGATION OF BUILDING CITIZENS?

A. These competencies come from the functions of the citizen in our democracy — obey the laws, vote, pay taxes, serve in the armed forces, serve on juries, and uphold the Constitution. Such competencies could very well be provided a child through formal schooling up to and including the eighth grade — what was formerly called a "common school" education.

The Courts and Education

Q. WHAT IS MEANT BY THE STATEMENT: "WE ARE A LITIGIOUS PEOPLE"?

A. The statement means that Americans are overly inclined to litigate rather than compromise. Almost a century and a half ago de Tocqueville noticed this tendency at work when he visited America. "Scarcely any political question arises in the United States," wrote de Tocqueville, "that is not resolved, sooner or later, into a judicial question." The statement is equally true today. Judge-made law plays a larger part in our society than in any other.

Q. WHAT IS MEANT BY "JUDGE-MADE" LAW?

A. That part of the unwritten law which results from decisions of our courts of law, including those of the court of final jurisdiction, the United States Supreme Court, are referred to as "judge-made" law.

Q. HOW DO CASES GET TO THE SUPREME COURT FOR REVIEW?

A. By two routes: 1) On appeal, which is review by right; and 2) On *certiorari* (a discretionary review granted or denied by vote of the Supreme Court). Even under the appeal process, the Court may decide that the question presented is "insubstantial." The Court may also grant or deny *certiorari* (permission). The net effect of a denial of *certiorari* is to let stand the decision of the court immediately below, usually the circuit court of appeals.

Q. IS JUDGE-MADE LAW BINDING ON TEACHERS AND STUDENTS?

A. It all depends. Decisions of the United States Supreme Court are binding on all citizens of the United States and its possessions. State court decisions normally apply only to individuals in that particular state. The district and circuit federal courts below the Supreme Court level generally apply only to that district or circuit. Where, however, the Supreme Court lets stand a constitutional issue decided by either a district or a circuit court of appeals, that decision is generally held to be controlling until overthrown by subsequent litigation.

You should become familiar with decisions of your state courts in order to know your limits as a teacher. Ordinarily, a case decided in another state by a state court is not controlling in your state. The same is true of federal court decisions in a circuit other than your own. Where the circuit courts are not in agreement, the Supreme Court tends to settle the differences by accepting cases for review.

Q. WHAT MAJOR ISSUES HAVE THE COURTS RECOGNIZED IN EDUCATION?

A. Cases dealing with teachers and teaching have fallen into various categories, such as desegregation, separation of church and state, teacher loyalty, right to continuing employment, and exercise of constitutional rights of teachers and students (rights of assembly, privacy, and petition; protection against illegal search and seizure; and cruel and inhuman punishments).

Q. WHAT IS THE CURRENT MODEL FOR CHANGE IN OUR SOCIAL INSTITUTIONS?

A. When the Warren Court began handing down judge-made law in the 1950's, the Court instituted a model which has become the process we now follow in the law. There are three steps in this change process.

1. A minority individual or class of individuals goes to court and wins protection of a right guaranteed under the United States Constitution. 2. A period of time passes during which the general public must make adjustments to come into line with the Court's decision. 3. Over time, the new value is accepted by the majority and enacted into law through majority legislation in the states.

Q. WHAT IS MEANT BY "JUDICIAL ACTIVISM"?

A. Judicial activism is one end on a continuum the other end of which is "judicial restraint." Ever since it was decided that the Supreme Court could review governmental actions, the role of the courts has been to balance the powers of the executive and legislative branches and to prevent government from invading individual rights. Former Justice William O. Douglas put it succinctly: "The purpose of the Bill of Rights is to keep the government off the backs of the people." The pendulum from time to time swings from one extreme to the other depending on the membership of the Court.

Q. WERE THE WARREN AND BURGER COURTS JUDICIALLY ACTIVE?

A. Yes. The Warren Court decided thirty-six school law cases between 1953 and 1969. The Burger court was no less active. What was taken for granted in education for many years has been held up for critical re-examination — church-state relations, teacher loyalty, desegregation, civil rights of students, and teachers' rights to be first class citizens, for example. Such a flood of cases, however, caused the Burger Court to say that insofar as possible, the states should solve their own educational problems, leaving to the federal courts those cases in which there was the question of unconstitutionality "so clear that it is not open to rational question." From the end of the Civil War till 1910 the Supreme Court practiced judicial restraint. The Court since 1925 has almost complete discretion to choose among the many cases presented for review.

Q. IS THERE DANGER IN ALLOWING THE COURTS TO BECOME TOO POWERFUL?

A. There are those who believe that the courts go too far and are actually invading the realm reserved for the other two branches of government. It is true that Supreme Court justices are not elected, and that they hold office for life. But if the purpose of the balance-of-power clauses is to prevent any one branch from becoming too powerful, it is necessary that each branch (including the Supreme Court) exercise its constitutionally granted powers in the interests of the general welfare. Justices must give reasons for their decisions, and these reasons are public records. Another advantage is that a group decision probably produces a final judgment having a viewpoint of greater breadth and depth, and fewer extremes, than most individual decisions. Control over judicial activism is potentially possible through executive appointment of new members and enactment of new laws by the legislative branch.

Q. SHOULD JUDGES BE MAKING EDUCATIONAL DECISIONS?

A. Some people feel that educational decision making should be done as close to the problem as possible. They point to our long history of local control of education to show that educational problems are best dealt with at the local level. On the other hand, many of the problems boards deal with are national in scope; nation-wide guidelines are therefore necessary to provide stability and predictability to our educational decision-making processes. Some judges are asking local boards to settle their problems at home rather than take them to court, pleading that they know they "do not write in granite, but on occasion, merely trace patterns in the sand." If local boards do not use their power, they tend to lose their power by default. Ideally, local boards and administrators are in a better position to make educational decisions than are judges.

The Federal Government and Education

Q. DOES THE FEDERAL CONSTITUTION NOT GUARANTEE EQUAL EDUCATIONAL OPPORTUNITY TO ALL CHILDREN?

A. No. That question was before the Supreme Court in 1973 (*San Antonio School District v. Rodriguez*). The Court, by a vote of 5-4, held that so long as the State of Texas was providing a minimal "schooling" to a child living in a poor district, it was not a violation of the Constitution to allow more prosperous districts to spend more per child per year on public education. Thus, by deduction, the educational birthright of each child must be found in the state constitution of that state in which the child lives.

Q. DOES THAT MEAN THAT SOME CHILDREN WILL BE DISCRIMINATED AGAINST BECAUSE OF WHERE THEY LIVE?

A. Yes. The amount and quality of the state's minimal program for its children varies from state to state according to the benefits that each state sees fit to provide for each of its children. There is a very real effort within the states, however, to equalize educational opportunity, or more precisely, to avoid discriminating between and among children because of some factor such as location of residence, wealth of the district, sex, religion or country of origin of the family. It does appear, furthermore, that once the state has provided the minimal competencies essential to good citizenship, it is meeting its constitutional obligations.

Q. IS NOT THE RIGHT TO ATTEND SCHOOLS A "PROPERTY" RIGHT PROTECTED BY THE U.S. CONSTITUTION?

A. Yes. The Supreme Court said in 1975 that the right to attend public schools is a protected right under the Fourteenth Amendment. "In these days, it is doubtful that any child may reasonably be expected to succeed in life if he is denied the opportunity of an education," said the Court in 1954 *(Brown v. Board of Education).* Thus, separate but equal facilities for the races are inherently unequal. "Where the State has undertaken to provide (education for all) the right to attend school is a right which must be made available to all on equal terms." The state is therefore prohibited from discriminating within its borders and must provide equal treatment in the distribution of the benefits of education.

Q. ARE THE RIGHT TO EQUAL TREATMENT AND THE RIGHT TO TREATMENT AS AN EQUAL THE SAME?

A. No. *Equal treatment* means that the benefits which the state provides must be equally distributed — that is, the right to vote, to hold office, to be represented by counsel, and to be free from illegal searches and seizures must be available to all equally. On the other hand, *treatment as an equal* means that the state may not set up a double standard, such as one set of rules for children, another for adults.

Q. DO CHILDREN HAVE THE RIGHT TO TREATMENT AS AN EQUAL IN PUBLIC SCHOOLS?

A. Yes. The Supreme Court in 1967 and again in 1969 held that due process of law is not for adults alone. "State-operated schools may not be enclaves of totalitarianism," said the Court. "In our system, children in school as well as out are 'persons' and do not shed their constitutional rights at the schoolhouse gate." The protections of the Constitution have thus been extended into your classroom.

Q. HOW HAS THE SUPREME COURT'S DECISION THAT CHILDREN HAVE THE RIGHT TO TREATMENT AS EQUALS CHANGED THE WAY WE RUN OUR SCHOOLS?

A. More will be said in later sections of this book on the total effect such declarations have had on eliminating the double standard in schools. Suffice it to say at this point that the introduction of constitutional rights into the schools dramatically changed how the schools are managed. These changes extend to all concerned — teachers, pupils, parents, board members, non-certificated employees and the general public served by the schools. The relationships are not the same; they have been transformed. In effect, running the schools is a whole new ball game.

Answers to the Cases Illustrating the Need

Case No. 1 — BIRDS OF A FEATHER

The jury found for the teacher, and awarded her $33,000 compensatory damages, $5,000 punitive damages, and $5,800 attorney fees. The judge upheld the compensatory damages on the ground that a teacher "has the right to be free from unwarranted governmental intrusions into one's privacy." Such right of privacy extends, said the court, to the right to attend church or not, to determine his or her own physical proportions, and to determine with whom he or she will associate. The judge, however, denied the award of *punitive* (to punish) damages and attorney's fees on the grounds that although the board members did invade the teacher's privacy, they had not acted maliciously in so doing (*Stoddard v. School Dist. No. 1,* 429 F.Supp. 890 Wyo. 1977).

Case No. 2 — THOSE DIR-R-R-TY BOOKS

The board won. Ordinarily, said the court, the selection of high school English textbooks lies within the protection of the First Amendment. While academic freedom is everywhere a protected value, it must always be tempered by professional responsibility. The only justification for restricting academic freedom is that the particular conduct or activity is inconsistent with or counterproductive to the objective of producing effective citizens. But teachers may bargain away the freedom to communicate by joining a bargaining unit and voluntarily submitting themselves to the negotiations processes. Thus, the clause in question yielded final authority to the school board for the choice of instructional material, and the teachers could not plead the denial of a constitutional freedom to avoid such contractual agreement (*Cary v. Bd of Educ.*, 427 F.Supp. 945 Colo. 1977, *affirmed on different grounds* 598 F.2d 535, 10 CA 1979).

Case No. 3 — PRACTICE MAKES PERFECT

The teacher-coaches had to face trial for negligence. The court held that the district, the superintendent, and the principal were immune. But the teacher-coaches could still be liable if the jury found negligence on their part. "The liability of teachers is not based on negligence imputed to them as public functionaries," said the court, "but rather it arises from their individual conduct. They must be held accountable for their own actions" (*Lovitt v. Concord School Dist.*, 228 N.W.2d 479 Mich. 1975).

Case No. 4 — YOU'RE IN GOOD HANDS...

The Supreme Court ruled (6-3) that the board was within its rights in discharging the teachers. The teachers, said the Court, did not come into equity with *clean hands* since they had disobeyed the law by striking. Also, it is better for the Supreme Court to keep *hands off* in local school matters; the legislature has decided that schools are *in good hands* with boards of education and the courts should not try to second-guess them. If teachers want to act like blue-collar *hands*, then they will be treated as such before the law. Nor is the board a biased tribunal just because it was familiar with the facts. The board members did not have a personal or official stake in making the decision they did sufficient to disqualify them as a hearing tribunal. The majority held that the teachers by going on strike had breached their contracts and could not be heard to complain that they had been denied due process of law by their firing (*Hortonville S.B. v. Hortonville Tea. Assn.*, 426 U.S. 482, WI. 1976).

Case No. 5 — KER-R-R CHOOOO!

Milly Twilly could not recover damages from her teacher, Maude Casey. The court held that a teacher who had a reasonable ground to believe she would be assaulted had the right to use a "sneeze gun" on a girl who was much larger than the teacher, who was in a school where attacks had been made on teachers by students, and where the student had been belligerent and had made a move toward the teacher (*Owens v. Commonwealth of Kentucky,* 473 S.W.2d 827, 1972).

Chapter Two Your Employment Security

No one, no matter how well qualified, has a right to work for the government. Teaching in a public school is a *privilege,* and is extended only to those who have become qualified to hold that high honor. Once employed, however, individuals have rights, chief among which is the right not to be discriminated against in employment benefits, promotions, or in other aspects of your job. Teacher employment/dismissal/non-renewal cases continue to outnumber by far all other educational cases combined.

Some of your rights to work have been secured by means of the various civil rights acts by the Congress as well as through decisions of the United States Supreme Court. While your relationship to your employing board may rest initially on contractual law, there may be a constitutional dimension if the board dismisses you or otherwise punishes you for the exercise of a constitutionally protected right, such as freedom of speech, association, and petition.

The Civil Rights Act of 1964 made it illegal for any district to discriminate against its employees on account of race, religion, ethnic origin, sex, or language. Hence, a whole new dimension was added to the traditional relationship between teacher and board of education — that of the constitutional dimensions of the job, not its contractual arrangements alone. This new dimension has led to larger volumes of litigation than before 1964, and continues to prove to be a fertile field for teachers, both as defendants and as plaintiffs.

Ordinarily, unless the board can show the deleterious effects of your lifestyle, your sexual preferences, or other personal habits on *your teaching efficiency,* the courts will tend to uphold the teacher. As we have seen at the start of Chapter One, in one case, the board sought to dismiss a teacher for "immorality" because she was an avowed lesbian. It lost its cause when the board president said, in public, "But she's one of our *best* teachers!" Unable to show that her lifestyle was deleterious to the teacher's effectiveness in the classroom, the board was ordered by the court to pay her for the remainder of her contract. (The court did not order reinstatement.)

Following are some additional sample cases. Read the fact situations carefully, then decide how you would have judged the case had you been on the bench. Then turn to the end of this chapter to discover how the cases turned out.

Cases in Point

Case No. 1 — LETTER TO THE EDITOR

An Illinois teacher wrote a letter to a local newspaper which the paper published in its "Letters to the Editor" column. The letter was critical of the way the board had been handling prior bond issues and contained certain false statements. The board dismissed the teacher on the grounds that the letter would damage the professional reputations of the school's administrators and tend to foment controversy and conflict among the teachers, the administrators, the board of education and the citizens. The teacher sued the board for reinstatement. The board had held a hearing and had acted only after it found some statements were false. Was the teacher legally dismissed?

Case No. 2 — PREGNANCY LEAVE

The board had a mandatory maternity leave policy that compelled female teachers who were pregnant to quit their jobs without pay several months before the expected birth of their children. Was the policy constitutional?

Case No. 3 — THE UNION FOREVER

Peters and Epperson were president and president-elect, respectively, of the local branch of the National Education Association and were involved in some rather heated negotiations with the board. Therefore, when the board notified them they would not be rehired because of budgetary problems, the teachers went to federal court claiming denial of due process of law. Peters had taught in the district eleven years, Epperson seventeen years. Kansas law provided for annual contracts to continue unless written notice of an intention to terminate was furnished by March 15. The district served notice on February 9. Were the teachers entitled to a hearing before being terminated?

Case No. 4 — NEVER WAIVER

The board of trustees refused to renew an elementary school teacher's contract for another year, and she requested a hearing before the board, which was granted. However, when time for the hearing came, the teacher did not appear. The board then proceeded to notify the teacher that she was no longer on the faculty. She appealed to a federal district court for relief. Does the teacher who requests a hearing then fails to appear lose his/her right to be heard?

Case No. 5 — AH, COMMUNAL LIVING!

A teacher and her husband lived at Koinonia Farms, an interracial, religiously oriented communal farm. After an interview for a school position, the superintendent hesitated to hire her because of her place of residence. The teacher did, however, substitute; finally, she was denied even that job because some parents objected. She filed an action in federal court claiming that although she was competent and qualified for the job, she was being denied employment because of her free exercise of a constitutionally protected right. Could the board refuse to hire a teacher under these conditions?

Certification

Q. WHO MAY TEACH?

A. No person, no matter how well qualified, has an inherent *right* to teach in the public schools. Rather, teaching is a *privilege* extended to those who fully qualify under the certification rules of each state. Thus, there may be health requirements such as a chest x-ray, the completion of a designated course of study including the history of the state, an oath of allegiance, or a recommendation by the preparatory college or university. Most states have a minimum-age limit for teachers, and most of the states require the candidate "to be of good moral character," whatever that means.

Q. WHAT IS THE LEGAL STATUS OF THE TEACHING CERTIFICATE?

A. Your teaching certificate or credential is merely your state license to practice. It does not guarantee you a job; in effect, it is a hunting license. And you must first obtain the certificate in the state in which you will be employed.

Q. WHAT IS THE PURPOSE OF THE TEACHING CERTIFICATE?

A. It may have many purposes. Chief among the reasons for certification of teachers is to avoid having unqualified persons come into contact with the young. Another reason is to protect the public treasury — no board may pay out money to anyone who is not the holder of a certificate without running the risk of having to make up the losses from their own pockets. Certification standards tend to upgrade the profession of teaching over time, as well as contribute to the individual improvement of the teacher. Finally, certification tends to protect society against false prophets and quacks who profess to know how to teach but do not. While the state in effect issues a monopoly to a professional, it may also hold that professional responsible for his/her performance on pain of non-renewal of the certificate to teach.

Q. IS THE TEACHING CERTIFICATE A LIMITED DOCUMENT?

A. Yes. Since it is merely a license, it only proves that at the time of issuance the holder was qualified for it. But there are time limits, subject limits, and other qualifications which limit the document. And the state may revoke the certificate under certain conditions. The continuing validity of the certificate is usually conditioned on the successful completion of a certain number of months of teaching. And when the certificate lapses, it is completely annulled and is subject to renewal only upon full compliance with certification standards in effect at the time of renewal.

Q. DOES A CERTIFICATED TEACHER HAVE THE RIGHT TO EMPLOYMENT BY THE GOVERNMENT?

A. No person, no matter how well qualified, has a legal right to governmental employment. Working for the government is considered a privilege, not a right. However, once you are employed and have entered upon your duties, you do have a protected right not to be discriminated against in promotion, fringe benefits, retirement considerations, and other conditions of employment.

Q. WHAT IS THE LEGAL STATUS OF ONE WHO TEACHES WITHOUT HAVING A VALID TEACHING CREDENTIAL?

A. In the eyes of the law, such an individual is a "mere volunteer" and cannot be paid for teaching services performed without a credential.

Q. WHEN MUST I HAVE MY TEACHING CREDENTIAL — WHEN I SIGN A CONTRACT, WHEN I BEGIN TEACHING, OR WHEN I GET PAID?

A. States vary on their statutory requirements relative to when the certificate is necessary to the contractual relationship. In Colorado, for example, it is sufficient that you have the certificate before you receive pay for teaching (in fact, boards may be personally liable if they pay out public funds to anyone not holding a valid Colorado teaching certificate). In other states, you must have the certificate at the time you sign the contract, while in others you need have it when school starts. You should become familiar with your own state's requirements on when to obtain the certificate to teach.

Q. HOW DOES CERTIFICATION DIFFER FROM ACCREDITATION?

A. Certification is the legal device by which the state licenses those individuals who are qualified to teach in the state. Certification applies to a *person,* and a certificate is not transferable. Accreditation, on the other hand, is a control exercised by the state or a voluntary organization for the overall improvement of an *institution.* Thus, we say that a teacher is certificated (or has a credential) to teach, while this high school or that college or university is accredited by some regional or national accrediting agency or organization, such as the North Central Association of High Schools and Colleges.

Q. HAVE THE STATES CEASED ISSUING "LIFE" CERTIFICATES?

A. Most of them have done so. The life certificate which was issued earlier entitled the teacher to continue to teach without having to renew the certificate, in effect, as long as the teacher lived. However, due to rapid changes in methodology and in the fund of knowledge, states have gone to a system whereby the teacher must take certain courses or have certain in-service experiences to continue to be certified.

Q. MAY A STATE REQUIRE A MINIMUM SCORE ON THE NATIONAL TEACHERS EXAMINATION (NTE) AS A REQUIREMENT FOR THE ISSUANCE OF A TEACHING CERTIFICATE?

A. Yes. By a divided vote (7-2), the U.S. Supreme Court ruled without a hearing that despite a "disparate racial impact," the practice was not a violation of the equal protection clause of the Fourteenth Amendment nor a violation of Title VII. The State had not intentionally discriminated against blacks in issuing certificates and setting teacher pay scales based on NTE scores, and had shown that it was a more efficient system for determining teacher competency than the plaintiffs' alternative of graduation from an approved teacher education program. *United States v. South Carolina*, 445 F. Supp. 1094, (D.S.C. 1977), aff'd., 434 U.S. 1026 (1978).

Q. MAY THE STATE REVOKE A TEACHER'S CERTIFICATE?

A. Yes. Most states provide for revocation of the teaching certificate on the grounds that the power to issue the certificate implies the right to revoke it. The revocation must occur, however, only for just cause and is limited to the state board of education or the state credentialing board's discretion. Such grounds as immorality, conduct unbecoming a teacher, conviction of a felony, or other similar grounds are the bases on which most revocations take place. In California, the state board of education is empowered by the Education Code to revoke a teacher's certificate "for evident unfitness for service."

Q. IF I AM CERTIFIED IN ONE STATE, CAN I BE CERTIFIED IN THE OTHERS?

A. Under a system of reciprocity, many states now issue you a certificate if you have qualified in one of the states recognized by that state. But this practice is by no means universal. You should write to the state education agency or state department of education (sometimes called the state board of public instruction) in the capital city of the state in which you wish to teach to find out what must be done to obtain the certificate there.

Contracting and Tenure

Q. WHAT ARE THE ELEMENTS OF A VALID CONTRACT?

A. There are five elements of a valid contract: 1) it must be between competent parties (teachers must be certified or certifiable, for example); 2) there must be a meeting of the minds (sometimes called mutual assent); 3) it must contain a valid consideration (a contract to pay "the going wage" would be unenforceable); 4) it must be sufficiently specific in detail as to time and the rights of the parties as to be enforceable; and 5) it must not be illegal or against public policy. Since those who deal with boards of education do so at their own peril and are assumed to know the law, you should, if possible, have your contract examined by your attorney to see that it is valid in every one of these five respects.

Q. WHEN DOES MY CONTRACT ACTUALLY BECOME BINDING?

A. You may have signed a contract to teach, but it isn't binding until the board, in a regular or special meeting, has *ratified* it, that is, has officially accepted the conditions. What you signed was a mere offer, but there must be acceptance by the opposite party before there is a valid contract.

Q. CAN I BE REQUIRED TO SIGN A LOYALTY OATH AS A CONDITION OF EMPLOYMENT IN A PUBLIC SCHOOL?

A. Yes, but the loyalty oaths now in use are much toned down from those of the 1960's, which required that teachers not belong to or believe in organizations which had as their object the "violent overthrow of the government." The Supreme Court declared most of these statutory requirements unconstitutional on the grounds they were too vague — the teacher could not tell whether he or she was within the requirements or not. The states hastily re-enacted their loyalty oath statutes to fall within the constraints of the Constitution. For example, the original teacher loyalty oath in Colorado was declared unconstitutional. The state now requires that teachers take the following oath as a condition of employment: "I solemnly swear (affirm) that I will uphold the Constitution of the United States and the Constitution of the State of Colorado, and I will faithfully perform the duties of the position upon which I am about to enter."

Q. CAN THE BOARD REQUIRE TEACHER CANDIDATES TO TAKE A PHYSICAL TEST BEFORE BEING HIRED?

A. Yes, but only if the board can show a reasonable relationship between the test and the work to be done if the candidate were to be offered employment. In New York, a school board required that a visual aids technician must pass a test to lift twenty-five pounds with one hand and twenty pounds with the other. The court upheld the test where it was shown that the one hired must lift heavy audio-visual equipment as a part of the job. Nor would the court say that the test discriminated against women, since if hired, a woman would have to be able to lift the equipment the same as a man. Also, one of the western states where people go who have tuberculosis could legally require a chest x-ray in order to keep diseased persons from coming into contact with youth.

Q. MAY A TEACHER BE DISMISSED FOR DELIBERATELY FALSIFYING AN APPLICATION FOR A POSITION?

A. Yes. Falsification of a record is not only fraudulent but also, in the words of one court, "a continuing deception" (*Negrich v. Dade Co. Bd. of Ed.*, 143 So.2d 498, Fla. 1962). In one case, a teacher claimed to be a citizen and repeated the statement in a loyalth oath. The court upheld his dismissal for fraud. Another teacher who wrote on his application that he was not a homosexual but later did "come out of the closet" was legally dismissed by the board, not because of his homosexuality, but for fraud (*Acanfora v. Bd. of Educ. of Montgomery Co.*, 491 F.2d 498 4CA, 1974; cert. denied, 419 U.S. 836, 1974).

Q. WHAT IS THE DISTINCTION BETWEEN DISMISSAL AND NON-RENEWAL OF THE TEACHING CONTRACT?

A. *Dismissal* refers to steps being taken against you to remove you as a teacher *during the life of the contract.* If you are dismissed, you are entitled to 1) a statement of the reasons; 2) a notice of a hearing at which you can respond to the stated reasons; and 3) the actual holding of a hearing. (A meeting with the board has sometimes been held by the courts to constitute a "hearing" if it had all the earmarks of fundamental fairness.) *Non-renewal* of the contract means that the board gives you timely notice that *your contract will not be renewed.* In most of the states, the board does not have to give reasons if the teacher is on probationary status. Where the teacher is tenured, however, he/she is entitled to a hearing on the merits of the board's good and just cause reason for non-renewal.

Q. WHAT ARE SOME OF THE GROUNDS WHICH JUSTIFY DISMISSAL?

A. The most common grounds for dismissal of teachers are incompetency, immorality, insubordination, physical or mental disability, unfitness or inadequate performance of duties, services no longer needed due to unavoidable reductions in enrollment, conviction of a felony or a crime involving moral turpitude, failure to show normal improvement in professional training and growth, and any cause which constitutes grounds for the revocation of your teaching credential. There is normally an "elastic" clause which adds to this list the words, "or other good and just cause." The burden of proof of any of these charges is with the board of education, which must show that you failed to do something which you should have done or did something which you should not have done.

Q. IF I AM ILLEGALLY DISMISSED, WHAT DAMAGES ACCRUE?

A. You are entitled to damages equal to the amount of your actual loss. Thus, where a teacher was illegally dismissed but found another teaching job at a higher salary, the court held the board could settle for nominal damages of $1. You are required to accept employment when waiting for litigation to run its course or at least to seek comparable employment. If the board's action in dismissing you has been heavy-handed and deprives you of a civil right, you may be awarded "punitive" damages ("smart money") as well as attorney's fees. Normally, the court will rule the board must pay back wages from the date of your suspension or dismissal if you have not found work in the meantime. But you must "mitigate the damages" by looking for other work as you wait for resolution of your case.

Q. AM I BOUND BY BOARD RESOLUTIONS AND POLICIES THAT ARE ADOPTED LONG AFTER I HAVE BEEN ON THE JOB?

A. Yes. Your original contract of employment may undergo many changes as time goes on. This is not, however, a breach of contract on the part of the board, since the courts hold the board must be free to make changes that it can prove are necessary. For example, the City of Cincinnati enacted a policy that all teachers hired after a certain date must reside in the district. The court upheld the policy. *Wardwell v. Bd. of Educ. of Cincinnati*, 529 F.2d 625, Ohio 1976; accord, *McCarthy v. Phila. Civil Serv. Comm.*, 424 U.S. 645, 1976. Similarly, a school board's rule establishing contract nonrenewal as the sanction for not complying with a continuing education requirement was held to be constitutional. *Harrah Ind. Sch. Dist. v. Martin*, 440 U.S. 194, Okla. 1979.

Q. DOES THE TEACHER'S CONTRACT CONTAIN PROVISIONS DESCRIBING ALL THE TEACHER'S OBLIGATIONS?

A. No. Teaching contracts are usually of the short form, in contrast with the more lengthy, nitty-gritty contracts of earlier times. Today's contract ordinarily shows only the name, length of time the contract is to run, the general teaching area (such as English or elementary), and whatever state requirements must be included, such as an oath of loyalty. In addition, it includes *by implication* all subsequent policies adopted by the board, all state laws governing teaching contracts, and the by-laws adopted by the board at a later date. That is why there is so much litigation in this area — because your duties are not spelled out in detail, you sometimes have to ask the judge to interpret them.

Q. DOES THE CONTRACT IMPLY THAT I MAY BE ASSIGNED TO EXTRA-CURRICULAR DUTIES OR OTHER GENERAL RESPONSIBILITIES NOT SPECIFICALLY LISTED IN THE CONTRACT?

A. Yes. You may be assigned to certain duties, such as sponsorship of a class, or club, but the courts say that there must be a reasonable relationship between your classroom duties and your assigned sponsorship. For example, where a teacher was assigned sponsorship of a bowling club that was not associated with the school, and which practiced after school or on Saturday, and which did not enter into interscholastic competition the court ruled it was not sufficiently germane to the academic program as to be "reasonably related" to the program of studies. Therefore, the teacher could refuse to take a sponsorship where it in effect amounted only to "baby sitting."

Q. WHAT IS MEANT BY BREACH OF CONTRACT?

A. Breach of contract is failure to live up to the conditions in the contract. For example, teachers in the Hortonville schools (see Case No. 4, Ch. 1) who went out on strike in violation of state law were considered to have breached their contracts. Boards of education may breach the contract where they precipitously dismiss a teacher without a hearing. One who signs up to teach school but who leaves the state to teach elsewhere is breaching the contract unless a release is obtained exonerating the person from the obligation.

Q. WHO DETERMINES WHETHER THE CONTRACT HAS BEEN BREACHED?

A. The court. A party to a contract who feels that the other party has broken the contract may appeal to a court of law to uphold his interests. The court must first determine whether there has indeed been a breach. If there has been, then the court must also determine what must be done to make the injured party whole again.

Q. DOES A TEACHER WHO IS ARRESTED OR WHO IS CONVICTED OF A MISDEMEANOR BREACH HIS CONTRACT?

A. Courts vary on this as do the states. Ordinarily, the teacher who is found guilty of a felony (which is much more serious than a misdemeanor) will be considered to have breached the contract of employment (teachers are expected to be exemplars to their students). Nor is the teacher subject to double jeopardy merely because he is tried both in a criminal court and in a civil hearing before the board. Double jeopardy applies only to criminal actions, not civil. But being arrested for drunkenness, for fighting, for petty theft, or some similar misdemeanor does not mean that the teacher has breached the contract, unless the board can show that what happened did prove to be deleterious to the teacher's effectiveness as a teacher.

Q. WHAT PENALTIES ARE LEVIED AGAINST THOSE WHO BREACH A CONTRACT?

A. For teachers, the penalties range all the way from formal censure through having to pay a penalty or suspension of the teaching certificate in some states. Normally, the opposite party must show that it has lost valuable considerations (money, time) through the breach. Where boards breach the contract, they may have to pay back wages, attorneys' fees, and even punitive damages where the actions are arbitrary, capricious, or illegal in nature. If the board members acted in a conspiratorial way, and there is a deprivation of a civil right, or if the board acted knowing that what it was doing would deprive someone of a civil right, the individual members may be held liable in damages under the Civil Rights Act of 1871 (42 U.S.C. Sec. 1983).

Q. IS THE CONTRACTUAL RELATIONSHIP THE ONLY CONTROLLING ELEMENT IN TEACHER-BOARD OF EDUCATION DEALINGS?

A. No. At one time, contractual relationships were big — in fact, all inclusive. But when the civil rights movement gained momentum, there arose another dimension, that of the Constitution. This latter relationship now far outstrips contractual questions in the amount of litigation which it generates. The new rules require that the board conduct its contractual relationships with teachers wholly within the constraints of the United States Constitution. These include, but are not limited to, due process of law, equal protection of the laws, the rights of privacy, speech, press, and religion, and all the other liberties contained in the Bill of Rights.

Q. WHAT LEGAL RIGHTS ACCRUE TO THE TEACHER ON TENURE?

A. Tenure granted by the state generally means at least these two things: 1) continuing employment without the necessity of notification each year during good behavior; and 2) if employment is to be terminated, the board must provide the teacher with an impartial hearing having the attributes of fundamental fairness. Some states provide only for continuing contracts of the "spring-notification" type. These would not be considered "tenure" under this definition because they would lack the very important consideration of a due process hearing on the merits before termination could legally be completed.

Q. WHAT DUE PROCESS PROCEDURES ARE NORMALLY GUARANTEED UNDER STATUTORY TENURE?

A. States differ in how the local board must proceed in terminating a tenured teacher. Whatever the statute says must be followed to the letter in order for the board to succeed in attempts to fire a teacher. Generally, there must be a written notice specifying grounds on which the board is basing its action and a due process hearing before an impartial tribunal. The board must then base its decision on the facts found at the hearing, and there is always the right of appeal from the board's decision.

Q. FOR TEACHERS ON CONTINUING CONTRACT, WHEN MUST THE BOARD NOTIFY THEM IF THEY ARE NOT REHIRED?

A. States vary on this requirement. Usually, the board must notify the teacher of non-renewal sometime in the spring, say, by March 15, or April 1. Failure to notify the teacher in the manner specified (by registered mail, for example) will result in the teacher's being re-employed for the coming year. You should find out what the cut-off date is in your own state and govern yourself accordingly.

Q. DO I, A CERTIFICATED TEACHER, HAVE A *CONSTITUTIONAL* RIGHT TO TEACH SCHOOL?

A. No. Working for the government is considered a privilege, not a right. But you do have the right once employed to be free from harassment, coercion, or other types of discrimination because of sex, religion, country of origin, race, or age. Many of the cases which now arise call for the court to determine whether a teacher has been discriminated against in employment.

Q. IF I TEACH FOR ONE YEAR, DO I HAVE A REASONABLE EXPECTANCY OF CONTINUING EMPLOYMENT IN THE DISTRICT?

A. No. One who is on probationary status has no vested interest in continuing employment in the district, except that one cannot be discontinued because of the exercise of a protected constitutional right, such as freedom of speech, or the right to join a teacher's organization and be active in it. Some states call for a legal hearing on non-renewal of the probationary teaching contract, while other states say the board does not have to give reasons. But where the teacher claims that a constitutional reason exists, the board ordinarily must hold a hearing to determine whether such a reason exists, or whether it is merely a case of "dismissal or non-renewal for just cause."

Q. DOES A NON-TENURED TEACHER WHO TAKES MATERNITY LEAVE HAVE THE RIGHT TO RETURN TO DUTY?

A. Boards of education normally have policies covering what to do if a teacher desires to return to active employment after the expiration of a certain number of days following delivery. Since practice varies widely from district to district, you should acquaint yourself with the policy in force in your district of employment.

Q. ARE MALE TEACHERS ENTITLED TO *PATERNITY* LEAVE?

A. Yes. The courts are saying that what is provided in the way of parental leave for women teachers is also due male teachers if they so desire. A teacher who adopts an infant one year old or less may also be entitled to such fringe benefit. You should peruse your school board's policies to determine what the policy is on such leaves of absence.

Q. WHAT CONSTITUTES A "STIGMA" IN TEACHER TERMINATION?

A. Stigma is defined as a stain or reproach to one's reputation or good name by what the state is doing to him. When applied to teachers who are terminated, the school board may deprive the individual of the freedom to seek future employment opportunities, and thus deprive that individual of "liberty" under the Fourteenth Amendment by reason of the stigma which attaches to being sacked. When applied to students, stigma may attach where the student is grouped into a mentally retarded class, or is labeled in such a way as to limit his or her future educational or employment possibilities. Where the state has acted in either instance "to foreclose a range of opportunities in a manner that contravenes due process," said the Supreme Court, "the teacher may have recourse to the Fourteenth Amendment" (*Bd. of Regents v. Roth,* 92 S.Ct. 2701, Wisc., 1972; *Perry v. Sindermann,* 92 S.Ct. 2694, Tex., 1972).

Q. CAN A TEACHER GAIN A VESTED RIGHT TO FURTHER EMPLOYMENT EXCEPT THROUGH STATUTORY TENURE?

A. Yes. The Supreme Court held that one who works in a position for a length of time (here ten years or more) may have a vested right to a hearing before termination of employment, even though his state doesn't have statutory tenure. Such a vested right is referred to as "constitutional tenure" because it is a "property" right protected under the Fourteenth Amendment (*Perry v. Sindermann,* 408 U.S. 593, Texas, 1972). In this case, the teacher's right was not so much to the job or to continuing employment as to not be discriminated against because he chose to exercise a constitutionally-protected right (freedom of expression). He could still have been fired, but only after a full and legal due process hearing.

Q. MAY A TEACHER BE DISCHARGED BECAUSE OF A DECREASE IN ENROLLMENTS OR A LACK OF MONEY?

A. It all depends. If the teachers' union has negotiated a clause which allows the board to terminate tenured teachers under these circumstances, then the board can proceed on these grounds. In the absence of such a negotiated agreement, however, the board cannot plead these two "just causes" for non-renewal or discharge without showing that it has indeed experienced a drop in enrollment or that it can no longer find the money for the teacher's salary. And then, it would have to show the court that it uses some systematic way of determining who stays and who goes — such as last-hired, first-fired (seniority) as a base for its decision.

Q. CAN THE BOARD USE THE NATIONAL TEACHERS' EXAMINATION (NTE) AS GROUNDS FOR RETAINING TEACHERS?

A. Yes, it is possible that results of the NTE might be used, but retention or dismissal could not be based on this *single* test alone. However, in *United States v. South Carolina,* 445 F.Supp. 1094, (D.S.C. 1977), aff'd. 434 U.S. 1026 (1978) the U.S. Supreme Court upheld the State of South Carolina which for over 30 years had used scores on the NTE to certify teachers and determine the amount of state aid payable to local school districts. Despite the fact that the NTE had a disproportionate impact on blacks, the defendants proved through an exhaustive validity study that the test was a valid, reliable and economical means for measuring one element of effective teaching: the degree of knowledge possessed by the teacher.

Q. IS "REVERSE DISCRIMINATION" ALLOWED IN HIRING AND PROMOTING PUBLIC SCHOOL PERSONNEL?

A. It all depends. Where a district is under an affirmative action order from the court, it must move as quickly as it can to remove all traces of racial discrimination in its employment practices. In San Francisco, some white plaintiffs brought a suit in federal court claiming "reverse discrimination" because they were being passed over for administrative appointments which went to minority applicants (*Anderson v. San Francisco Unified Sch. Dist.*, 357 F.Supp. 248, 1972). In upholding the plaintiffs, the court said that "preferential treatment under the guise of 'affirmative action' is the imposition of one form of racial discrimination in place of another. There is no place for race or ethnic groupings in America. Only in individual accomplishment can equality be achieved." Thus, any classification based on race is "suspect" unless the board can justify it on the grounds of an overriding public purpose to be served.

Q. HAS THE SUPREME COURT LAID DOWN GENERAL STANDARDS BY WHICH TO JUDGE ALL CASES INVOLVING TEACHERS' FREEDOM OF EXPRESSION?

A. No, In *Pickering v. Board of Education* (Sample Case No. 1, this chapter) the Court held that a teacher has the right to write and have published a letter critical of board policies in a bond election without fear of retaliatory dismissal. In 1979, the Court assessed damages and attorneys' fees against a board that fired a teacher for her "petty and unreasonable communications" to her principal about board policies which the principal described as "hostile," "loud," and "arrogant." The Court held that a public employee does not forfeit his First Amendment protection when he communicates privately with his boss. *Givhan v. Western Line Consol. Sch. Dist.*, 439 U.S. 410, Miss. 1979.

Q. ARE TEACHERS AS A CLASS PRECLUDED FROM SPEAKING OUT ON PUBLIC ISSUES EVEN THOUGH THEIR VIEWS MAY DIFFER FROM THE BOARD'S?

A. No. In *Pickering,* the Supreme Court said that of all citizens, teachers are, as a class, "the members of a community most likely to have informed and definite opinions as to how funds allotted to the operation of the schools should be spent. Accordingly, it is essential that they be able to speak out freely on such questions without fear of retaliatory dismissal." This is a protected right, even though a mistake in facts is included therein, so long as the mistake is an honest one.

Q. MAY A TEACHER BE DISCIPLINED OR FIRED FOR WEARING A BLACK ARMBAND IN SCHOOL TO PROTEST U.S. ENGAGEMENT IN A WAR?

A. No, unless there is a disruption of the school program, or a clear and present danger, or invasion of the rights of others. For example, a teacher who was suspended for wearing a black armband in school and who refused to take it off when asked by the principal to do so was held to have been denied a civil right in the absence of a finding that discipline or sound education was materially and substantially jeopardized (*James v. Board of Education*, 461 F.2d 566, 2CA, 1968).

Q. INTO WHAT GENERAL CATEGORIES DO CASES INVOLVING DISMISSAL OR NON-RENEWAL OF THE TEACHING CONTRACT FALL?

A. There are four general classes of dismissals of teachers: those cases where the charge is incompetency but where the teacher may be salvageable; cases where the teacher is incompetent and no amount of help will cure the defect (unsalvageable); cases where the teacher is competent in the classroom but is considered deficient in some other category (what he does is "counter-productive"); and cases where the teacher is competent and what he or she is doing is protected.

Q. WHAT RIGHTS DOES THE TEACHER HAVE WHO IS INCOMPETENT YET SALVAGEABLE?

A. The courts are saying that the teacher whose performance is deemed unsatisfactory is entitled to notification of what is wrong. Such notification must be made early enough so that remediation can take place. Further the teacher is also entitled to assistance from the school district in the form of supervisory help, conferences, visitation, and all the other in-service aids which the district can muster before a declaration of incompetency is made. Since first-year teachers sometimes run into difficulty making adjustments, the probationary teacher is entitled to assistance along the way. Each teacher has the right to succeed, and the district cannot fail to notify the teacher of any remediable defects, then fire the teacher for incompetency at the end of the year.

Q. WHAT RIGHT DOES THE TEACHER HAVE WHO IS BOTH INCOMPETENT AND UNSALVAGEABLE?

A. Such teachers are entitled to all the help mentioned above, plus a hearing on the merits before non-renewal or dismissal. The burden of proof that the teacher is indeed incompetent is upon the board of education and the board must cite facts, not opinions, in supporting its case. One board finally dismissed a "lovely lady" who was just too gentle to clamp down on students who took advantage of her, concluding that her incompetency was unsalvageable (*Stroman v. Bd. of Educ.*, 300 A.2d 286, Pa., 1973).

Q. WHAT RIGHT DOES THE TEACHER HAVE WHO IS COMPETENT IN THE CLASSROOM BUT WHOSE BEHAVIOR IS COUNTERPRODUCTIVE?

A. Again, the burden of proof rests with the board of education. The board must prove that, although the teacher is competent to teach, his or her behavior, life-style, activity, or pronouncements detract so much from his or her effectiveness as a teacher as to be controlling the situation. For example, teachers competent in the classroom have been legally dismissed for making students write a vulgar word 1,000 times for having said the word (*Celestine v. Lafayette Parish Sch. Bd.*, 284 So.2d 650, La., 1973), for molesting or "touching" students in class, for administering corporal punishment in violation of a board policy, and for refusing to take a physical examination as required by the board. A California teacher claimed her membership in a "swingers" club had nothing to do with her teaching competency. The court could not agree and held she had been legally dismissed "for counterproductive behavior."

Q. WHAT RIGHT DOES THE TEACHER HAVE WHO IS COMPETENT AND ACTING WITHIN THE CONSTITUTION?

A. It is now well-settled law that the teacher who is competent and who exercises a constitutional right may not be punished for doing so. Non-renewal of even an untenured teacher may not be predicated on exercise of a First Amendment right (*Gray v. Union Co. Interm.Ed.Dist.*, 520 F.2d 803, Or., 1973). In Wyoming, a non-tenured teacher was denied another contract after she encouraged students to start their own underground newspaper, although she was a capable teacher in the classroom. The federal district court ruled that her right to procedural due process had been violated by the board. The Court of Appeals affirmed the court below and remanded the case with directions to reinstate the teacher (*Bertot v. Sch. Dist. No. 1,* 522 F.2d 1171, Wyo., 1977).

Sex Discrimination in Education

Q. HAS EDUCATION BEEN A FIELD WHERE SEX DISCRIMINATION HAS BEEN ROUTINELY PRACTICED?

A. Yes. Sex discrimination in education begins in the primary grades ("wanted: female kindergarten teacher") and grows increasingly worse the higher one goes through the system (only fifteen percent of all full professors are women). Phi Delta Kappa, the most "prestigious" educational fraternity, was sued to admit women since membership in that organization opened doors to employment of men while women were denied that privilege. Women were routinely paid less to teach in universities even though they did the same work as men. We have mentioned elsewhere how women were discriminated against by being forced to take maternity leave without pay until the Supreme Court threw out this practice. One employer was censured for willingness to hire men with pre-school-age children but not women (*Phillips v. Martin-Marietta Corp.,* 416 F.2d 1257, 5CA, 1969).

Q. TO WHAT EXTENT WAS THERE SEX DISCRIMINATION IN EDUCATION?

A. In 1970, a study was made which showed that women superintendents in the United States comprised only 0.6 percent of the total of all superintendents; 67.2 percent of all teachers were women; 91.4 percent of all librarians; and 99.2 percent of all nurses were women. Women made up twenty-eight percent of all college and university faculties, and sixty-three percent of these were paid at a rate less than that enjoyed by their male counterparts. Only nine percent of all full professors were women (now somewhere around fifteen percent). In the public schools girls were not allowed to take boys' courses and *vice versa;* girls were barred from boys' sports; there were higher standards for women than for men teachers; some positions were closed to women entirely; and women were discouraged from advancing up the leadership ladder. Maternity leave policies were discriminatory and there were inequities in assignments. Even the textbooks (remember Dick and Jane?) were suspect. There have been some adjustments made since 1970 but there is still a long way to go to reach that equality of opportunity envisioned by the Congress and the President in 1972.

Q. WHAT IS MEANT BY A DISTRICT'S AFFIRMATIVE ACTION PROGRAM?

A. An affirmative action plan for a district or an educational institution such as a college is a scheme to erase all semblance of racial or sex discrimination, which assesses the current status of these two variables, sets time tables for erasure, and contains quotas and goals for attainment at some future date by the district. Title IX guidelines deal with correction of problems of sexual discrimination while Title VII deals with eradication of discrimination in employment opportunities. A district may be ordered by a court to draw up an affirmative action plan, or it may voluntarily proceed to set its house in order.

Q. MAY THE BOARD HIRE A LOWER-SALARIED MAN INSTEAD OF FILLING THE POSITION WITH A WOMAN?

A. The courts are reluctant to interfere in the decisions that local boards make unless there is a clear sign that some constitutional right is being denied. In Wyoming, a female teacher brought charges of discrimination on the basis of sex because the board hired a man who would enter the district at a lower salary than she would have received had she been employed. She claimed violation of the Fair Employment Practices Act. The court held that "in determining which teaching applicant shall receive a particular position a school board is not required to line up all applicants, place their degrees, teaching experience, and amount of expertise in some sort of order and mechanically pick the one that has the highest degree, the greatest amount of experience and the most on-paper expertise (*Shenefield v. Sheridan County School Dist. No. 1*, 544 P.2d 870, Wyo., 1976).

Q. CAN THE BOARD ADVERTISE FOR A MALE COACH OR A FEMALE DRAMA INSTRUCTOR?

A. Under the Equal Employment Opportunity Act, the board or any other employer is barred from specifying the sex of teachers unless sex is a *bona fide occupational qualification* (BFOQ). There are very few teaching positions where BFOQ claims are supportable by the board. For example, there are now male kindergarten teachers, women football coaches, and female superintendents of schools. Where qualifications are the same, the board may choose to have a female coaching the girls' swim team, but it had better be ready to defend its selection on some factual grounds rather than on its preference. And of course a board cannot deny qualified candidates of the female gender from filling administrative posts on the grounds that women cannot become leaders, or that teachers will not perform well for a woman principal. These are mere opinions, and not factually validated conclusions, something that boards have found out about to their sorrow.

Q. ARE TEACHERS PROTECTED AGAINST DISCRIMINATION BECAUSE OF SEX?

A. Yes. For example, in Mississippi, two unwed mothers brought an action seeking to have declared unconstitutional a board rule which made unwed mothers ineligible to be hired as teachers aides. The teachers aides attacked the rule on the grounds that it did not treat unwed fathers in the same way. The court held that the rule had no rational relationship to any objective sought to be achieved by the board and was fraught with invidious discrimination. It was constitutionally defective in that it was a denial of both equal protection of the law and due process of law (*Andrews v. Drew Municipal Sep. Sch. Dist.*, 507 F.2d 611, Miss., 1975).

Q. MAY A FEMALE TEACHER CLAIM REJECTION OF SEXUAL ADVANCES BY HER SUPERVISOR AS BASIS FOR DISCRIMINATORY ACTION BY THE BOARD?

A. Courts are divided on the question of whether sexual advances to female employees by supervisory personnel amount to sex discrimination in employment. In *Cochran v. Odell* (334 F.Supp. 555, Tx., 1971), plaintiff Cochran alleged that she had been dismissed because she would not submit to advances from supervisory personnel. However, her case was dismissed because she had accepted and cashed a check that bore a notation that upon her acceptance the check was a waiver of any right to notice or hearing. In other cases, the courts have held there is no recovery under the Civil Rights Act of 1964, but implied that since the employer was not liable, the action should be against the individual involved (*Corne v. Bausch and Lomb,* 390 F.Supp. 161, Ariz., 1975).

Q. CAN A BOARD PAY ITS WOMEN EMPLOYEES LESS FOR DOING THE SAME WORK AS MEN?

A. No. Several school districts have been ordered by the Office of Civil Rights or the Justice Department to pay back wages to women custodians who were paid less per hour than men, even though there were two different job descriptions in use in the district. The court held that such "subterfuge" was obviously an "excuse" to pay women less than men for doing essentially the same kind of work, and amounted to a form of invidious discrimination which is outlawed in the civil rights acts (*Marshall v. Marshalltown Sch. Dist.,* Case 74-271-2, Iowa, 1977).

Q. WHAT IS MEANT BY EQUAL EMPLOYMENT OPPORTUNITY?

A. In 1972, as part of the Equal Employment Opportunity Act of 1972, Title VII of the Civil Rights Act of 1964 was extended to include public schools. The purpose was twofold: to encourage employers to hire and promote women, and to encourage women to seek training and apply for those jobs which had theretofore been closed to them. Title VII prohibits employment discrimination based on race, color, national origin, religion, or sex. In June of 1972, Congress prohibited sex discrimination against both students and employees in federally assisted educational programs. Titles VI and IX are administered by the Office of Civil Rights (OCR) of the Department of HEW, Title VII by the Equal Employment Opportunity Commission (EEOC). All three titles provide for investigation of complaints related to discrimination in hiring, classification, compensation, promotion, duties, fringe benefits, and termination, as well as the whole spectrum of student affairs, including course selection, grading, athletics, and school-related activities.

Q. WHAT IS THE DIFFERENCE BETWEEN A QUOTA AND A GOAL?

A. Both terms are in use in affirmative action programs to remedy past discrimination in schools on account of race or sex. The term "quotas" is generally applied to racial balance within the faculty of the district, while "goals" are hoped-for achievement levels in providing equal job opportunities for women.

Q. HOW ARE RACIAL QUOTAS DETERMINED FOR PUBLIC SCHOOL FACULTY?

A. An early racial norm for the racial composition of the faculty was to achieve the same racial composition as was to be found in the student body as a whole. This was called the *Singleton* rule from a case by that name (*Singleton v. Jackson Mun.Sep.Sch.Dist.*, 419 F.2d 1211, 5CA, 1969). Later, the Supreme Court decided that the correct statistical measure of a violation of Title VII is the relation between the racial composition of the school district's staff and that of the relevant labor market (*Hazelwood Sch.Dist. v. U.S.*, 433 U.S. 299, Mo. 1977). The relevant labor market differs from area to area, but generally a metropolitan area including the inner city and the suburban schools must be taken together in answering the question of whether a district's faculty is indeed integrated.

Q. WHAT ARE THE TRENDS IN STAFFING THE PUBLIC SCHOOLS?

A. The nation's 2.2 million elementary and secondary teachers are younger and better educated than ever before, but less satisfied with their choice of a career and the support they receive from school administrators. The average age for teachers dropped from forty-one in 1961 to thirty-three in 1976, the lowest ever. During this time, the collective experience of teachers dropped from an average of twelve years to ten years of experience. Only about half of those who graduate as teachers each year are able to find jobs as teachers. Non-degree teachers have all but disappeared from the scene, while the proportion with master's degrees rose to thirty-seven percent. About six out of ten say they will remain until retirement, while five percent plan to leave as soon as they can. Only three out of eight say they would certainly teach again if they had the choice to make, a decrease from fifty-four percent in 1966. Further information is to be found in NEA's *Status of the American Public School Teacher 1975-76.*

Q. MAY TWO PERSONS OF THE SAME SEX LEGALLY MARRY?

A. The courts have not permitted interpretation of marriage to mean two persons of the same sex. In *Jones v. Hallahan* (501 S.W.2d 588, Ky., 1973), the court held that such a union was not a "marriage" even though the couple pled religious freedom as their rationale. "This would make professed doctrine superior to the law of the land and in effect to permit every citizen to become a law unto himself," said the court. However, such a marriage would not constitute grounds for dismissal of a teacher unless the publicity surrounding it had ruined the effectiveness of the teacher as a teacher. (See *McConnell v. Anderson,* 451 F.2d 193, 8CA, 1971; cert. denied, 405 U.S. 1046, 1972, where a male librarian who sought to marry another man was precluded from employment with the University of Minnesota because his campaign as an activist homosexual had embarrassed the university.)

Q. IF I AM CONVINCED THE DISTRICT IS DOING SOMETHING WHICH DEPRIVES ME OF MY CIVIL RIGHTS, WHAT SHOULD I DO?

A. There are many avenues open. One is to contact your own teacher's organization which represents teachers in your district. They may support you in filing a grievance. Another way is to go directly to the state's civil rights commission (it will be listed in the telephone directory). They will make an investigation of the charge, then, if grounds are found for supposing that you are indeed being denied a civil right, they will mediate between you and your employer seeking to settle the condition found. If the employer still is adamant, they have the power to hold a hearing and execute a cease and desist order. Another way is to file suit in a federal district court. But this latter way is costly, takes time, and the loser pays the costs of the action. In any event, you should have legal counsel since the federal equal employment opportunity maze is a veritable thicket. One who is not familiar with it is easily lost.

Resolution of Cases in Point

Case No. 1 — LETTER TO THE EDITOR

The Supreme Court of the United States ordered the teacher reinstated. Although the teacher had some of the facts mixed up, the board had not proved that the letter was "detrimental to the best interests of the schools," the grounds on which it had based dismissal. Quoting from an earlier Supreme Court case, the Court reiterated that "the theory that public employment which may be denied altogether may be subjected to any conditions, regardless of how unreasonable, has been uniformly rejected." One does not become a second-class citizen merely because he works for the government. And a board may not retaliate against an exercise of First Amendment rights by denying employment to a teacher even though he may have some of his facts wrong unless it can prove that he acted with malicious intent to harm (*Pickering v. Board of Education,* 88 S.Ct. 1731, Ill. 1968).

Case No. 2 — PREGNANCY LEAVE

The board's policy was held by the Supreme Court to deny "freedom of personal choice in matters of marriage and family life" and was based on a false premise — that all female pregnant teachers are disabled and so must take leave without pay (*Cleveland Bd. of Educ. v. LaFleur; Cohen v. Chesterfield Co. Sch. Bd.,* 414 U.S. 632, 1974). The Court did hold, however, that a board would be within its rights in requiring a doctor's certificate of fitness for the job. To hold that every woman who is pregnant becomes unable to teach is "an irrebuttable presumption of physical incompetency," and is a form of sex discrimination which violates the due process clause of the Fourteenth Amendment. "The Court recognizes higher values than speed and efficiency," said the Court. "Administrative convenience alone is insufficient to make valid what otherwise is a violation of due process of law."

Case No. 3 — THE UNION FOREVER

The court upheld the teachers, saying that they had been denied due process in the board's failure to provide them with a due process hearing before termination. The jury found that their non-renewal had in fact been necessitated by budgetary reductions and not on account of exercising their constitutional right to freedom of association. But the courts would not grant reinstatement, instead remanding the case to the lower court with directions that it determine the damages fairly attributable to the failure of the board to afford Peters and Epperson their Fourteenth Amendment right to a pre-termination hearing (*Unified School Dist. No. 480 v. Epperson,* 551 F.2d 254 10CA, 1977).

Case No. 4 — NEVER WAIVER

The teacher lost. By failing to appear at a hearing which she had requested, she had waived her right, said the court, to a hearing (*McCullough v. Bd. of Trustees of North Panola Consol. School Dist.,* 424 F.Supp. 616 Miss., 1976).

Case No. 5 — AH, COMMUNAL LIVING!

Although the court upheld the right of the school board to hire and fire, it cautioned the board that its discretion in such matters is not unlimited. The standards that boards use in the evaluation of prospective teachers must be reasonably related to teaching competency and effectiveness and must be applied in a uniform fashion. The board's interest in keeping farm residents out of the school system was not more compelling than protection of the teacher's right to free association. She was not entitled to back pay, but was granted attorney's fees plus the offer of a job (*Doherty v. Wilson,* 356 F.Supp. 35 Ga., 1973).

Chapter Three: Student Discipline and Control

Historians have neglected children in writing their record of mankind's accomplishments; only in the last half-century have psychologists undertaken a systematic study of the young.

When the history of childhood is finally written, it will be no pretty picture. Heartlessness, starving, beating, solitary confinement — these and other instances of man's inhumanity to children have made this history a nightmare. It has been only since the early 1950's that any serious attempt has been made to remove the stigma which has traditionally attached to being a child. Once started, the movement toward freedom for children accelerated, so that one may now say that children have moved from a position as *chattels* to *persons* in our time.

This chapter is about how a single class of individuals, namely the nation's children, has, since 1954 (*Brown v. Board of Education of Topeka,* 347 U.S. 483, Kans., 1954), won undreamed of freedom both in and out of school. So far-reaching has been the civil rights movement as it affects children that teachers now must know with some certainty what they can and cannot do with the children under their care and supervision. Because teachers as a class have also won important civil rights, the problem becomes one of how two liberated groups can live together in harmony under the same roof.

Curiously, the Supreme Court has continued the Ichabod Crane image of teaching by upholding the right of the teacher, using reasonable force, to administer corporal punishment without first providing due process of law. That leaves the public schools as the last bastion of the idea that children are born in sin (a la Calvin), that is that parent and teacher must literally "beat the Devil out of them, or suffer the decline of all future generations of adults."

In effect, despite the liberating influences of such ideas as progressive education, child psychology, and the concept that school should be fun, the fact remains that the nation is divided into two opposing camps with respect to how children should be disciplined and controlled.

On the conservative side are those who say, "Clamp down," "run a tight ship," "get back to the fundamental values." Proponents of more repression of children point to rising crime rates, vandalism in schools, and a lack of respect for others as evidence that children must be "broken" before they can be led. At the other extreme are others — perhaps a majority of the populace — who recommend giving children all the freedom they can safely handle. The federal courts have joined this latter group, holding in 1969 that "children are 'persons' under our Constitution, and do not shed their constitutional rights at the schoolhouse gate" (*Tinker v. Des Moines School Board,* 393 U.S. 503, Iowa, 1969).

Yet the Supreme Court has steadfastly refused to deny school officials the right to use corporal punishment, "the rod," in running their schools. The remedy if punishment is excessive, say the courts, is in an action for recovery of damages where injuries occur. More will be said on this topic in Chapter 4, "Teacher Liability for Pupil Injury."

It seems evident that the best solution in raising children is not more repression or more freedom but a proper balancing of both these elements within the school setting. School officials must maintain sufficient law and order so that instruction is not hindered. But students should likewise be allowed to enjoy certain freedoms within the school — freedoms of expression, religion, right to due process, to petition the government for a redress of grievances, and the right to peaceably assemble. It is this "razor's edge," with the interests of the state on the one side and the individual citizen on the other, that becomes the focus of our inquiry in this chapter. In effect, we are trying to achieve "attainment of freedom for the individual" at the same time that we are hoping to accomplish "containment of the awesome power of the government." That this is not an easy task goes without saying.

Here are five cases which illustrate the dilemma. After you have read and discussed the cases, turn to the end of this chapter to find out how the courts ruled in each instance.

Cases in Point

Case No. 1 — CORPORAL PUNISHMENT

A teacher in North Carolina administered a mild paddling to a sixth grader. The boy's mother argued that the state statute empowering school officials to "use reasonable force in the exercise of lawful authority to restrain or correct pupils and to maintain order" was unconstitutional insofar as it allowed corporal punishment over parental objection. A federal district court had the case. Do you feel that, despite protestations from the American Civil Liberties Union, child psychologists and others, the state should be free to employ corporal punishment at the judgment of the teacher and principal? If so, should teachers who paddle students first follow the dictates of due process of law, which would be necessary under the Constitution if the child had "a legitimate interest in avoiding unnecessary or arbitrary infliction of a punishment"? And finally, what relief has the student who has been *excessively* punished?

Case No. 2 — EXPULSION

What started out as a prank to spike the punch at a school function turned out to be a major Supreme Court case. Three sophomore girls admitted they mixed malt liquor, fruit juices, and water to make the punch served at a meeting. The board had a rule that intoxicating beverages could not be served at school affairs and expelled the girls for three months. Even though the girls admitted their misdoing, they maintained that they had been denied due process of law and sued the board. They also claimed that school board members, as individuals, are not immune from liability under the Civil Rights Act of 1871, which says that "any person . . . who deprives another . . . of a civil right shall be liable to the party injured in an action at law, suit in equity or other proper proceedings for redress." Were the girls denied due process of law, and may school board members, as individuals, be held personally liable when they deprive someone of a civil right?

Case No. 3 — SUSPENSION

Ohio had a law permitting principals to suspend a student for up to ten days without a hearing. During racial tensions in the Columbus schools, several students were suspended without advance notice of the charges against them and without affording them the opportunity to defend themselves. Dwight Lopez and others brought an action to test the validity of the Ohio statute. The case finally reached the Supreme Court. Do students facing suspension have interests qualifying for protection of the due process clause of the Fourteenth Amendment? If so, what are the minimal requirements in order to meet due process guarantees? Is ten days too long a period of time to be out of school? Is the right to go to school a "property" right for which due process is required?

Case No. 4 — COMPULSORY ATTENDANCE

An Amish farmer in Wisconsin sought to have his son, who had passed the eighth grade but was under sixteen, exempted from the compulsory attendance law which required children to attend school until they reached the age of sixteen. Yoder gave as his reasons that the Amish do not believe in high schools and that further knowledge of "the world" would cause his son to reject the rural life espoused by that religious belief. Also, he feared censure by the elders of his religion as well as loss of salvation for his son. The Supreme Court had twice upheld compulsory attendance laws as being in the interest and within the competency of the state. Should the state's interest in an enlightened citizenry transcend the right of a parent to decide what type of education he wants for that child? Did the Wisconsin law invade the right of the parent to "free exercise of religion"? If one parent is allowed to avoid compulsory attendance laws, will there not be others who will attempt to do so on "religious" grounds?

Case No. 5 — EXCLUSION

A high school senior was excluded from spring baseball under a board rule excluding married high school students from participation in extra-curricular activities. He was an honor student, an excellent baseball player, and a good prospect for an athletic scholarship in several colleges. In the past, many state courts had upheld board rules of this kind. The boy, however, claimed a constitutional question (invasion of his marital privacy rights) and sought relief from the federal district court. The board defended itself on the grounds that it intended the rule to discourage teenage marriages and that the boy was not excluded from regular classes, only extra-curricular activities. He could go to classes, and could and did graduate with his class. Did the board overreach its authority? Is baseball an important part of high school? Did the board's action put an unendurable strain on the marriage? Does one have a constitutional right to engage in extra-curricular activities?

The *In Loco Parentis* Doctrine

Q. WHAT IS MEANT BY THE TERM "STUDENT DISCIPLINE AND CONTROL"?

A. There is no specific meaning in the law for the term "student discipline and control." Historically, it meant that the teacher stood *in loco parentis* (i.e. in the place of the parent) to the child and had the same rights to regulate the student's behavior as the average parent would under similar circumstances. But in a more permissive setting, regulatory teacher actions have given way to attempts to help students participate in making decisions affecting their lives in school. Students in school are "persons" under the Constitution, and do not shed their rights to constitutional guarantees at the schoolhouse gate, said the Supreme Court in *Tinker v. Des Moines* (393 U.S. 503, Iowa, 1969). With this new dimension, students now often take the teacher to court to let the court determine just how much authority school officials can exercise without infringing upon the constitutional rights of children.

Q. WHERE DID THE DOCTRINE OF *IN LOCO PARENTIS* ORIGINATE?

A. Greek slave teachers were used by Roman parents to instruct their young. Because the master must outrank his student, the legal fiction of *in loco parentis* was invented and has come down to us through the British system of education. William Blackstone advised that "a parent may delegate part of his parental authority, during his life, to the tutor or schoolmaster of his child; who is then *in loco parentis,* and has. . .a portion of the power of the parent, viz.,. . .restraint and correction, as may be necessary to answer the purposes for which he is employed" (*Blackstone's Commentaries,* p. 453). The key to the law is the last part of that quotation: *as may be necessary to answer the purpose for which he is employed.* This means that the teacher does not have absolute control over the student, but only over his educational needs while in school.

Q. WHAT IS MEANT LEGALLY BY THE TERM "RESTRAINT AND CORRECTION AS MAY BE NECESSARY TO ANSWER THE PURPOSES FOR WHICH THE TEACHER IS EMPLOYED"?

A. It means that the teacher is entitled to use the force necessary to get the job done. Frank Rolando, a sixth-grade teacher in Oglesby, Ill. had trouble maintaining order. His students would not remain in their seats, they made noises — at times standing on their desks and screaming — and they threw paper wads, pencils, and erasers. Rolando told the parents but nothing happened. He asked the principal what to do. She said, "Handle it the best way you know how." So that's just what Rolando did. He went to a specialty store and bought a two-foot electric cattle prod. When one of the frisky little calves misbehaved: Zap! He gave him a goose which those who were so goosed described as making them "shaky," or "it stung." Word got around that Rolando was administering cruel and inhuman treatment to his students. He was dismissed. Undaunted, he brought an action for reinstatement. The court upheld the teacher — there was no permanent injury, and it worked. Would a hickory stick have been any better? The board should thank him, not fire him, said the judge (*Rolando v. Sch. Directors,* 358 N.E.2d 945, Ill., 1976).

Q. DOES THE *IN LOCO PARENTIS* DOCTRINE IMPOSE LIABILITIES ON TEACHERS?

A. Yes. The doctrine has two sides. One side of the coin is labeled "rights," the other side "liabilities." Since the public school teacher is a foster parent standing in place of the natural parent, he or she has certain privileges — to direct the child's learning experiences, in short, to exercise the control and discipline over the child which the average, normally prudent parent would exercise under similar conditions. But the other side of the coin imposes certain responsibilities upon the teacher. The child is expected to be in a safe place, is expected to learn something while under the teacher's care and supervision, and is entitled to the protection of his constitutional rights while in the teacher's care. This side of the coin, which relates to negligence and deprivation of civil rights of the student by teachers will be more fully covered in Chapter 4.

Q. DOES THE PARENT RETAIN CONTROL OVER CERTAIN AREAS OF THE CHILD'S LIFE?

A. Yes. Even though the child is in school, the parent still retains three very important prerogatives: 1) to determine which religion if any the child shall embrace; 2) to say who shall treat him medically; and 3) to guard against invasions of his inner mind. Thus, the parent still retains substantial control over the child: his soul, his body, and his mind. This leaves the teacher with only that part of the child's life which the state considers essential to his becoming a good citizen, i.e., his educational needs. Because children who are taught to behave well learn better, it is then the teacher's prerogative to expect him to conduct himself in a peaceable manner, to show respect for the teacher and others, and to apply himself to his learning duties as best he can. If he does not do so, the teacher, like the parent, may apply measures to attain these objectives the same as the normally prudent parent would apply under the circumstances.

Q. IN WHAT WAY HAS THE LAW PROTECTED THE PARENT'S RIGHT TO CONTROL HIS CHILD'S RELIGIOUS UPBRINGING?

A. In 1925, the Supreme Court held that the parent has the right to decide whether to send his child to public or private schools (*Society of Sisters v. Pierce,* 45 S.Ct. 571, Oregon, 1925). In 1943, the Court ruled that students who object to saluting the flag because of religious reasons may not be expelled for refusal to salute the flag (*W.Va.St.Bd. of Educ. v. Barnette,* 319 U.S. 624, 1943). Children may be released from school to attend religious instruction of their choice (*Zorach v. Clauson,* 343 U.S. 306, N.Y., 1952). In 1962 and 1963, the Court held that no state, board of regents, or school board may compose a prayer and require it be recited as a part of the school day (*Engel v. Vitale,* 370 U.S. 421, N.Y. 1962; *Abington Twp. v. Schempp* [Pa.] and *Murray v. Curlett,* 83 S.Ct. 1560, Md., 1963). And in 1968, the Court ruled that no state may limit its teaching of science to that theory of the origin of man contained in the Book of Genesis (*Epperson v. Arkansas*, 393 U.S. 97, 1968).

Q. IN WHAT RESPECT IS PARENTAL CONTROL OVER MEDICAL ATTENTION CONTROLLED BY LAW?

A. The Supreme Court twice held that compulsory vaccination required by state or local officials was not unconstitutional (*Jacobson v. Massachusetts*, 197 U.S. 11, Mass., 1905; *Zucht v. King*, 260 U.S. 174, Texas, 1922). Nor does the absence of an epidemic for the past fifty years bar the state's right to work for a disease-free populace. (*Wright v. DeWitt School Dist.*, 385 S.W.2d 644, Ark., 1965). Most school districts have forms for parents to fill out designating whom to call when the child is in need of medical attention. Aside from vaccination, the school usually recognizes the right of parents to decide who shall attend to their child's medical needs. In the absence of the parent or guardian, teachers may administer first aid only to an injured or sick child, but are held personally liable should their aid cause further injury.

Q. TO WHAT EXTENT MAY PARENTS BLOCK IN-DEPTH TESTING WHICH INVADES THE INNER MIND OF THE CHILD?

A. School psychologists need not obtain prior parental consent to administer school tests which do not probe deeply into the inner mind of the child. They are expected, however, to obtain parental permission where in-depth testing is to take place. Failure to do so may result in an action for invasion of the child's privacy.

Some states have enacted legislation outlining the extent to which the school may administer brain-probing tests. In the absence of such a statute, it is wise to work closely with parents in administering psychiatric or other in-depth tests because of the legal hazards involved.

Q. MAY THE PARENTS EDUCATE THEIR OWN CHILD AT HOME?

A. There seems to be a growing tendency on the part of the courts to permit parents wider latitude in educating their own children at home. Ordinarily, the parent must demonstrate that the child is receiving an education "equivalent" to that he/she would receive if attending the public schools. (*Scoma v. Chicago Bd. of Educ.*, 391 F.Supp. 452, Ill., 1974.) Some states have legislation controlling home instruction, and permit parents to teach their youngsters even though they are not certified teachers; others prohibit such a practice. The lack of peer contact for the child may not be considered in determining equivalency, nor may the reasons why parents want to keep their children at home be inquired into. You should become familiar with the laws of your state governing home instruction to make sure that parents are not needlessly prosecuted for non-compliance with the compulsory attendance statute. The state's interests in an enlightened citizenry must be balanced with the parents' interests in the upbringing of their progeny.

Q. DOES THE *IN LOCO PARENTIS* DOCTRINE PROTECT THE TEACHER OR PRINCIPAL WHO PLACES CHILDREN IN VARIOUS STUDY GROUPS OR CLASSES FOR STUDY PURPOSES?

A. The law recognizes the need to separate children into groups for instructional purposes so long as there is no discriminatory action on the part of school officials. You must be prepared, however, to prove that what you are doing in separating children into groups does not create a stigma which will stay with the child, that will discriminate against him on account of race, sex, religion, language or nation of origin, or that will deprive the child of a civil right. This is not always an easy burden, but school districts have now adopted due process procedures, and the special-education, handicapped children's program has done a lot to provide the protection school personnel need in order to avoid legal pitfalls in the placement of children.

Q. WHAT IS THE CLASSIC SUPREME COURT CASE INVOLVING STIGMATIZING ONE'S GOOD NAME WITHOUT DUE PROCESS OF LAW?

A. Parents and others who claim that a child has been stigmatized because of his placement in a group at school often quote *Wisconsin v. Constantineau* (400 U.S. 433, 1971). A Wisconsin law required the posting in taverns and packaged liquor stores of the names of "problem drinkers" without a hearing first on the merits. The Supreme Court held that the State of Wisconsin denied such persons procedural due process of law by posting their names in public view, and that the stigma that attached thereby might stay with a person permanently. The statute was therefore declared to be unconstitutional.

Q. WHAT TYPES OF GROUPING PATTERNS HAVE BEEN DECLARED UNCONSTITUTIONAL ON THE GROUND THAT THEY TEND TO DENY CHILDREN THEIR CIVIL RIGHTS?

A. In *Hobson v. Hansen* (269 F.Supp. 501, D.C., 1967), the court held a "tracking" plan in use in the District of Columbia locked-in some children and prejudiced some school personnel against them. Tracking itself is not illegal; what is illegal is grouping which denies due process of law or tends to stigmatize a student. In some instances, boys and girls may be separated for instructional purposes but there are no longer boys' and girls' courses. Any grouping pattern which results in a high proportion of any racial minority being lumped together may also be "suspect," and subject to explanation by the district (*Larry P. v. Riles,* 502 F.2d 963, 9th CA, 1974). And the Buckley Amendment directs that pupil records shall be open to inspection by parents or students eighteen years old or over.

Q. MAY PUPILS BE EXCLUDED FROM SCHOOL BECAUSE THEY ARE HANDICAPPED?

A. No. Beginning with the PARC case in 1972, the courts have uniformly upheld the right of a handicapped pupil to be admitted to the public schools no matter how severe the handicap (*Pennsylvania Association for Retarded Children v. Commonwealth,* 343 F.Supp. 279, Pa., 1972). "All mentally retarded persons are capable of benefitting from a program of education or training," said the court in a consent decree. "Placement in a regular classroom in public school is preferable to placement in a special education class, and placement in a special public school class is preferable to placement in any other type of program of education and training. And any district which provides free preschooling to normal children under six is prohibited from denying such schooling to retarded children under age six." A similar ruling was made in *Mills v. Bd. of Educ. of D. of C.* (348 F.Supp. 866, D.C., 1972).

Q. WHAT IS "FUNCTIONAL EXCLUSION" OF A CHILD IN SCHOOL?

A. The term was coined by civil rights lawyers to denote a condition where the child is physically present in the classroom yet is unable to profit from the environment in which he has been placed. Courts are now holding that the district is under an affirmative duty to place the child in the best environment for that particular child — in effect, giving the child the right to his or her own individual program of study. Nor may the district plead that it has no program nor any money to found one. The child is also entitled to "mainstreaming" which means that except for certain kinds of specialized handicaps, the child is entitled to be in the regular classroom at least a part of the day. Although special "adjustment" classes are legally possible, these assignments must not become permanent. The schools may test children, but the tests must meet certain very rigid constitutional standards before being accepted by the courts.

Q. WHAT FOUR HURDLES MUST THE TESTS CLEAR IN ORDER TO BE CONSIDERED CONSTITUTIONAL?

A. In *Griggs v. Duke Power Co.* (401 U.S. 424, 1971), the Supreme Court dealt with the problem of pre-employment tests. The standards applied there have now been transferred to educational problems. To meet constitutional constraints, the schools must: 1) show that the test being used has *differential* validity, that is, it has separate validation scores for all minorities on which it is used; 2) bring the level of confidence up to the .05 level, which is the same as saying that the probability of obtaining the same test results through mere chance must be no greater than one in twenty; 3) demonstrate that the testing procedure contains an adequate sample; and 4) demonstrate that the test has been administered to all testees under uniform testing conditions which correlate with the test conditions under which the test was validated.

Q. MAY A TEACHER INCUR CIVIL RIGHTS DAMAGES BECAUSE HE/SHE STANDS *IN LOCO PARENTIS?*

A. Yes. Although remote, there is that possibility. Liability attaches where anyone acting as an agent of the state and under color of state law does know or reasonably should know that he or she is depriving a student of a civil right. In *Wood v. Strickland* (95 S.Ct. 992, Ark., 1975), the Supreme Court held that school "officials" may be held personally liable under the Civil Rights Act of 1871 (42 U.S.C., Sec. 1983). If a teacher knew of child abuse, for example, and failed to report such to the proper authorities, liability might accrue on the grounds that his or her role as a child advocate was not being sufficiently played. The first type of damages may occur where civil rights are denied; the second type of damages (liability for negligence where a child is injured) will be more fully discussed in Chapter 4.

Q. MAY TEACHERS CONTROL THE APPEARANCE OF THEIR PUPILS?

A. Yes. Such a right comes with the *in loco parentis* role. Scores of court cases recently have dealt with student appearance, particularly with long hair for boys. In *Leonard v. School Comm. of Attleboro* (349 Mass. 704, 212 N.E.2d 468, 1965), the court held that a school regulation on hair length for boys did not invade the domain of family privacy as charged by the parent. About half the 100-plus cases on boys' hair have upheld school regulations, while the other half have been won by parents. The difference seems to be in whether a board can demonstrate that as a matter of fact, wearing long hair by boys resulted in disruption of the school program or was dangerous, as in shop classes. Many of the courts following 1969 have cited *Tinker v. Des Moines,* in which it was ruled by the Supreme Court that students in school may not be punished for communications "akin to pure speech," such as wearing black armbands in school or other forms of symbolic speech, in the absence of substantial disruption of the academic program of the school.

Student Discipline and Control

Q. OF THE MAJOR PROBLEMS CONFRONTING THE PUBLIC SCHOOLS WHICH ONE IS MENTIONED MOST FREQUENTLY?

A. The Fourteenth Annual Gallup Poll of the Public's Attitude Toward the Public Schools (1982) reports that "lack of discipline" was cited by more respondents than any other problem as their most pressing concern. (Lack of financial support gained most in mentions over the previous year.) Also prominently listed in the survey were items akin to discipline, such as the use of drugs (third), truancy (eighth), parents' lack of interest (ninth), crime/vandalism (twelfth), and drinking and alcoholism (thirteenth). Overall, slightly more than one-third of the respondents gave the schools A or B, while one-sixth gave the public schools a rating of D or Fail.

Q. WHAT ARE THE MAIN REASONS WHY TEACHERS ARE LEAVING THEIR JOBS?

A. The 1982 Gallup Poll discovered that the public gives "discipline problems in the schools" as the major reason why teachers are leaving their classrooms for other pursuits. The reason selected by the next highest number of respondents was "low teacher salaries," followed in turn by "students are unmotivated/ uninterested in school." It takes no Solomon to conclude that teacher burnout is caused in large part by problems of pupil discipline and control, the subject of this chapter.

Q. MAY THE CHILD BE PUNISHED FOR THE ACTS OF HIS PARENT?

A. No, apparently not. Eartha St. Ann, a mother, belted the assistant principal, and the Orleans (La.) Parish School Board successfully prosecuted her for assault and battery. However, when the school suspended her two children for her behavior, Mrs. St. Ann hired a lawyer and took her case to court. The district had a regulation which provided that children would be liable to suspension or other punishment "should the principal or teacher be called to account or be reproved in an offensive way in the classroom or elsewhere." The court held the rule unconstitutional. "Freedom from punishment in the absence of personal guilt is a fundamental concept in the American scheme of justice," wrote Circuit Judge Walter Pettus Gewin. "To intrude upon this fundamental liberty governments must satisfy a substantial burden of justification. The board has failed to satisfy this requirement" (*St. Ann v. Palisi*, 495 F.2d 423, La., 5CA, 1974).

Q. ARE PARENTS GENERALLY HELD FINANCIALLY LIABLE FOR VANDALISM OF THEIR OWN CHILDREN?

A. No. Studies on school vandalism show that the English law tends to predominate here — that each individual is responsible for his own unlawful acts. Attempts to make parents legally liable for misconduct of their children have not met with outstanding success. One deterrent to such legislation is that it places a heavy burden on low-income families. Another bar is that it would place stress and strain on families where relationships are already tense and might even give troublesome delinquents a weapon against their parents which they would not hesitate to use (See Michael Severino, *School Vandalism: Legal Implications*, Denver, Unpublished Ed.D. dissertation, University of Denver, 1971.)

Q. SHOULD TEACHERS BE MADE LEGALLY ACCOUNTABLE FOR THE LEARNING OF CHILDREN IN SCHOOL?

A. Organizations of teachers have uniformly resisted such an accountability system, in part because of widespread disagreement over what yardstick should measure teacher competence. Many of the problems that children have in school are traceable to lack of home support of the educational enterprise, and there is also some question about the efficacy of testing instruments. Some educators say that testing is an unfair and simplistic means of finding out what a student has learned and what a teacher has taught. In *Scheelhaase v. Woodbury Community School District* (488 F.2d 237, 8CA, 1973), a teacher was legally fired where her students' low achievement scores were used as the basis for her dismissal. The Eighth Circuit Court of Appeals held that such action by the board did not violate her substantive due process rights, and upheld the board's action.

Q. DO SOME STATES HAVE "MINIMUM COMPETENCY TESTING REQUIREMENTS" FOR GRADUATION FROM HIGH SCHOOL?

A. Yes. However, lengthy court battles have ensued on whether these tests are "curriculum related." In Florida, white students failed the tests at a 1.9 per cent rate while 20.0 per cent of blacks failed it. A class action suit was filed alleging multiple due process violations. *(Debra P. v. Turlington,* 644 F.2d 397, 5CA 1981) While a competency test has a "rational relation to a valid state interest," the court decided that the record "is simply insufficient in proof that the test administered measures what was actually taught in the schools of Florida," and stayed use of the test for four years. Similarly, other tests being used challenged the court *(Anderson v. Banks,* 520 F.Supp. 472, S.D.Ga. 1981) *(Bd. of Educ. v. Ambach,* 436 N.Y.S.2d 564, N.Y. 1981).

Q. IS DETENTION A LEGALLY ACCEPTABLE MEANS OF CONTROLLING STUDENTS?

A. Yes. The courts have upheld reasonable detention of students, nor has there been a ruling that students must be given due process of law before detention is imposed. In Nebraska, students objected to a school rule specifying periods of detention after school for unexcused absenteeism and tardiness on the grounds that the rule was "unconstitutionally vague," hence unenforceable. The court could not agree (*Fielder v. Bd. of Education,* 346 F.Supp. 722, Nebr., 1972). No constitutional issue is at stake in detaining a child in order to make up for lost time, said the court.

Q. MAY A TEACHER OR PRINCIPAL SEARCH A STUDENT TO DISCOVER STOLEN ARTICLES?

A. It all depends. A dime was missing from the classroom; Billy Marlar, eleven, had violated a school rule by returning to the room during recess. He denied taking the dime, so the teacher searched his pockets not so much to find the missing dime as to vindicate the boy from suspicion. In an action for assault and battery, the court upheld the teacher's action (*Marlar v. Bill,* 178

S.W.2d 634, Tenn., 1944). However, where a policewoman called by the principal to find a girl's stolen ring had the girls strip down to their bras and panties, the court held that school officials could be held liable only if "they participated with the police in taking actions, or if the evidence establishes an understanding and agreement between school officials and the police to deny plaintiffs their constitutional rights" (*Potts v. Wright*, 357 F.Supp. 215, Pa., 1973).

Q. MAY A TEACHER OR PRINCIPAL SEARCH A STUDENT FOR SUSPECTED CONTRABAND?

A. Only when there is reason to believe that the student has contraband concealed on his person, or where there is justifiable "plain view" cause. The Georgia Supreme Court refused to suppress, in a pending criminal prosecution, evidence of possession of marijuana found upon a student by an assistant principal conducting a personal search, not without cause but with less than enough cause for a search warrant required of a law enforcement officer (*State v. Young*, 216 S.E.2d 586, 1976). And seizure of exposed leaflets which contained false information that classes were cancelled was held justified where they were in plain view and seizure did not abridge the student's constitutional rights (*Speake v. Grantham*, 317 F.Supp. 1253, Miss., 1970). Also, where a principal was informed by the chief of police that certain students would be carrying marijuana into school, the principal was within his rights in searching them bodily for suspected contraband (*State v. McKinnon*, 558 P.2d 781, Wash., 1977).

Q. MAY A TEACHER OR PRINCIPAL SEARCH A STUDENT'S LOCKER WITHOUT A WARRANT?

A. Yes. The courts have held that the principal not only has the right but the duty to see that student lockers, which belong to the school and are rented to students, are free from contraband. Evidence obtained in this way is admissible in court even though the principal does not have a warrant. The *in loco parentis* doctrine protects school personnel from liability for an illegal search since it is their duty to protect other students from dangerous drugs, liquor, or explosives (*In re Donaldson*, 269 ACA

593, Calif., 1969; *State v. Stein*, 456 P.2d 1, Kans., 1969). In *Stein*, the Kansas Supreme Court held that although a student may have control of his school locker as against fellow students, he does not have exclusive control as against the school and its personnel, which includes, presumably, teachers.

Q. DO SCHOOL PERSONNEL HAVE THE RIGHT TO SEARCH STUDENT AUTOMOBILES?

A. No, not without a warrant, unless, of course, some contraband is in "plain sight." Even though the student's car is in the school parking lot, it is private property and a warrant must be issued before it can be searched. But if there is probable cause to suspect something (car is weaving; it is a stolen car; car seems central to suspected drug traffic), a warrantless search may be permitted. The Fourth Amendment does not outlaw all searches, only *unreasonable* searches and seizures. In one instance, a student was driving without a license, whereupon the police searched the vehicle and found dangerous drugs. The Supreme Court upheld (6-3) the search as constitutionally sound. "If there is probable cause to take a person into custody," said Justice William Rehnquist for the majority, "the fact of lawful arrest establishes the authority to search." However, since school personnel ordinarily do not make arrests (but can make a citizen's arrest under extreme circumstances), searching a student's car usually requires a valid search warrant.

Q. WHAT DETERMINES WHETHER THE TEACHER WILL BE PROTECTED UNDER THE *IN LOCO PARENTIS* DOCTRINE WHEN TAKING ACTION IN SEARCH AND SEIZURE CASES?

A. The teacher may play three roles: 1) as the teacher, standing *in loco parentis*, for which there is an immunity granted by the common law; 2) as a private citizen, for whom a warrant to search is needed; and 3) as a state agent, acting under color of state law, or willfully participating with the police in joint activity (*Potts v. Wright* 357 F.Supp. 215, Pa., 1973), where the principal and assistant principal were bound over to the jury because they took part in a "strip" search of girls who were suspected of stealing a ring. See also *U.S. v. Price* (383 U.S. 787, 1966), where the court held that "it is enough (to have action under color of state law) that the defendant is a willful participant in joint activity with the State and its agents." It is the nature of the act taken by school officials and not the status of the person as a state official which provides the element of "under color of state law." You should therefore protect the child's interests at all times to act out your role as the foster parent acting *in loco parentis*.

Q. DO SCHOOL PERSONNEL GENERALLY HAVE A GREATER AUTHORITY TO CONDUCT SEARCHES OF STUDENTS THAN OTHER GOVERNMENTAL AGENTS?

A. Yes. The *in loco parentis* doctrine protects the teacher or principal in that he or she is standing in place of the parent. It would be for the jury to decide whether the teacher acted as the normally prudent parent would act in similar circumstances. But where the teacher steps outside this protection, and becomes in effect a state agent seeking evidence on which to convict the student, he or she must become subject to the due process and the illegal searches and seizures sections of the U.S. Constitution. The courts will make a careful analysis of the factors that justify school searches on less than probable cause: child's age, history, and record in school, prevalence and seriousness of the drug traffic in the building, and, of course, the exigency to make the search without delay (*People v. D.*, 358 N.Y.S.2d 403, N.Y., 1974).

Q. MAY A STUDENT BE REQUIRED TO EMPTY HIS POCKETS?

A. The courts are not in agreement on this point. In Texas, a principal got a tip that a student was in possession of marijuana. Calling the boy into his office, the principal requested him to empty his pockets; upon being informed that his father would be called if he did not comply, the boy complied. The procedure produced two marijuana cigarettes, marijuana and some marijuana seed. No force was used and the father later said he would have done the same (*Mercer v. State of Texas*, 450 S.W.2d 715, 1970). The court allowed the search on the ground that the principal is responsible for discovering and bringing under control drug traffic in the school. But where a uniformed school security officer who was searching for a stolen watch asked a boy to empty his pockets, the court held he had insufficient cause to search the boy and evidence obtained thereby (drugs) was not admissible in court (*People v. Bowers*, 339 N.Y.S.2d 783, 1973).

Q. MAY A STUDENT'S GRADES BE LOWERED AS PUNISHMENT FOR MISBEHAVIOR NOT OF AN ACADEMIC NATURE?

A. Courts are hesitant to review a teacher's decision whether a student deserves a better grade unless the student can prove that a lower grade was given for a non-academic reason. In one instance, a teacher was overheard to say that a certain student in his class would not get a passing grade no matter how hard he tried. The court was sympathetic to the student's plea for relief. Continued absence as it relates to low grades cannot bring an automatic penalty, such as "each day missed is a zero," since there may be extenuating circumstances which the student is entitled to tell to the teacher. Any "blanket" lowering of grades without chance to be heard is "suspect" and open to court challenge. A student's rights are prejudiced where he is given a zero for truancy and then given a make-up test, but the zero is weighed against the result (*Minorics v. Bd. of Educ.*, N.J. Comm. of Educ. Decisions, 1972).

Q. MAY A STUDENT BE PUNISHED FOR KEEPING BAD COMPANY?

A. No. Guilt by association is everywhere repugnant to the Constitution. In Iowa a boy who was riding in a car where beer was being consumed, but who was not himself consuming beer, was declared ineligible for interscholastic athletics under a high school activities association rule to that effect. He challenged the rule as one which featured guilt by association. His challenge was successful. The Iowa Supreme Court held that the rule denied the boy a valuable property right (to participate in athletics) without due process of law (*Bunger v. Iowa H.S. Ath. Assn.*, 197 N.W.2d 555, 1972).

Q. THROUGH WHAT STAGES HAS CORPORAL PUNISHMENT GONE IN PUBLIC SCHOOLS?

A. Under the common law, the teacher could administer reasonable corporal punishment to the student. But when the punishment was unreasonable and excessive, it was no longer lawful and the perpetrator could be held criminally and civilly liable (*Ware v. Estes,* 328 F.Supp. 657, aff'd. 458 F.2d 1360, Tex., 1971). A Pennsylvania federal district court experimented with allowing a parent to veto corporal punishment for his own child, but the decision was overthrown later by the Supreme Court (*Glaser v. Marietta,* 351 F.Supp. 555, Pa., 1972). In *Baker v. Owen* (395 F.Supp. 294, N.C.), which was affirmed by the Supreme Court without comment, the high court ruled that while a parent could not veto corporal punishment for his own child, he was entitled, if he requested it, to a written account of the punishment, together with the name of the adult observer who was present. In *Ingraham v. Wright* (97 S.Ct. 1401, 1977) the Supreme Court held that there was no violation of the Eighth Amendment's bar to cruel and unusual punishment where children in school were spanked, so long as the corporal punishment was reasonable under the circumstances.

Due Process and Equal Protection

Q. DOES THE FOURTEENTH AMENDMENT APPLY TO CHILDREN IN SCHOOL?

A. Yes. The Supreme Court has so ruled. "No state shall make or enforce any law which shall abridge the privileges or immunities of citizens of the United States; nor shall any State deprive any person of life, liberty, or property, without due process of law; nor deny to any person within its jurisdiction the equal protection of the laws." Children are "persons" under our Constitution, and do not shed their constitutional rights at the schoolhouse gate, said the Court in *Tinker v. Des Moines School Board* (393 U.S. 503, Iowa, 1969). Whereas during the first twenty years of the civil rights movement, different classes of individuals gained substantial liberties under the equal protection clause, the emphasis after 1970 has shifted to the due process clause as grounds for challenging what school boards are doing to children.

Q. IS A CHILD ENTITLED TO A FREE EDUCATION BY THE STATE UNDER THE UNITED STATES CONSTITUTION?

A. No. In 1973, the Supreme Court ruled (5-4) that there is no guarantee of equal educational opportunity under the federal Constitution (*San Antonio Indep. School District v. Rodriguez,* 411 U.S. 1, Tx., 1973). If there is a right to a free education at public expense, the parent must look to the state for it, said the Court. Most state constitutions provide for a "thorough and uniform" system of public education, but there is a wide variation in each state on how "equal" education is for each child. Rodriguez, who lived in a poor district, argued that the state denied him equal protection because it spent about half as much per pupil in his district as was being spent by wealthier districts in the same state. But the Court majority held that so long as the Rodriguez' child was receiving the same "minimal" education as other children in the state, he was not being denied equal protection of Texas laws.

Q. WHAT TESTS DOES THE SUPREME COURT USE IN DETERMINING WHETHER A STATE IS DISCRIMINATORY IN ITS PRACTICES TOWARDS CHILDREN?

A. The most severe test used by the Court is the "strict scrutiny" test which assumes that what the state is doing to the child is unconstitutional on its face and calls for the state to justify its actions, a difficult test for states to meet. In *Rodriguez,* the State of Texas admitted that it could not meet such a severe test, and asked the Court to use the "legitimate state interest" test instead, which the majority agreed to use. Under the "legitimate interest" test, the state must show that it is doing something which meets one or more of its legitimate state interests (here the education of its children for adult citizenship). A state is not required by the Constitution to provide free education for its children; when it does so, however, it must be offered to one and all on an equal basis. So long as the Rodriguez child was receiving the minimum "schooling" required of all children, he was not being discriminated against, even though wealthier districts could put the frosting on the cake.

Q. IS THERE A DIFFERENCE BETWEEN "SCHOOLING" AND "EDUCATION"?

A. Yes. In *Rodriguez* the Supreme Court majority held that the student is entitled to that level of educational opportunity (generally referred to as "common schooling") which will help the child perform what is expected of him or her as a citizen of the state: to obey the laws, serve in the armed forces, vote, pay taxes, serve on the jury, and earn a living. In education, promises have outrun performance, so that the public has come to expect an "education" through the university as a birthright of every child. In *Rodriguez,* the Court said each state must decide for itself what it will guarantee as the educational birthright of every child in that particular state. States have found that there is a practical limit to which they can go in affording free education to each child. Reduced to its lowest common denominator, the state's obligation can be as minimal as "schooling," which extends to about the sixth grade.

Q. IF A CHILD DOES NOT LEARN TO READ, CAN THE TEACHERS BE HELD LIABLE?

A. No, not to date. Peter W. Doe, a middle-class white, sued the San Francisco board for one million dollars because he was graduated from high school reading at a fifth-grade level. He charged fraudulent negligence on the part of the district, a tort (actionable wrong not involving breach of contract). His suit was unsuccessful (*Peter W. Doe v. San Francisco Unified Sch.Dist.,* 131 Cal.Rptr. 854, 1976). A similar result was obtained in *Donohue v. Copiague Union Free Schools* (N.Y., 1977). As a result of these cases, many states have enacted minimum competency legislation to stabilize the high school diploma and to set responsibility for educational accountability. The courts have said that with the nation's schools in financial straits, the consequences of a series of damage suits "in terms of public time and money would burden them beyond calculation." A university student was denied return of her tuition because the course was "a dud;" the agreement between a student and a school to provide an education cannot be viewed "in the same light as other consumer purchases," said the judge.

Q. WHAT IS MEANT BY DUE PROCESS OF LAW?

A. The Supreme Court has said that students facing punishment in school have the right to due process of law, without defining such a term in clearly stated rules. Here again the Court is saying that it will proceed on such cases on a case-to-case basis. So there is no overall, unequivocal definition of due process of law. All we can do is read the cases in which due process is the issue and then extrapolate from them what is or is not due process of law in dealing with students in public schools.

Q. WHAT IS THE DIFFERENCE BETWEEN *SUBSTANTIVE AND PROCEDURAL* DUE PROCESS OF LAW?

A. Due process has two dimensions: the substantive or *content* dimension, and procedural or *process* dimension. Under the substantive test, two questions are asked: Was the school rule fair under the circumstances, and did the school rule tend to deny equity to someone? Under the second dimension, procedural due process, the question is: Did the board or its agent(s) proceed with fundamental fairness in its handling of the punishment handed out?

In a suspension case arising in Chicago, the Supreme Court ruled that where a deprivation of a property interest (here the right to go to school) is substantively justified, but procedurally defective, plaintiffs are entitled to recover only nominal damages, usually $1.00 (*Carey v. Piphus,* 435 U.S. 247, 1978) in the absence of proof of actual loss or injury.

Q. UNDER SUBSTANTIVE DUE PROCESS, WHAT IS MEANT BY A *FAIR* RULE?

A. Some school rules are fair under the circumstances, others are not. If the rule itself is not substantively fair under the circumstances, it will be thrown out by the court. In Mississippi, two high schools had identical rules: freedom buttons could not be worn in the school — those who did not remove the buttons were sent home. In one high school, there was disruption, noisy demonstrations, and the end of learning. The court upheld the rule. "School authorities have not only a right but a duty to quell disruptions," said the court (*Blackwell v. Issaquena Co.Bd. of Educ.,* 363 F.2d 749, Miss., 1967). In the other school, there was no disruption. The court held that the rule was unconstitutional since it denied students their right to communicate "a matter of vital public concern," a right protected under the First Amendment.

"The Fourteenth Amendment," said the court, "protects the First Amendment rights of school children against unreasonable rules and regulations imposed by school authorities" (*Burnside v. Byars*, 363 F.2d 744, Miss., 1967).

Q. WHAT IS AN EXAMPLE OF A SCHOOL RULE THAT DENIES EQUITY?

A. Any school rule which discriminates against some persons but not others is unconstitutional, since it denies *treatment as an equal.* (Not the same as equal treatment, however). See page 22, Chapter 1. School rules which limit boys' hair length but not girls' deny equal protection of the laws, hence are devoid of equity (*Crews v. Cloncs*, 432 F.2d 1259, 7CA, 1970; *Dunham v. Pulsifer*, 312 F.Supp. 411, Vt., 1970). And requiring all boys to get their hair cut on the grounds that long hair in shop classes was dangerous militated against those boys who were not enrolled in shop. In Ohio, a federal district court threw out a school rule excluding long-haired males from school band but not girls (*Cordova v. Chonko*, 315 F.Supp. 953, Ohio, 1970). A rule which excluded girls from participating in boys' tennis where the high school had no comparable program for girls was declared to be unconstitutional since it lacked the elements of equity (*Brenden v. Ind.Sch.Dist.* 742, 477 F.2d 1292, Minn., 8CA, 1973).

Q. WHAT FUNDAMENTALLY FAIR PROCEDURE WILL MEET THE STANDARD OF DUE PROCESS OF LAW IN STUDENT DISCIPLINE CASES?

A. The more serious the possible penalty, the more careful must school officials be in providing the student his day in court. Any action by the state or its employees (teachers included) which looks to be arbitrary, capricious, or outside the power of the teacher to promulgate is immediately "suspect," and will raise the concern of a federal judge that someone is being denied a constitutionally guaranteed right. The right to go to school is both a "liberty" and a "property" right protected under the Fourteenth Amendment. Any denial of the right to go to school must be accompanied by a deliberate, fair, impartial hearing before final action is taken to impose the sanction. Lack of this process is interpreted as lack of procedural (as opposed to substantive) due process of law, a right protected under the Fourteenth Amendment. But each case must rest on its own peculiar set of circumstances — the question is did the state act at all times with fundamental fairness?

Q. DOES A STUDENT HAVE THE RIGHT TO A HEARING BEFORE A THREE-DAY SUSPENSION?

A. It all depends. In *Hillman v. Elliott* (426 L.W. 2134, Va., 1977), the court ruled that a student facing suspension has a constitutional interest in his good name and reputation. "A suspension is noted on a child's school records, and these records are often used by potential employers and admissions personnel at colleges and universities," said the court. "Any time a student misses his classes, he is deprived of a learning experience that cannot be repeated. Hence, a three-day suspension is not *de minimis* (small, unimportant) and a student is constitutionally entitled to a hearing." In *Goss v. Lopez* (95 S.Ct. 729, Ohio, 1975), the Supreme Court held that a student facing suspension has at least these three rights: 1) to know why he is being suspended; 2) to know the nature of the evidence against him; and 3) the right to tell his side of the story. (See Case No. 3 "Suspension," at the beginning of this chapter).

Q. DOES A RULE WHICH EXCLUDES PREGNANT GIRLS FROM SCHOOL DENY DUE PROCESS OF LAW?

A. Yes. The courts have held that in order to bar a pregnant unmarried girl from public school, the board must show that her presence would be a disruption to the school's program or that attendance would be injurious to her health. Here the fatal unconstitutionality would be in the lack of equity which would result were the board to deny attendance of the girl. In *Ordway v. Hargraves* (323 F.Supp. 1155, Mass., 1971), for example, the court held that the "board has not shown any danger to petitioner's (the girl's) physical or mental health, no likelihood that her presence will cause any disruption, nor any valid educational or other reason to justify her segregation and to require her to receive a type of educational treatment which is not the equal of that given to others." The girl was ordered reinstated.

Q. WHAT MUST GIRLS DO IN ORDER TO COMPETE ON BOYS' ATHLETIC TEAMS?

A. In *Brenden v. Ind. Sch. Dist. 742* (477 F.2d 1292, Minn., 8CA, 1973), the court said that a girl who wished to participate on a boys' tennis team must demonstrate that 1) she could compete on an equal footing with boys; and 2) that there was no comparable program for girls at her high school. In *Hoover v. Meiklejohn* (430 F.Supp. 164, Colo., 1977), the court held that the school district had three options: 1) it could decide to discontinue soccer as an interscholastic athletic activity; 2) it might decide to field separate teams for males and females, with substantial equality in funding, coaching, officiating and opportunity to play; or 3) it could decide to permit both sexes to compete on the same team. Any of these options would satisfy the equal protection requirements of the Constitution. What the school could not do was to continue to make interscholastic soccer available only to male students. There is no constitutional requirement that a school has to offer soccer; what is required is that whatever opportunity is made available be open to all on equal terms. There is no legal right to a position, only the right to compete on equal terms.

Q. IS THE PRIVILEGE OF PARTICIPATING IN ATHLETIC COMPETITION *PER SE* PROTECTED BY THE DUE PROCESS CLAUSE?

A. No. If the state or local district chose to eliminate interscholastic athletics entirely, no substantial federal question would be raised because the privilege of participating in athletic competition *per se* (in itself) is not protected by the due process clause (*Mitchell v. La. H.S. Ath. Ass'n,* 430 F.2d 1155, La., 5th CA, 1970). But the district may not discriminate against students in exercising this privilege (*Walsh v. La. H.S. Ath. Ass'n.,* 428 F.Supp. 1261, La., 1977).

Q. WILL THE COURTS INTERVENE TO PROTECT THE INTERESTS OF STUDENTS WHO ARE BEING PUNISHED ILLEGALLY?

A. Yes. One teacher required students to stand touching their toes for ten to twelve minutes. The court remanded her case to the trial court to determine the physical and mental effects of the punishment (*U.S. v. Coffeeville Consol. School Dist.*, 513 F.2d 244, Miss., 5CA, 1975). Another court interfered to protect students who were required to write a vulgar four-letter word 1000 times for having said the word (*Celestine v. Lafayette Parish Sch.Bd.*, 284 So.2d 650, La., 1973). One teacher was legally dismissed for taping a student's mouth shut, while a court held that due process was lacking in a board's determination that a high school athletic letter be revoked, where, after the season, and after he had won the letter, a boy's letter was revoked for beer drinking (*O'Connor v. Bd. of Educ.*, 316 N.Y.S.2d 799, N.Y., 1970).

Q. MAY THE DISTRICT INSTITUTE A PROGRAM TO SPOT POTENTIAL DRUG ABUSERS?

A. Probably not. In Pennsylvania, the district had a program called Critical Period of Intervention (CPIN) aimed at early identification of potential drug abusers. Some parents got wind of the program and sought to have it enjoined. Their suit was successful (*Merriken v. Cressman*, 364 F.Supp. 913, 1973). Such a program, said the court, is an invasion of student privacy, and further may result in labeling students as drug potentials, a self-fulfilling prophecy. Parents were not notified of the true nature of the program in advance. "The attempt to send the letters home to parents requesting consent similar to a promotional inducement to buy lacks the necessary substance to give a parent the opportunity to give knowing, intelligent and aware consent," said the court. "When a program talks about labeling someone as a particular type and such a label could remain with them for the remainder of their life, the margin of error must be almost nil. There is too much of a chance that the wrong people will be singled out for the wrong reasons and counselled in the wrong manner." However, if you can avoid the pitfalls illustrated here, you might still have such a program in your district, but burden of proof of its non-discrimination would be on you.

Q. MAY THE STUDENT WHO HAS FULFILLED GRADUATION REQUIREMENTS BE PROHIBITED FROM RECEIVING THE DIPLOMA?

A. No. Issuing the diploma is a ministerial duty over which there is no discretionary control by school officials. However, as punishment, the student may be barred from participating in the graduation exercises if there is evidence that disruption may occur. In New York, a student had completed her studies, but was denied participation in the graduation ceremony. The court said that there was no evidence of a threat to the orderliness and no disruption occurred. "Without due process, such a means of punishment may not be an appropriate regulatory act by the board of education" (*Ladson v. Bd. of Education*, 323 N.Y.S.2d 545, N.Y., 1971). And in Arizona, a girl who was prohibited from participating in eighth-grade graduation ceremonies because her dress was not of the prescribed color was able to recover damages from the principal who barred her from the ceremony.

Q. MUST TEACHERS BE AWARE OF RACIAL BIAS IN METEING OUT PUNISHMENTS?

A. Yes. In a Louisiana case, the statistician showed that blacks were being punished more frequently than their proportion in the student body might warrant. The court ruled that where the principal allegedly meted out punishment along racial lines, claimants for relief need not first go before a state administrative board but may go directly to the federal district court for relief (*Griffin v. DeFelice*, 325 F.Supp. 143, La., 1971). Disproportionate amounts of punishment of one race over the other are unconstitutional, and may subject the perpetrator to financial liability under the Civil Rights Act of 1871 (42 U.S.C. Sec. 1983).

Q. WHAT DRESS CODES WILL STAND CONSTITUTIONAL CHALLENGE?

A. Ordinarily, the less complicated the dress code, the more chance it has to pass constitutional muster. In *Jacobs v. Benedict* (316 N.E.2d 898, Ohio, 1974), the court said that "the hair regulations are not actually necessary for the government of the schools. Moreover, there is not, in point of fact, evidence that such regulations serve a useful purpose." Another court ruled that "school regulations, of whatever nature, must bear some reasonable relationship to the purpose of compulsory school attendance, education in the broadest sense of the term (*Graber v. Kniola*, 216 N.W.2d 925, Mich., 1974). An Idaho dress code which prohibited female students from wearing slacks, pantsuits, or culottes was held to be in excess of the school board's authority since the board had not shown that such dress was disruptive, nor that the code bore a reasonable relationship to the educational process (*Johnson v. Joint Sch.Dist.*, 508 P.2d 547, Ida., 1973).

Q. IS THE STUDENT FACING EXPULSION ENTITLED TO ATTEND SCHOOL PENDING THE OUTCOME OF HIS HEARING?

A. Courts generally agree that if the absence from school is more than three to five days, a student facing expulsion is entitled to attend school in the meantime. In Kansas the court held that a student in this situation is entitled to know with some degree of specificity what the charges against him are and who is the principal witness. His return to school pending any appeal or during time allowed for appeal from his order of expulsion lies within the sound discretion of the examiner (*Smith v. Miller*, 514 P.2d 377, Kans., 1973). And where Chicano high school students were allowed to wear black berets in school pending the outcome of their challenge to the principal's order that they must take off the berets, the students were allowed to be in school, minus the berets, pending the outcome of the federal district court's decision on their petition (*Hernandez v. Sch.Dist.No.1, City & Co. of Denver*, 315 F.Supp. 289, Colo., 1970).

Q. MAY THE LENGTH OF A BOY'S HAIR BE USED TO DENY HIM HIS LETTER IN FOOTBALL?

A. This question was before a court in West Virginia in 1973. The high school football coach had decreed that all members of the squad should observe a "hair code" prescribed by him, not merely during football season, but throughout the school year under penalty of being denied their "letter" for participation. Plaintiff, a student who during the football season had worn his hair short, and who had earned his letter, but who after the season, allowed his hair to grow beyond the prescribed length, was denied his letter and an invitation to a football banquet at the end of the year. He challenged the ruling in court. The federal district judge dismissed his action and he appealed. The Fourth Circuit Court of Appeals held the coach's rule was unfair and unlawful, and ordered the school to issue him his letter (*Long v Zopp,* 476 F.2d 180, W.Va., 4CA, 1973).

Q. WHAT ARE THE EXCEPTIONS TO THE RULE THAT A STUDENT HAS FREEDOM OF CHOICE IN LENGTH AND STYLE OF HIS HAIR?

A. In order for the state, in the form of school officials, to limit that individual right, the state must be prepared to show that it has a legitimate state interest justifying the regulation. Ordinarily, the courts will accept these reasons if the state can prove its point through sufficient factual evidence: 1) student's hair length caused disruption; 2) promotion of safety for boys; 3) promotion of a better "academic atmosphere" (a tough one to prove); 4) boys with short hair are more manly (Jesus and Thos. Jefferson wore long hair); 5) long hair is symbolic (rebellious) speech; 6) long hair shows disrespect for the establishment; 7) parents have requested that the boy wear short hair; and 8) long hair creates a clear and present danger to the educational process (not recommended). In any event, the student is entitled to due process on the merits before any punishment is handed down.

Q. WHAT ARE SOME CASES IN WHICH RULES HAVE BEEN DECLARED UNCONSTITUTIONAL "FOR VAGUENESS"?

A. Phrases like "wilfull disobedience" or "intentional disruption" are not clearly defined in the law, but have been held to be sufficiently clear as to be enforceable (*Murray v. West Baton Rouge Parish Sch.Bd.,* 472 F.2d 438, La., 1973). However, the terms "insubordination" and "disorderly" were upheld as grounds on which a board might legally suspend a boy so long as due process had been accorded the student in assessing the punishment (*Reid v. Nyquist,* 319 N.Y.S.2d 53, N.Y., 1971). One court held a blanket rule against distribution of "literature" at school to be too vague (*Vail v. Bd. of Educ.,* 354 F.Supp. 592, N.H., 1973). The general rule about vagueness was expressed by a California court thusly, "A statute which either forbids or requires doing of an act in terms so vague that men of common intelligence must necessarily guess at its meaning and differ as to its application violates first essentials of due process" (*People v. Barksdale,* 503 P.2d 257, Calif., 1972.)

Q. WHAT PUNISHMENTS CAN BE ASSESSED WHERE STUDENTS ASSAULT TEACHERS?

A. Serious assault and battery can be a criminal act for which the police will intervene. In civil suits, however, there are other forms of relief. In Oregon, a school board regulation providing for suspension or expulsion of students "for the commission of assaults" was not voided for vagueness (*Black Coalition v. Portland Sch.Dist.No. 1,* 484 F.2d 1040, Oreg., 1973). In Pennsylvania, the courts upheld a teacher in slapping a student in an effort to expel him from the classroom, and ruled that this act did not justify the student striking the teacher. The student's action amounted to misconduct warranting suspension for the balance of the school year (*Edwards v. Jersey Shore Area Sch.Dist.,* 301 A.2d 116, Pa., 1973). And in Texas, a student's suspension for the remainder of the school year was upheld where he threw a cup of hot coffee and the cup on the band director (*Greene v. Moore,* 373 F.Supp. 1194, Tx., 1974). The judge quoted from an earlier case, "We cannot forget that a public school principal retains considerable freedom to administer his realm. . . ." (*Murray v. West Baton Rouge Parish School Bd.,* 472 F.2d 438, La., 1973).

Q. CAN STUDENTS BE PUNISHED FOR ACTS CONNECTED WITH THE FLAG?

A. Students do not have to salute the flag as a condition of attendance in a public school (*W.Va.St.Bd. of Educ. v. Barnette,* 319 U.S. 624, W.Va., 1943). In Tennessee, a high school student was suspended when he refused to remove a rebel flag from his clothing, although students were allowed to wear peace and ecology symbols in school. Because of racial incidents which closed the school on two occasions the flag was in the principal's words "provocative" and amounted to "fighting words," (*Melton v. Young,* 465 F.2d 1332, Tenn., 1972). A similar finding occurred in *Augustus v. S.Bd. of Escambia County* (361 F.Supp. 383, Fla., 1973), where the Confederate battle flag caused racial tensions. In Colorado, a student appeared at school wearing a pair of blue jeans on the seat of which a portion of the American flag was sewn, and was arrested under a statute making it unlawful to mutilate, deface, and defile the flag. His use of the flag was held to be protected by the First Amendment even though it had the effect of inciting others to unlawful conduct (*State v. Vaughan*, 514 P.2d 1318, Colo., 1973).

In Colorado, near a military base, the speech teacher asked high school students to prepare short speeches on the subject of "symbols." One lad who brought with him a small American flag told the class that it was only a piece of cloth, a symbol of something having implicit value only in the eye of the beholder. He then tore up the small flag and stamped on it to illustrate his point. The school board heard of the incident and expelled the boy. The boy sought reinstatement in court. His case was successful. "The board produced no evidence whatsoever that the welfare, safety, or morals of any pupil was harmed by what the boy did," said the court, "or even that the class was distracted or the school disrupted by what he did. Some of the students were no doubt stunned or shocked or offended by what they heard, but behavior which only shocks, stuns or offends falls far short of behavior inimical to one's welfare, safety, or morals. The court finds the expulsion illegal" (*Canfield v. Sch.Dist.No. 8, El Paso County*, No. J-842, Dist.Ct., April 16, 1970).

Q. WHY ARE "AUTOMATIC PENALTIES FOR CERTAIN MISCONDUCTS" SUSPECT *PER SE?*

A. Americans like to believe that there are exceptions to every rule and that they are those exceptions. The Tyler, Texas board had a rule that any student who participated in a sit-in, walk-out, or other boycott would be automatically suspended from school. Following a walk-out, some black students were suspended for an indefinite period without proper notice or hearing. They brought an action for reinstatement, citing *Tinker* — children are "persons" — and *In re Gault* (87 S.Ct. 1428, Ariz., 1967) — due process is not for adults alone. The court held that the board's rule was unconstitutionally broad and vague — what did "participation" in a boycott of the school mean? Also, any rule which assesses an "automatic" penalty is *per se* suspect (in and of itself) because the student in an impartial hearing may well be able to show cause why he did what he did. While he may not be entitled to practice disruptive tactics in school, he is at least entitled to be heard, to face his accusers, and to tell his side of the story (*Dunn v. Tyler Ind.Sch.Dist.*, 327 F.Supp. 528, Tex., 1971).

Q. MUST A SCHOOL RECOGNIZE A GROUP EVEN THOUGH IT MAY BE CONTROVERSIAL?

A. "Absent a threat to the orderly operation of the school," said one court, "to deny recognition to a student group for the reason that it advocates controversial ideas is patently unconstitutional" (*Dixon v. Beresh,* 361 F.Supp. 253, Mich., 1973). In higher education, the cases are more numerous. Colleges are not *required* to allow student groups to organize; however, once they recognize one, and give it certain advantages, they must act constitutionally with all groups that apply. The U.S. Supreme Court held that a local chapter of Students for a Democratic Society (SDS) were entitled to a hearing before being refused recognition (*Healy v. James,* 92 S.Ct. 2338, Conn., 1972). The First Circuit Court of Appeals likewise held that once recognized, a campus organization is entitled to hold dances and other social functions in the absence of any illegal activity or conduct even though to do so may offend the community's sense of propriety (*Gay Students Org., U of N.H. v. Bonner,* 509 F.2d 652, 1CA, 1974).

Q. DO STUDENTS HAVE THE RIGHT TO PEACEABLY ASSEMBLE AND PICKET?

A. Yes. Freedom of expression is protected by the First Amendment as is the right to peaceably assemble and petition the government for a redress of grievances. Thus, the courts held that school authorities were wrong in suspending public school students for bringing onto campus and distributing to other students signs protesting the refusal of the board to renew the contract of an English instructor, despite the fact that there was potential for violence in the action taken by the student (*Karp v. Becken,* 477 F.2d 171, Ariz., 1973). In another case, because of the potential for violence (news stories had forecast a student demonstration; fifty students gathered together and got signs ready), the school officials were justified in taking the signs away from the students even though there was no school rule against having signs on campus. Also, when twenty boys who had been sent to get haircuts created a disturbance in the parking lot, school officials were barred from punishing them, since if it were not for the hair regulation, there would not have been any disturbance (*Seal v. Mertz,* 383 F.Supp. 945, Pa., 1972).

Sex Education

Q. WHAT OBJECTIONS HAVE BEEN RAISED BY PARENTS AND OTHERS WHO OPPOSE SEX EDUCATION IN THE PUBLIC SCHOOLS?

A. Parents have objected to an invasion of their religious freedom to teach sex education to their own children where schools have undertaken sex education for all. Both the right to free exercise of religion (the parents' right to raise their children) and the prohibition of an established religion have been pleaded. Other parents have charged a lack of due process in that sex education courses were established and operated in the schools without their prior knowledge or consent. Some have charged violation of state constitutional provisions (*Clemmer v. Unified Sch.Dist. No. 501,* Shawnee, Kansas 1970, Case No. 112,064). Still others claimed that the board had no power to carry on such a program, and that it was acting in an *ultra vires* (beyond its power) way. The responsibility and authority for educational matters in the states is implicitly given to the states in the Tenth Amendment, which gives states "police" power over health, welfare, and family matters.

Q. WHAT INTERESTS DO THE STATES CLAIM IN OFFERING SEX EDUCATION TO PUBLIC SCHOOL STUDENTS?

A. The police powers of the states charge the states with promoting the health, welfare, and general morality of the people of the state. Among the "interests" states have advanced in teaching sex education are these: 1) reduction of illegitimacy through increased knowledge among juveniles; 2) reduced incidence of venereal disease; 3) the promotion of better health through teaching physiology of the body; 4) the presentation of factual materials on human reproduction; 5) the providing of information where home and church have no longer proved able to do so; and 6) the promotion of healthy family life and the teaching of responsibilities associated with worthy home membership.

Q. DO PARENTS HAVE THE EXCLUSIVE RIGHT TO TEACH THEIR CHILDREN ABOUT SEX?

A. No. The state has a compelling interest, also. The Maryland State Board of Education passed a by-law that required each school district in the state to provide a comprehensive program on family life and sex education. The federal courts held that the by-law did not deny equal protection or due process because it applied equally to all children. Although it could not prove that a sex education program would do so, the Maryland Board hoped to head off school-girl pregnancies. Said the court, "There would appear to be just as much reason for the state board to provide sex education for the non-pregnant (and, incidentally, for the non-impregnating) as for those students who, owing to lack of information on the subject (or for other reasons), have become pregnant, or who have caused pregnancy" (*Cornwell v. St. Bd. of Educ.*, 428 F.2d 471, 4CA, Md., *cert. denied*, 400 U.S. 942, 1971).

Q. DO STATE-OPERATED SEX EDUCATION PROGRAMS INVADE THE RELIGIOUS FREEDOM OF PARENTS?

A. Apparently not. Nor is sex education by the state an invasion of the privacy of the parental domain. Fifth and sixth graders in Hawaii were shown a film series on family life and sex education via television. Parents challenged the plan on the grounds that it invaded their religious freedom and familial privacy. They argued they had the right to educate their children in the intimacies of sexual matters according to their own moral and religious beliefs without interference from the state. They were unsuccessful, chiefly because each parent had the option of viewing the films ahead of time, then sending written exclusion slips for those films they felt were objectionable. Since parents had an option, the program was held not to violate parental prerogatives (*Medeiros v. Kiyosaki*, 478 P.2d 314, Hawaii, 1971).

Q. HOW EFFECTIVE IS SEX EDUCATION IN THE SCHOOLS?

A. A Youth Poll conducted by the National Association of Secondary School Principals in 1977 showed that lack of sex education was the greatest problem perceived by the young people responding. Only one in ten said there was any meaningful sex education in the schools; most courses were late or tiptoed around the subject. Each year more than one-million teenage pregnancies occur, and 600,000 of these go full term; about 300,000 get abortions. There are more than 250,000 unwanted teenage births per year in our high schools — one every three weeks per high school.

Sex Discrimination in Education

Q. WHAT EFFORTS HAVE BEEN MADE TO END SEX DISCRIMINATION IN EDUCATION?

A. The Fourteenth Amendment says that "no state shall deny to any person within its jurisdiction the equal protection of the laws." Yet between 1868, when the Fourteenth Amendment was ratified, and 1971, not a single statute which discriminated on the basis of sex was found by the Supreme Court to be in violation of the Fourteenth Amendment. Efforts to eliminate sex discrimination in education are therefore of fairly recent origin. Title VI of the Civil Rights Act of 1964 prohibited sex discrimination in educational institutions receiving federal funds. Title VII of the same act as amended by the Equal Employment Opportunity Act of 1972 prohibited discrimination in employment because of sex. Title IX of the Education Amendments of 1972 outlawed discrimination in schools, and Executive Order No. 11246 (1965) as amended in 1967 prohibited all institutions with federal contracts over $10,000 from discriminating in employment on the basis of sex. There are also sets of federal regulations promulgated to enforce these directives in the schools of the nation.

Q. MAY THE STATE STILL MAINTAIN STATUTES WHICH GROUP WOMEN IN CERTAIN CATEGORIES OR IS GROUPING BY SEX "SUSPECT"?

A. Separate does not always mean unequal in the eyes of legislators and judges dealing with sex discrimination. There are two levels. The first is where the state may not maintain grouping "if the classification is totally irrational and arbitrary." A sterner test protects fundamental rights, and suspect classifications are subjected to "strict scrutiny" by the courts. A suspect classification of persons has these criteria: 1) Does the class have an immutable characteristic? 2) Has there been a history of invidious discrimination against the class? 3) Is the class a discrete and insular minority? 4) Is the class politically powerless? 5) Does the classification stigmatize members of the class as inferior? Race, color, and national origin are "suspect classifications" under these criteria, and except perhaps for questions three and five, sex is also "suspect" in itself as a classification unless the state can show cause why it wishes to group females or exclude females from some benefit or other.

Q. ARE CHILDREN (PUPILS) SUSPECT CLASSES OF PERSONS?

A. Using the criteria in the question above as a basis, children are a "suspect" classification, especially girls who have had to fight discrimination in admission, treatment not equal to that of males, and in employment. We are interested here with Title IX as it affects girls in public schools. The Dick and Jane syndrome meant that even reading literature was suspect, and there were other practices such as participation in sports which have had to be changed in line with Title IX "affirmative action" programs either by court order or through voluntary compliance in order not to lose valuable federal moneys. Affirmative action means taking steps to remedy a situation based on sex which was caused by past discrimination either by the school or by society at large, such as "girls' courses" and "boys' courses." Athletic scholarships, girls' teams, equal facilities for girls, entitlement to leadership roles, and similar problems still face the schools. Since a teacher is the child's advocate, you must govern yourself in such a way as not to discriminate in your classroom because of race, religion, country of origin, or sex.

Q. IN WHAT WAYS ARE COUNSELORS INVOLVED WITH SEX DISCRIMINATION IN SCHOOLS?

A. One area of possible discrimination is that of testing. If the counselor or teacher knew or reasonably should have known that the test would create a suspect classification, that individual can be held personally liable under the Civil Rights Act of 1871 (42 U.S.C. Sec. 1983). Counselors can no longer guide students into "boys' courses" or "girls' courses" nor discourage girls from taking such lines of work as engineering, medicine, law, or any number of formerly male-dominated careers. Schools may not require higher admission standards for girls than for boys, nor may girls be excluded from boys' sports if 1) the girl can demonstrate equality of skills with boys or 2) the school does not have a girls' team in that sport. But teachers must also be aware of "reverse discrimination" and guard against it in dealing with students under their care and supervision.

Q. DO MINORS HAVE THE RIGHT TO FAMILY-PLANNING ASSISTANCE?

A. Yes. In 1977 the U.S. Supreme Court ruled that a state cannot legally ban the sale of contraceptives to persons age 16 and under. Under a New York law, youngsters 15 years of age or younger could obtain contraceptives legally only from doctors (*Carey v. Population Services, International,* 97 S.Ct. 2010, N.Y., 1977). Justice Brennan wrote: "The right to privacy in connection with decisions affecting procreation extends to minors as well as to adults." A 3-judge panel sitting in Utah ruled earlier that minors must have free access to birth control information and services, including contraceptives, without parental consent. While HEW advocated such practices without parental consent, it did say that "the adolescent must bear some of the risks and consequences of an unintended pregnancy and should be permitted to avoid the pregnancy." The court rejected the argument that the right to privacy was outweighed by the state's "substantial" interest in protecting minor females "from the evil effects and unsuspected harm of actions which go against the mores of society" and in enforcing the right of parents to control the family (*T. H. v. Jones,* July 23, 1975).

Q. IS A STATE STATUTE REQUIRING PARENTAL PERMISSION FOR AN ABORTION UNCONSTITUTIONAL?

A. Yes. Colorado had a statute requiring single girls under the age of 18 who were unmarried and pregnant to first obtain permission of their parents or guardians before legal abortions could be performed. Fatima Foe, who had a small child, was on her own, wanted to continue her education, and was unmarried and pregnant, challenged the statute (*Foe v. Vanderhoof,* 389 F.Supp. 947, Colo., 1975). She had discussed an abortion with her doctor, and had been apprised of the social consequences through discussions with social workers. Her case was successful. "Just as the state has no authority to interfere with a woman's right of privacy in the first trimester of pregnancy," said a Florida court, "it likewise may not constitutionally require by statute that a physician obtain the consent of the husband or parents of a pregnant woman before terminating the pregnancy during that period (*Coe v. Gerstein,* 376 F.Supp. 695, Fla., 1976).

Resolution of the Cases in Point

Case No. 1 — CORPORAL PUNISHMENT

The court held that the North Carolina paddling law was constitutional, so long as teachers first afford the student three due process rights: 1) they must forewarn their students of behavior punishable by paddling; 2) another school official must be present; and 3) parents must be furnished a written account of the punishment although they may not veto the punishment itself. At all times, the teacher must not administer other than reasonable punishment; if this occurs, the student and his parents may institute an action for damages (assault and battery). The Supreme Court affirmed, without comment, the ruling of the federal district court (*Baker v. Owen,* 395 F.Supp. 294, N.C., 1975, affrmd., 96 S.Ct. 210, Oct. 20, 1975).

Case No. 2 — EXPULSION

The Supreme Court held that any student who is faced with expulsion (and the subsequent loss of a very important "property") is entitled to the full panoply of due process guarantees — written notice, an impartial hearing, right to representation by counsel, and the right of appeal. The girls had not been accorded such consideration, which the board members should have realized was a denial of their constitutional rights. With respect to the liability of board members as individuals, the Court said, "We hold that a school board member is not immune from liability for damages under Sec. 1983 (42 U.S.C. Sec. 1983) if he knew or reasonably should have known that the action he took within his sphere of official responsibility would violate the constitutional rights of the student affected, or if he took the action with malicious intention to cause a deprivation of constitutional rights or other injury to the student." The opinion has subsequently been broadened to include principals and teachers (*Wood v. Strickland,* 95 S.Ct. 992, Ark., 1975).

Case No. 3 — SUSPENSION

Dwight Lopez and other students who were suspended under the Ohio law were held to have been denied constitutional rights to due process of law. The right to attend school is a "property" right under the constitution, and cannot be taken away by the state without a hearing, even for so short a time as ten days. The Supreme Court declared the Ohio statute unconstitutional and held that students facing suspension for short periods of time are entitled to at least these minimal constitutional guarantees: 1) the student must be told why he is being suspended; 2) he is entitled to know the nature of the evidence against him (whether circumstantial or who his accusers may be); and 3) he is entitled to tell his side of the story, all within minutes after the incident occurs. Suspensions longer than five or six days must be followed by an impartial hearing on the merits; the school is under an affirmative duty to see that this is afforded the student (*Goss v. Lopez,* 95 S.Ct. 729, Ohio, 1975).

Case No. 4 — COMPULSORY ATTENDANCE

Yoder won. "However strong the State's interest in universal compulsory attendance," said the Supreme Court, "it is by no means absolute to the exclusion or subordination of all other interests." A state's interest in universal education, no matter how highly we rank it, is not totally free from a balancing process when it impinges on fundamental rights and interests, such as those included in the First Amendment and the rights of parents to control the religious upbringing of their children. "The right of parents (to bring up their children as they see fit) is now established beyond debate as an enduring American tradition" (*Wisconsin v. Yoder,* 406 U.S. 205, 1972).

Case No. 5 — EXCLUSION

Federal courts took a different tack from state courts, which tended to uphold the board's right to limit married students from participating in extra-curricular activities. "Marriage is an accepted and highly honored institution in our society," they said. "What greater invasion of marital privacy can there be than one which could totally destroy the marriage itself?" (*Davis v. Meek,* 344 F.Supp. 298, Ohio, 1972). Also courts have begun to recognize that extra-curricular activities such as baseball are "generally recognized as a fundamental ingredient of the educational process" (*Moran v. School Dist., Yellowstone Co.,* 350 F.Supp. 1180, Mont., 1972).

Chapter Four Teacher Liability For Pupil Injury

A *tort* is defined as a legal wrong or injury, not involving a breach of contract, for which a civil suit can be brought. Teachers are *not* immune from tort liability if their negligence leads to an injury to a student or students under their care and supervision.

Governmental units in this country were at first exempted from tort liability, but that immunity has largely disappeared. Now, only half a dozen states still maintain legal protection for school districts on the grounds they are performing a public service and cannot spend money raised for educational purposes for other claims, such as damages in tort.

Teachers, as individuals, have never been completely immune from having to pay damages where students under their care have been injured. But no teacher, no matter how serious the injury, can be held liable in damages unless there is evidence that he or she acted in a negligent manner and the negligence was the main cause of that injury.

Teachers enjoy a limited, or conditional immunity because they stand *in loco parentis* to the child. You cannot guarantee that a child will not be injured while under your care — to do so would amount to an insurer's bond. Your standard of care is that which the average, normally prudent parent would have exercised under the same or similar circumstances. The jury is empowered to decide whether you met that standard of care as a matter of fact under instructions from the judge, who handles points of law. If your standard of care is less than what the jury thinks the average, normally prudent parent would have exercised, you (or your insurer) may be held personally liable in damages for the pupil's injury.

School board members also enjoy a limited immunity, not because they stand *in loco parentis,* but because they are public officials protected under a sovereign status. Your status as a teacher is that of a public employee, who, like all other citizens, is responsible for his or her own acts of tort.

"All of the paths leading to the origin of governmental tort immunity converge on *Russell v. Men of Devon* (100 Eng.Rep. 359, 2 T.R. 667, England, 1788)," said the Minnesota Supreme Court in striking down that state's immunity doctrine for local governmental units (*Spanel v. Mounds View Sch.Dist.,* 118 N.W.2d 795, Minn. 1962). When Russell's horse fell through a bridge that was in disrepair, the courts of England were unwilling to assess "the men of Devon," who were unincorporated, and therefore had no treasury out of which to pay damages, with tort liability for Russell's injury. "This product of the English law (governmental immunity) was left on our doorstep to become the putative ancestor of a long line of American cases beginning with *Mower v. Leicester* (9 Mass. 247, Mass., 1812)," said the Minnesota court. Since liability insurance is readily available, and is not costly, the Minnesota court held that after 1962 school districts in that state could be held liable in damages if what they did amounted to negligence. Other states have followed suit, either by judicial fiat or by statutory enactment, until now only a handful of states still permit their local governmental units to hide behind the doctrine.

Read the cases (and there have been thousands — you couldn't possibly read all of them) which illustrate how you, as an individual teacher, may be held liable in damages if you are negligent. These cases rest upon a common basic assumption: the child is not voluntarily in school but is there at the insistence of the state; his natural parents cannot be present, so you are standing in their stead *(in loco parentis);* the child is expected to be "in a safe place" while attending school; you are not expected to guarantee that no child will ever be hurt — that would be too much to expect, too high a standard of care; you may purchase liability insurance or be covered by a blanket insurance policy; your state may have a "save harmless" statute which passes the liability along to your employer, the school district; your expected standard of care is only that which the average, normally prudent parent would have exercised under the same or similar circumstances. You will be held personally liable only if your actions fail to come up to that standard of care.

Following are five cases which illustrate how teachers may or may not be held personally liable for pupil injury. The solution to the cases is included at the end of this chapter. Discuss them with others, then turn to the back of the chapter and find out how the cases turned out. The situation is very important in tort liability cases. Applying the basic assumptions above, see how many of the cases you can solve successfully before looking up the answers.

Cases in Point

Case No. 1 — FIRST AID TURNS SOUR

A ten-year-old boy had an infection on the little finger of his right hand, but the condition did not prevent him from playing baseball during the noon recess. Two teachers detained the boy after school for the purpose of giving him medical attention. One heated a pan of water to the boiling point and with the assistance of the other immersed the boy's hand in it for ten minutes. The boy's hand was permanently disfigured. The parents brought suit for damages from the teachers as joint tort-feasors (wrong-doers). Would the teachers be liable for damages under these conditions? Why or why not? Would each be equally at fault? Suppose one were the principal and the other a teacher. Would this change their relative culpability for the injury? Was their action what one would expect from the average, normally prudent parent under the same or similar circumstances?

Case No. 2 — TEACHER'S ABSENCE

The children began arriving in the classroom about 8:30 a.m., and soon the room was buzzing with talk and laughter. By 8:45, all the children had arrived, but Miss Jones was nowhere to be seen. The noise became louder. Among the students was a boy, who in the back of the room began brandishing a knife. Just before the nine o'clock bell rang, he stabbed another student in the hand. The teacher had not yet arrived. Would the teacher be held liable for negligence in the injury since she was not present in the classroom at the time of the injury? If her presence would have prevented the injury, was her absence the proximate cause of the student's injury? Were others responsible for the accident? Suppose she had a flat tire on the freeway and could not phone in notice that she would be late? Is the principal also not negligent in allowing this condition to get out of hand?

Case No. 3 — LAYING ON OF HANDS

A twelve-year-old seventh grader brought a suit for damages against the coach for assault and battery. The teacher admitted pushing the student against the backstop on the baseball field but he claimed he had that right to discipline the boy for using unacceptable language. (The boy had been called "out" by the coach-umpire. "Like hell I'm out," returned the boy; the pushing followed.) The boy claimed the coach had taken him by the throat and slammed him into the backstop. No permanent injury resulted, only embarrassment before the other students on the field. Was the coach's disciplinary action protected under the circumstances? Or did his actions amount to assault and battery? What consequences might have flowed from the boy's kicking the dirt if the coach had not done what he did?

Case No. 4 — SCHOOL DISTRICT LIABILITY

Plaintiff was a fifteen-year-old student whose arm was caught in a shredding machine in an upholstery class. As a result, his arm had to be amputated. He charged negligence in failing to supervise the class, in supplying the machine for use without a proper safety device, in maintaining it in a dangerous and defective condition, and in failing to warn children of the dangerous situation. The defendant school district objected on the grounds that school districts were protected under the doctrine of governmental immunity. Three questions were raised: 1) was supervision lacking in the class? 2) was the equipment dangerous and faulty? and 3) was the district immune from tort liability?

Case No. 5 — WRONGFUL DEATH?

A high school student who was out for football suffered heat stroke. The incident occurred about 5:20 p.m., and although the coaches administered first aid, they did so in a negligent manner by placing a blanket over the boy. At 7:15 p.m., the boy was finally taken to the hospital where he later died. His parents brought an action against the district and the coaches claiming wrongful death of their son. The record showed that the coaches did not halt the practice although it was very hot, and it was early in the season (Louisiana in August). Louisiana was one of the states where the doctrine of governmental immunity had been judicially abrogated earlier. Would the district or the coaches be held liable? What is a reasonable settlement in the event of negligent wrongful death? Would medical testimony be necessary to prove the negligence (if any) of the coaches? And finally, does not a student who goes out for football *assume* some risk, which would exonerate the coaches from tort liability?

Negligence

Q. WHAT IS THE THREE-TIERED COURT TEST FOR NEGLIGENCE IN TORT LIABILITY CASES?

A. In order to find negligence on the part of the defendant, the following three questions must be answered in the affirmative: 1) Did the defendant owe the plaintiff a duty? 2) Did the defendant breach the duty owed the plaintiff? 3) Was the breach of the duty owed the proximate cause of plaintiff's injury? These so-called "common law" questions grew out of our heritage in English jurisprudence. Negligence is a matter of fact and must be decided by the jury on instructions from the judge, who notes points of law. For example, where a teacher has been charged with failure to provide proper supervision and a child is injured, the court would first ask whether the teacher owed the child a duty, a question which is normally answered in the affirmative. Did the teacher breach that duty owed (did he or she do something or fail to do something) which in turn became the causal link between the breach of duty and the pupil's injury? If all questions are answered in the affirmative, then the judge will instruct the jury to find negligence.

Q. WHAT IS AN EXAMPLE OF A CASE IN WHICH THERE WAS NO DUTY OWED?

A. In Case No. 2 ("Teacher's Absence") at the head of this chapter, the principal did not owe the students a duty for their safety, or if he did, he had discharged it by appointing a teacher to assume the *in loco parentis* role for that group of children. Another case in point was one in which a boy was electrocuted during a letterman's club initiation when an electric charge was passed through his body. The court ruled that the coach could be held liable if negligence was proved, but that the principal and superintendent, who were not present, had discharged their responsibility to the deceased by seeing that the coach, a qualified teacher in every respect, was present during the ceremonies (*DeGooyer v. Harkness,* 13 N.W.2d 815, S.Dak., 1944). But where a school principal did not warn a substitute teacher concerning known misconduct of students, who later assaulted her in class, the principal was held to have failed in his duty to warn of any dangerous conditions (*Ferraro v. Bd. of Ed. of City of N.Y.,* 212 N.Y.S.2d 615, 1961).

Q. DOES THE TEACHER OWE THE DUTY OF CARE TO SEE THAT THE STUDENT LEARNS TO READ?

A. Apparently not, unless the student can prove individual educational malfeasance. In *Doe v. San Francisco Unified Sch.Dist.* (131 Cal.Rptr. 854, 1976), the appellate court had before it the question of whether a high school graduate who could read at only the fifth-grade level could claim tort injury against the school district. The court held that the school district had no "duty of care," as that term is used in negligence tort law, and therefore the plaintiff's complaint was dismissed. As to the plaintiff's claim of "false and fraudulent" representation (as demonstrated by assurance to parents their son was doing all right and the fact he was promoted year after year), the court held that the plaintiff had not relied on misrepresentation, a necessary prerequisite to recovery and that he could not introduce it after not including it in his original complaint. His petition for a hearing before the California Supreme Court was denied on September 30, 1976. (But a teacher might be held to have such a duty on an individual basis.)

Q. DOES THE TEACHER OWE A STUDENT THE DUTY TO WARN AGAINST POSSIBLE CONSEQUENCES OF AN ACTION WHICH WOULD BE FORESEEABLE BY THE AVERAGE PERSON?

A. Yes, definitely. Some eighth graders were preparing for a science exhibit. Plaintiff's daughter was injured when a fellow student struck a match and an open container of alcohol ignited, causing serious burns. The question was whether the teacher should have warned the students prior to the exhibit that there might be an explosion if a match were to be lit. The real negligence, which the jury found against the teacher, was in keeping alcohol in an open container instead of in a sealed bottle. The science teacher's negligence was therefore the proximate cause of the student's injury (*Station v. Travelers Insurance Co.*, 292 So.2d 289, La., 1974).

Q. ARE SCHOOL BOARD MEMBERS AS INDIVIDUALS GENERALLY HELD LIABLE IN DAMAGES FOR INJURIES TO STUDENTS IN SCHOOLS?

A. Ordinarily, no. But if the board knew or reasonably should have known that the district was maintaining a dangerous condition (nuisance) on school property, and did nothing about it, there is the possibility that individual members of the board might be liable in the suit. In *Carroll v. Fitzsimmons* (384 P.2d 81, Colo., 1963), a child was injured when a rock was thrown in the school yard during noon recess. The parents sued board members, the county superintendent, the district superintendent, the principal, and a teacher for damages. The court held that all these would be liable in damages only if the teacher were held to have been negligent. Since the plaintiff could not bear the burden of proof, all were exonerated and the case was dismissed. Since supervision in general was adequate, there would be no finding that the teacher in charge of the playground was negligent, said the court.

Q. CAN A TEACHER GUARANTEE THAT NO CHILD WILL BE INJURED?

A. No. That would be too high a standard of care. Where large numbers of children are brought together in close proximity, it is inevitable that accidents will happen, or that some student will deliberately injure another. Where supervision in general is adequate, the teacher in charge will not be responsible. "There is no requirement that the teacher have under constant and unremitting scrutiny the precise spots wherein every phase of play activity is being pursued," said the court in *Carroll v. Fitzsimmons* . "Nor is there compulsion that the general supervision be continuous and direct, so long as it is otherwise adequate."

Q. MAY THE DUTY TO SUPERVISE STUDENTS BE DELEGATED TO ANOTHER?

A. Dozens of cases on this question show that a teacher may not depend on a student teacher, a teacher's aide, another teacher, or older students to supervise where the teacher has a clear duty. The duty cannot be abrogated merely by assigning it to another. A child was hurt when a school janitor was left in charge. The court held that a janitor is not qualified to supervise play (*Garber v. Central High School,* 295 N.Y.S.2d 850, 1937). An exception to the rule of delegation of the duty owed is where a principal or superintendent, who stands *in loco parentis* to the child, assigns the duty to a teacher for the class. This places the duty owed at the teacher-student level where decisions must be made concerning the child's safety. The parent, however, can assume the risk of injury for the child but usually this must be done on a temporary basis, such as where the parent takes his own child in his car to a school activity.

Q. SHOULD TEACHERS ANTICIPATE THAT CHILDREN WILL INJURE THEMSELVES?

A. Yes. The teacher is expected to have normal, average foresight in anticipating that an injury might occur. In Washington, students had rigged a teeter-board across the playground swing, and children were seen swinging and teetering at the same time. One child was injured when he fell from the board. The parents were able to recover damages from the teacher. "If the teacher knew it (that pupils used the teeter-board as they did), it was negligence to permit it, and if she did not know it, it was negligence not to have observed it," said the court on that occasion (*Bruenn v. North Yakima School Dist. No. 7,* 172 Pac. 569, Wash., 1918). On another occasion, a teacher continued to teach while a boy played with a knife, flipping it into the ground (the class was outside on the lawn). The knife hit a student in the eye, putting it out. The court held that the teacher should have been able to predict that this dangerous practice would result in injury and his failure to stop it amounted to a breach of the duty owed (*Lilienthal v. San Leandro Unified Sch. Dist.,* 293 P.2d 889, Calif., 1956).

Q, WHAT LEVEL OF FORESIGHT IS LEGALLY ADEQUATE?

A. The law does not anticipate clairvoyance, only "average" foresight that would have been present were the parent present instead of the teacher. An Oregon teacher took her small children to the beach on an outing. She took along some of the mothers, in anticipation that kids on an outing will need closer supervision than at school. She posed some of the children on a log to take their picture. With her back to the ocean, she neglected to notice a large wave which knocked her down, then lifted the log and injured the children when they were pinned underneath. The jury found that she should have known and protected her small charges against unusual wave activity along the Oregon coast. Her failure to foresee that such a thing might happen made her and her district liable for damages (*Morris v. Douglas Co. Sch. Dist.*, 403 P.2d 775, Ore., 1965). But where someone substituted loaded cartridges instead of blanks in a school play and a student was hurt, the principal was not negligent (*Ferreira v. Sanchez,* 449 P.2d 784, N. Mex., 1969).

Q. WHAT CASES ILLUSTRATE TEACHER'S BREACH OF THE DUTY OWED?

A. There are many such cases on record. Many of the cases deal with the reasonableness of leaving a class unsupervised. It is one thing to leave the classroom where the class is busy studying; quite another where the students are engaged in rowdy play, as in a gymnasium. In general, the smaller the children, the greater the duty to see they are in a safe place, but even older students need supervision depending on the activity. A high school club was initiating a student into the club. The sponsor could not be present so he turned the initiation over to the father of the host student. The court held that the district could not escape liability where as here the sponsor had breached his duty to the student, even though the initiation was held off school grounds and outside school hours (*Chappel v. Franklin Pierce School Dist.*, 426 P.2d 471, Wash., 1967). In an unsupervised gymnasium during the noon hour, the district was held liable where two boys engaged in "slap boxing" and one of them fell causing his death. The district was ruled to have failed in its duty owed (*Dailey v. L.A. Unified Sch. Dist.*, 470 P.2d 360, Calif., 1970).

Q. WHAT CASE ILLUSTRATES PROXIMATE CAUSATION BY OTHER THAN THE TEACHER?

A. In New York, the teacher was absent from the classroom storing instructional materials. One student was injured when another student threw a pencil intended for a classmate. The classmate ducked, and the pencil entered the first student's eye, permanently injuring him. "Whether tossing the pencil was done mischievously or wantonly or with the serious purpose of returning the pencil to its owner, it was the act of an intervening third party which under the circumstances could hardly have been anticipated in the reasonable exercise of the teacher's legal duty toward the plaintiff. A pencil in the hand is not a dangerous instrumentality. This is one of those events which could occur equally as well in the presence of the teacher as during her absence." The teacher had a duty to the pupil, and she may have breached the duty owed, but the proximate cause was an intervening third party and not the teacher's absence from the room (*Ohman v. Bd. of Educ. of City of N.Y.*, 90 N.E.2d 474, 1949).

Q. IN WHAT WAYS IS THE INSTRUMENTALITY WHICH CAUSES THE INJURY A DEFENSE AGAINST TORT LIABILITY OF THE TEACHER FOR PUPIL INJURY?

A. In the *Ohman* case cited above, the teacher was not held to the high standard of foreseeing that a *pencil* would cause permanent injury to a pupil. Other cases have been to the same effect where the instrumentality causing the injury was a finger in the eye, a ball, a rock, or the corner of a notebook. If an accident has never happened before where that instrumentality is involved, the teacher is legally entitled to assume that it will not happen. For example, an elementary student watered the plants using a glass milk bottle. The pupil, with the teacher's knowledge, took a chair on which to stand while watering the plants. The child fell from the chair and was severely cut on the broken bottle. The Supreme Court of Michigan ruled the teacher had not been negligent because children had been watering the plants for years without an accident. (*Gaincott v. Davis,* 275 N.W. 229, Mich., 1937).

Q. IN WHAT WAY DOES THE TIME ELEMENT INFLUENCE TORT LIABILITY OF TEACHERS?

A. Injuries occur either *instantaneously* or *gradually.* Normally, those which occur instantaneously, and which could occur as well during a teacher's presence as her absence, do not submit the teacher to tort liability. A good example is *Carroll v. Fitzsimmons* (384 P.2d 81, Colo., 1963), where a student was injured when hit by a rock thrown by an unknown student on the playground. The court held that the injury could have occurred even though the teacher had been standing near the injured pupil, since one cannot stop a rock in its flight. The teacher was not negligent. On the other hand, those cases in which events "build up" gradually, as in Case No. 2 ("Teacher's Absence") at the head of this chapter, the teacher can be held liable because he or she would have taken steps under the developing circumstances to stop the build-up and thus would have prevented the accident had he or she been present (*Christofides v. Hellenic E. Orthodox Christian Church,* 227 N.Y.S. 2d 946, 1962).

Q. WHAT IS MEANT BY "A KNOWN HAZARD"?

A. There are places in schools where the reasonable adult will anticipate that an accident might happen which would injure an individual. The rule is that in such instances, the pupils are *entitled to be warned* of the "known hazard" so that they will be on the alert. Such known hazards as buzzsaws in the school shop, slippery stairs, shaky railings, and wobbly scaffolding have been pointed out by teachers. Where students were later hurt on these hazards, it was held that the teacher had discharged his duty to the pupil by telling him of the hazard, and the student was then on his own. However, failure to notify the students and instruct them how to avoid injury on a known hazard subjects the teacher to possibility of negligence where the average adult would have foreseen that some condition in the school would cause injury to pupils. Safety instruction is a part of each teacher's duty to the pupil; a jury might find that failure to instruct him about a known hazard amounted to a breach of the duty owed, from which flowed the injury.

Q. WHAT CASES ILLUSTRATE FAILURE OF THE TEACHER TO INSTRUCT PUPILS ON A KNOWN HAZARD?

A. A boy in an auto mechanics class was welding an automobile gasoline tank, when the tank exploded, killing one of the boys and seriously injuring another. The teacher was held negligent for failure to supervise the activity and in not warning the boy that what he was doing would most likely lead to dire consequences (*Butcher v. Santa Rosa High School Dist.*, 290 P.2d 316, Calif., 1955). To the same effect was a case arising out of an explosion in a chemistry class where the teacher was demonstrating the production of explosive gases. One student was permanently injured. In holding the teacher liable, the court pointed out that the teacher knew of the dangerous nature of the gases, and should therefore have exercised greater caution in conducting the experiment (*Damgaard v. Oakland High Sch. Dist.*, 298 Pac. 983, Calif., 1931). But where a student sneaked chemicals out of an unlocked cupboard and made a rocket which injured him, the teacher was not held liable because the teacher had first instructed the students about the dangerous nature of the chemicals.

Q. WHAT IS MEANT BY "DUE CARE"?

A. Before liability can attach, a teacher must first have been found wanting in "due care" for the safety of the student. Sometimes this is called "the standard of care" and is measured by what the parent would do under the same circumstances. A state board of education regulation required that eye goggles be worn by students participating in hazardous experiments in chemistry class. A student was injured in general science class; the students were not wearing goggles. The students were making cloud formations when a flask exploded. The teacher was found negligent for using glass not designed for the experiment, for not using goggles even though this was not a chemistry class, and for failing to establish proper procedures and a pressure gauge, in effect, not using "due care" (*Maxwell v. Santa Fe Public Schools*, 534 P.2d 307, N.Mex., 1975).

Q. WHAT IS MEANT BY A DISTRICT "MAINTAINING A NUISANCE"?

A. It means knowingly allowing an unsafe condition to exist over a period of time. A student was injured while climbing a flight of marble steps; the steps were worn and had grooves in them making them slippery. Holding to the rail, the student slipped, and as she fell, the rail separated from the wall. It was established that the rail had been loose for several months prior to the accident. The district was held liable (*Wiener v. Bd. of Educ. of City of N.Y.*, 369 N.Y.S.2d 207, 1975). For ease of moving it from room to room, the school piano was mounted on a low platform. As the piano was shaky, the teacher had to be careful not to rock it too violently, because it might topple from the dolly. The piano was usually kept in the gymnasium. One day, the physical education teacher was leading a drill in the gym in which the students jumped up and down. Suddenly, the piano fell backwards without warning, pinning a girl's ankle to the floor. She was able to recover damages for the maintenance of a nuisance since it was well known around the school that the piano was wobbly and might fall (*Dawson v. Tulare Union Dist.*, 276 Pac. 424, Calif., 1929).

Q. IS THE TEACHER LIABLE FOR MAINTENANCE OF A NUISANCE?

A. Ordinarily, no, so long as you have notified the administration that a hazardous condition exists, and you can prove that you have so notified it. These conditions have been declared nuisances in court: maintaining a junk pile on school grounds, maintaining broken slides and other play equipment, slippery floors, unprotected stairwells, and jagged holes in fences. But where some boys slipped and fell on a wet lavatory floor, the court held that the school did not maintain the nuisance, since the pupils had splashed the water and wet towels on the floor, and thus had contributed to their own injuries (*Jones v. Kansas City*, 271 P.2d 803, Kans., 1954). Also, a "nuisance" legally must be a *continuing* condition, sometimes called "chronic," which is known to exist, and which for some reason or another has not been remedied in time to prevent injury to students or visitors while on school property.

Q. WHAT CONSTITUTES LEGALLY ADEQUATE SUPERVISION BY A TEACHER?

A. No one can give you an unequivocal rule which will apply in all instances because the facts in each case are different. But if supervision *in general* is adequate, it is immaterial that injuries will occur; you cannot insure that no accident will happen. You can reduce hazards: 1) inspect the area to be supervised for possible hazards such as junk, rusty nails, obstructions, and broken equipment; 2) instruct your pupils of known hazards and warn them of impending dangers; 3) report to the authorities all defective equipment or possible nuisance hazards; 4) separate children into groups so larger ones will not injure smaller ones; 5) choose points of vantage from which you can see all the children, and move from point to point; and 6) secure a supply of first aid materials in case they are needed. You are not expected to exercise extraordinary caution, but should ask, "What would the parent do in such a situation?" The answer to that question will constitute legally adequate supervision for those under your care and keeping.

Q. WHAT IS "AN ATTRACTIVE NUISANCE"?

A. In legal parlance, an attractive nuisance is a site which attracts children — such as a swimming pool, playground equipment, or other situation which might lure children. Ordinarily, courts have not required supervision of pupils before or after formal class hours, except for loading of buses or when students congregate to skate, throw snowballs, swim in the pool, hold pep rallies or school carnivals, or similar activities. A teacher is duty-bound to break up groups of rowdy children on school property, or at least report what is going on to the administrator in charge. A junior high school student brought an action against the district and the principal alleging that he could not get into the building until 7:15 a.m. and that he was beaten up by some rowdy kids on unsupervised school grounds while waiting for the doors to open. The court found that it was the willful act of a third party, and not the teacher or principal, who was the proximate cause of the boy's injury (*Sly v. Bd. of Educ., Kansas City, Kans.,* 516 P.2d 895, Kans., 1973).

Q. MAY A PHYSICAL EDUCATION TEACHER BE HELD LIABLE FOR REQUIRING TOO MUCH OF HIS STUDENTS?

A. Yes. There are several cases on this point of law. In Seattle, for example, a student was injured in gym class while attempting to perform acts which the teacher required of all students. She brought an action for damages against the teacher, charging that the teacher knew she could not perform the exercise, that she protested, that the teacher failed to show her how to do it, and that the teacher was negligent in directing her to do the exercise knowing she could not do it. The Supreme Court of Washington held that the teacher was negligent in her supervision of the class where she required too much of the student and would not pay heed to her protestations (*Rodriguez v. Seattle Sch. Dist. No. 1,* 401 P.2d 326, Wash., 1965). A doctor requested a list of exercises which the physical education teacher required but received none. His client, a student in the class, was required to perform a jump from an elevated board and was injured. The jury found the teacher negligent for not knowing that the girl had a back condition and in not furnishing the doctor a list of exercises so he could judge what she should undertake and what she should avoid (*Summers v. Milwaukie Union High School,* 481 P.2d 369, Ore., 1971).

Q. DOES THE DUTY TO PROTECT CHILDREN EXTEND BEYOND THE SCHOOL YARD AND SCHOOL HOURS?

A. Yes. But it is not so strictly enforced as is the duty to students during school hours and on school property. In Kentucky, an eighteen-year-old senior drowned while swimming in a lake while on an outing with his class. The lake was posted. The student was guilty of contributory negligence and the jury exonerated the teacher in charge (*Cox v. Barnes,* 469 S.W.2d 61, Ky., 1971). Likewise, a sixteen-year-old sophomore who broke his leg while on an outing in the mountains with his coach and fellow lettermen was deemed responsible enough to look out for his own safety (*Arnold v. Hafling,* 474 P.2d 638, Colo., 1971). However, where a student was injured at a school carnival when struck by two seventeen-year-olds, the evidence showed that no teachers were around either before or after the attack. The school district was held liable for what amounted to a lack of supervision (negligence) on the part of the district (*Beck v. San Francisco Unified School District,* 37 Cal. Rptr. 471, 1974).

Q. WHAT DIFFERENT TYPES OF DAMAGES DO COURTS AWARD TO PLAINTIFFS?

A. There are several different kinds of damages courts award plaintiffs. Here are the most common kinds: *Compensatory* ("actual") damages are such as will merely compensate the injured party for his loss and nothing more (medical expenses, court costs, loss of pay). *Exemplary* ("punitive," "vindictive") damages are awarded where defendants have shown violence, oppression, malice, fraud, or wanton or reckless disregard for plaintiff's safety. They are "smart money" to prevent defendants from doing the same thing again. *Nominal* ("in name only") damages are a trifling sum awarded plaintiff where there is technically little or no loss but plaintiff has been negligently dealt with. Sometimes appellate courts rule that the jury award was *excessive* (grossly in excess of the amount warranted by the facts). Damages in general are the court's way of making plaintiff "whole again," and are compensation to one who has suffered loss to his person, property, or rights through unlawful acts of another. Ordinarily, damages are *pecuniary* ("measured in terms of money") but may also include other hidden costs such as the attorney's fees, court costs, and similar costs of pursuing relief.

Q. WHAT CASES ILLUSTRATE THE DIFFERENT KINDS OF DAMAGES AWARDED TO STUDENTS WHO WERE INJURED AND/OR THEIR PARENTS?

A. In Louisiana, a new student was injured in a game of touch football when he plunged into a ditch overgrown with weeds. There were no barriers or warning signs near the ditch. The student was awarded punitive damages of $5,000, while the father was awarded actual costs of $651 (*Sears v. City of Springfield,* 303 So.2d 602, La., 1974). The punitive damages were assessed because the board had done nothing to reduce danger from a known hazard, the weed-covered ditch. In one of the largest tort damage awards in history, the court awarded a father and his son who was injured in a summer playground program jointly sponsored by the district and city, the sum of $4 million (*Niles v. City of San Rafael,* 116 Cal. Rptr. 733, 1974). As to nominal damages, the teacher who is illegally dismissed, but who obtains a job teaching at a higher salary is entitled to the sum of $1.

Defenses Against Charges of Negligence

Q. WHAT ARE SOME OF THE DEFENSES TEACHERS CAN USE AGAINST TORT LIABILITY?

A. Beginning with the three-tiered test, the teacher may say that a) he did not owe the student who was injured a duty; b) or if he did, he did not breach the duty owed; or c) that despite the fact that (a) and (b) are stipulated, there was an intervening force which was the proximate cause of the injury. Other defenses are: 1) an unavoidable accident which could not be foreseen by the average, normally prudent parent; 2) assumption of risk by the student when he undertook the activity, such as athletic competition; 3) contributory negligence, in that the student brought about his own injury or contributed to it in some way; 4) that the student or his parents had waived liability through signing a release slip; and 5) comparative negligence, in which the culpability for the injury is shared between the student and the teacher in charge. In rare instances, defendant teachers have pleaded that the injury was an act of God, but this is related to unavoidable accident.

Q. WHAT CASES ILLUSTRATE THE DEFENSE OF UNAVOIDABLE ACCIDENT?

A. A student was injured when hit by a bicycle on the playground. The teacher defended that it was an unavoidable accident. The court, however, said that permitting pupils to ride bicycles on the playground where other students were playing constituted inadequate supervision (*Buzzard v. East Lake Sch. Dist.*, 93 P.2d 233, Calif., 1939). The teacher who was bowled over by a wave while posing children on a log near the ocean defended on the grounds that the injury was a result of an unavoidable accident. The court could not agree, saying that adults should know of unusual wave activity along the Oregon coast, and protect their charges against it (*Morris v. Douglas Co. Sch. Dist.*, 403 P.2d 775, Ore., 1965). Still another student was injured during the summer when school was not in session. Three boys playing on school grounds threw a glass bottle at the basketball goal; it shattered and flying glass hit the plaintiff. The court held that the injury was caused by intervening acts of third parties, not by the teacher or principal (*Crossen v. Bd. of Educ. of City of N.Y.*, 359 N.Y.S.2d 316, 1974).

Q. WHAT CASES ILLUSTRATE THE DEFENSE OF ASSUMPTION OF RISK?

A. Athletic activities produce a plethora of injuries to students each year. The courts have tended to protect coaches and school officials from liability on the grounds that one who undertakes a hazardous activity in school *assumes some risk*. Some cases, such as *Vendrell v. Sch. Dist. No. 26C* (376 P.2d 406, Ore., 1962), turn on whether the injured student was "overmatched." The coach needs merely to show that the equipment was adequate, and that he had given instructions and coaching pointers to the players in order to avoid negligence. Gymnasium injuries where instructors require too much from their students may not be protected if physical education is a required subject since there is an element of voluntary choice in going out for a sport not present in the required gym class. But even playground activity may be subject to assumed risks where students are old enough to know better. A boy was shoved by another boy into a basketball goalpost. He lost both his front teeth. The cause of the injury, said the court, was an intervening classmate, and not a lack of supervision on the part of the teacher (*Woodsmall v. Mt. Diablo Unified Sch. Dist.*, 10 Cal. Rptr. 447, Calif., 1961).

Q. WHAT CASES ILLUSTRATE CONTRIBUTORY NEGLIGENCE AS A DEFENSE FOR THE TEACHER?

A. Contributory negligence depends on the age of the child; if the child is too young to apprehend the danger of his act, he cannot be held to have contributed to his injury. There is no legal age at which children are supposed to reach "reason." An eight-year-old boy was injured when he swung up on the moving bus as it pulled into the school yard. The court held that a sense of danger from impact with a moving bus is not wanting in a school child of eight years; he had contributed to his own injury (*Weems v. Robinson*, 9 So.2d 882, Ala., 1942). Other pupils have been similarly held to have contributed. A fifteen-year-old boy asked permission to set up chemistry apparatus for the day's lesson. An explosion occurred. The court held he had contributed to his own injury by mixing ingredients not called for in the experiment (*Decker v. Dundee Central Sch. Dist.*, 167 N.Y.S.2d 666, 1957). But where the principal employed a minor who slipped on the wet grass and his foot went under the mower, the defense of contributory negligence was not allowed (*Smith v. Uffelman*, 509 S.W.2d 229, Tenn., 1973). The boy's father did not know that his son was doing odd jobs at school presumably to earn lunch money. The court held that the principal was negligent in letting the boy mow the grass while it was wet. The case was remanded for determination of the amount of damages to the boy and to his father for medical bills.

Q. HOW EFFECTIVE ARE WAIVERS OF LIABILITY SIGNED BY THE PARENT?

A. They have high public relations but very little legal value. Schools sometimes make it a practice to send home waiver slips to parents when students are about to go on field trips or undertake hazardous activities in school. While these waiver slips may exonerate the school of any liability from suit by the parent (actually, in some states they do not) they still do not mean that the student has signed away his right to sue. The student may later sue in his or her own name. The greatest use of waiver slips is in their public relations value — they let you know that the parent is aware of the impending trip or hazardous activity, and to some extent that he is assuming some risk or the student is knowingly assuming some risk by allowing the student to be a part of that activity. You should check the law in your own state to determine the legal value, if any, of the liability waiver form in your jurisdiction.

Q. MAY THE TEACHER PLEAD SOVEREIGN IMMUNITY AS A DEFENSE?

A. No. Sovereign immunity extends only to governmental units, such as the board of education. The Supreme Court of Ohio, for example, ruled that the immunity of school districts from liability for negligence does not extend to teachers, who must exercise reasonable care in the performance of their duties (*Baird v. Hosmer*, 347 N.E.2d 533, Ohio, 1976).

Q. WHAT CASES ILLUSTRATE THE DEFENSE OF COMPARATIVE NEGLIGENCE?

A. Some of the states have adopted legislation whereby in cases where contributory negligence has been proved, liability is assessed in direct proportion to fault. If the plaintiff's fault is found to be about equal to the defendant's, for example, then the plaintiff will recover one-half the damages and must bear the remainder of the loss himself. The rationale for this is that the plaintiff, even though he is partly to blame for his own harm, will not be totally barred from recovery. (See *Nga Li v. Yellow Cab Co. of Cal.*, 532 P.2d 1226, 1976, in which the Supreme Court of California ruled that contributory negligence is no longer applicable in that state; and *Farley v. M. M. Cattle Co.*, 529 S.W.2d 751, Tex., 1976, in which the Texas Supreme Court abolished the doctrine of assumption of risk insofar as it relates to contributory negligence.)

Q. SHOULD TEACHERS EXPECT THE SCHOOL'S ATTORNEY TO PROVIDE DEFENSES AGAINST CHARGES OF TEACHER NEGLIGENCE?

A. Ordinarily, no. Each teacher should have legal counsel on an individual or group basis, either through private employment of an attorney, or through provision of counsel via a teachers' association. The school district's attorney (most districts now employ legal counsel) sometimes has a conflict of interest where the district acts as an employer, but this is not always so. You should consider negotiating for the use of the school's attorney in certain types of cases, such as in student injury cases, or negotiate some kind of "save harmless" clause in the negotiated agreement with the board, so that the board will come to the legal aid of a teacher who has suit brought against him or her over pupil injury. Also, there is a blanket liability insurance which members of certain teachers' organizations can obtain which will provide legal counsel in case you are hauled into court to face a suit for damages involving student injury.

Q. SHOULD THE TEACHER CONSIDER COVERAGE FOR LIABILITY THROUGH INSURANCE?

A. No teacher should be without adequate liability insurance coverage, even during vacation periods. An insurer will soften the blow should you be found personally liable for negligence while on the job. The largest area of "blind-side" liability lies in injury to students who may be transported in the teacher's car. Although "guest statutes" vary from state to state, you should become thoroughly familiar with the requirements for coverage of teachers in case you take a student to the doctor, or home because of illness, or to a school function somewhere such as to a game or meeting. The usual personal car insurance policy does not cover the transportation of students. Ordinarily, students riding with the teacher are not considered "guests" in the legal meaning of that term, and so can bring suit if the teacher is negligent. (A "guest" statute merely says that anyone riding with someone else as a non-paying guest cannot bring suit in case of injury except for certain overt circumstances.)

Q. WHAT CASES ILLUSTRATE LIABILITY OF TEACHERS WHO WERE TRANSPORTING STUDENTS?

A. Perhaps the best known is an Idaho case. The football coach borrowed a fellow-teacher's car to transport players to a game. On the trip, the coach missed a turn and was killed and some of the boys riding in the teacher's car were injured. Since the coach was not around to sue, the boys brought suit against the teacher, claiming the coach was her agent, and that she was liable. Their suit was successful. Idaho at the time had a "guest" statute, but the court held the boys were not "guests" within the meaning of that term (*Gorton v. Doty*, 69 P.2d 136, Ida., 1937). (The law of agency operates on the theory that one person, here the coach, becomes the "agent" for another, here the "principal" in the agency relationship, the teacher.) When you supervise a school bus loaded with boosters, the district ordinarily has insurance covering everyone, but with your own car, or in another teacher's car, it's different. So be sure that when you take students on a trip, your car is fully covered with a rider specifying that students under your care and supervision are included in the coverage. You may even be liable if you let students ride with some driver who has a reputation as a "harum-scarum" driver (*Hanson v. Reedley Jt. Sch. Dist.*, 111 P.2d 415, Calif., 1941).

Q. DOES THE USUAL LIABILITY INSURANCE POLICY COVER "WRONGFUL ACTS" TORTS?

A. No. Liability insurance coverage extends to persons, such as parents and students, who may be injured due to the negligence of the teacher. There is a type of insurance that covers "wrongful acts of school officials" (sometimes called "deprivation of civil rights insurance"). The name of this type of insurance is *indemnity* insurance, meaning that if you as the covered party are ever held to pay damages for your wrongful acts, the company will *indemnify* you, either by paying your attorney's fees or any damages which are won in court against you or both. More will be said on this topic in a following section of this chapter entitled "Constitutional Torts."

Assault and Battery

Q. LEGALLY, WHAT IS AN "ASSAULT"? CAN AN ASSAULT OCCUR WITHOUT TOUCHING?

A. An assault is an illegal attempt or offer (without actual contact) to beat or touch another person in such a way as to cause that person to apprehend immediate peril. Thus, the attempt must be coupled with the ability or what the person believes to be the ability to execute the threat. Assault may involve words, actions or both. But not all verbal attacks are classified as assaults. A parent brought suit against a teacher for intentionally "abusing, attacking, embarrassing, and intimidating" her children. She cited possible injury to their nervous systems, their learning abilities, and their later earning capacities. The court held that a teacher has the right to chastise the child verbally as well as corporally. Furthermore, a teacher cannot be sued unless there is evidence of malice which was not shown here (*Gordon v. Oak Park School Dist.*, 320 N.E.2d 389, Ill., 1974).

Q. WHAT IS A "BATTERY"? MUST THERE BE CONTACT IN A BATTERY?

A. A battery is the willful touching of another person by the aggressor or by some substance put in motion by him; or, as it is sometimes expressed, a battery is the consummation of the assault. A sixty-nine-year-old teacher worked in a tough school. Secretly, she armed herself with a "sneeze-gun" which emitted a spray designed to cause the eyes to water and to temporarily put a person on the defense. When a large girl in her class resisted her attempts to lead her to the principal's office, the teacher shot her with the sneeze-gun. The girl brought suit for assault and battery against the teacher for $50,000 damages. Her suit failed. The court found that a teacher who has reason to believe that she will be assaulted by a student has the right of self-defense (*Owens v. Commonwealth of Kentucky*, 473 S.W.2d 827, 1972).

Q. IN WHAT AREA DO MOST STUDENT-INITIATED SUITS FOR ASSAULT AND BATTERY ORIGINATE?

A. In the area of corporal punishment. Most state statutes say nothing about corporal punishment. A few states prohibit it while others make it available. But there is a basis for a tort action only if the punishment is excessive or unreasonable, a question for the jury (*Baker v. Owen*, 395 F.Supp. 294, affirmed, U.S. S.Ct. 44 L.W. 3235, Oct. 20, 1975). "Administering corporal punishment without due process of law is not inherently unconstitutional," said one court, "because if the punishment is unreasonable and excessive, it is no longer lawful, and the perpetrator of it may be criminally and civilly liable" (*Ware v. Estes*, 328 F.Supp. 657, affirmed, 458 F.2d 1360, Tex., 1971, *cert. denied*, 409 U.S. 1027, 1973). Nor does the reasonable use of corporal punishment violate the Eighth Amendment's prohibition against cruel and unusual punishment (*Ingraham v. Wright*, 97 S.Ct. 1401, Fla., 1977).

Q. WHO DETERMINES WHETHER ASSAULT AND BATTERY HAVE OCCURRED?

A. The question of assault and battery is for the jury to decide on instructions from the judge. In corporal punishment cases, the question is whether the teacher, acting *in loco parentis*, attained that standard of care which the average, normally prudent parent would have reasonably exercised in the same or similar circumstances. Failure to live up to that standard amounts to negligence, and the three-tiered test for negligence would be the points of law on which the judge would base instructions to the jury. Factors in the case — age, sex, strength, health, and similar characteristics of the child, the teacher's size, age and general health, the chronological events — all are pertinent. Once these are established, it then becomes the duty of the jury to determine whether the teacher acted as the reasonable parent would have acted or stepped outside the protection of the *in loco parentis* role, and administered excessive punishment under the circumstances.

Q. DOES THE EIGHTH AMENDMENT APPLY TO CORPORAL PUNISHMENT OF STUDENTS?

A. No. The Eighth Amendment's prohibition against cruel and unusual punishments applies only to *criminals,* said the Supreme Court in *Ingraham v. Wright* (97 S.Ct. 1401, Fla., 1977). "The openness of the public school and its supervision by the community afford significant safeguards against the kinds of abuses from which the Eighth Amendment protects the prisoner," said the Court. "Public school teachers and administrators are privileged at common law to inflict only such corporal punishment as is reasonably necessary for the proper education and discipline of the child; any punishment beyond the privilege may result in both civil and criminal liability. As long as the schools are open to public scrutiny, there is no reason to believe that the common law constraints will not effectively remedy and deter excesses such as those alleged in this case."

Q. WHAT CASES ILLUSTRATE ASSAULT AND BATTERY OF SCHOOL STUDENTS?

A. Where two school board members accused a fifteen-year-old girl of unchastity, as a result of which she suffered great mental anguish and nervous shock, her suit for damages was upheld (*Johnson v. Sampson,* 208 N.W. 814, Minn., 1926). "To be guilty of an 'assault and battery,'" said one court, "a school teacher must not only inflict on the pupil immoderate chastisement, but he must do so with legal malice or wicked motives, or he must inflict some permanent injury" (*Suits v. Glover,* 71 So.2d 49, Ala., 1954). Where a principal weighing 190 pounds knelt on a pupil weighing 89 pounds and caused permanent injury, the student was able to recover (*Calway v. Williamson,* 36 A.2d 377, Conn., 1944). And in Illinois, where a teacher bloodied a student's nose and put him in the hospital with a swollen eye, the jury found the corporal punishment unreasonable and excessive (*People v. Smith,* 335 N.E.2d 125, Ill., 1975).

Q. WHAT CASES ILLUSTRATE "REASONABLE" CORPORAL PUNISHMENT SHORT OF ASSAULT AND BATTERY?

A. Only near-shocking behavior of teachers in administering corporal punishment will give rise to liability. In Illinois, a student charged malice and abuse, and presented evidence of malicious physical and emotional actions, possibly motivated by anti-Semitism. The court, however, issued summary judgment in favor of the teacher (*Gordon v. Oak Park Sch. Dist.,* 320 N.E.2d 389, Ill., 1975). In an Oregon case, a student was being forcibly removed from a classroom when his arm was cut when it accidentally went through a window in a door. Although school regulations prohibited the use of corporal punishment "except in the event of forcible and physical resistance to the teacher's authority," the court found what it considered to be substantial evidence that the teacher was justified under the regulation. "A teacher under the regulation is not required to attempt all other means including suspension, expulsion, or detention in an effort to control the student's behavior," said the court (*Simms v. School Dist. No. 1 of Multnomah County,* 508 P.2d 236, Ore., 1973).

Q. IS THE TEACHER ENTITLED TO THE DEFENSE OF SELF-DEFENSE IN ASSAULT AND BATTERY CASES?

A. Yes, if it can reasonably be deduced that the student is about to attack the teacher. The teacher has the same right as any other citizen to protect himself or herself from attack. But the teacher can use only that force as is reasonably necessary to end the threat. If the teacher responds with force that is excessive under the circumstances, or continues to use force after the pupil has submitted or attempts to flee, the teacher steps outside the protection of *in loco parentis* and loses the defense of justification for self-defense in an assault and battery suit. The teacher is also expected to protect other students against physical attack by one of the members of the class or an outsider. Nor will the teacher be held liable for a mistake as to which one is the aggressor.

Defamation

Q. CAN TEACHERS "DEFAME" (LIBEL OR SLANDER) THEIR STUDENTS?

A. Teachers come into possession of critical information about their students, so it is only natural that there is the risk that some of this information may be communicated to others in such a way that an action in defamation of character is justified. Defamation is defined in the law as those words which tend to bring a person into public hatred, contempt or ridicule, cause him or her to be shunned or avoided, or injure him or her in his or her business or occupation. If the words are written or broadcast, the tort is called *libel;* if spoken, *slander.* These two components make up defamation of character, a very old tort (Moses commanded: "Neither shall you bear false witness against your neighbor"). Redress for injury to reputation is therefore one of the most cherished legal rights, a right which incidentally is not barred to children. More will be said in Chapter 5 on defamation of character in connection with student published newspapers.

Q. IS LIBEL AN OCCUPATIONAL HAZARD FOR TEACHERS?

A. Yes, particularly since the passage of the Buckley Amendment (Family Educational Rights and Privacy Act, P.L. 93-380, 1974) which was designed to protect the privacy of parents and students. As a result of this law, most school districts prepared a set of guidelines for release of information about students; these should be carefully followed by teachers in order to avoid liability. The act governs access to records — keeping the records, storing them, and releasing them to interested persons. Parents of students must have access to official records and an opportunity to challenge inaccurate or misleading information; parents and students must be notified of their rights; these rights transfer to the student at certain points, particularly at age eighteen; and due process of law must be observed in keeping, storing, and releasing the records of all students. Thus, an anecdotal record from a teacher that "this kid would be all right if it weren't for his dad" would become an "open record" and would constitute actionable words against the teacher.

Q. MAY THE TEACHER BE LIBELED BY STATEMENTS MADE BY PARENTS?

A. In California, some parents wrote a letter to the principal that a teacher "displayed an utter lack of judgment and respect, had been rude, vindictive and unjust, misused her authority and had given failing grades to students she did not like." The court used the following words in disallowing her claim for defamation of character: "One of the crosses a public school teacher must bear is intemperate complaint addressed to school administrators by overly-solicitous parents concerned about the teacher's conduct in the classroom. Since the law compels parents to send their children to school, appropriate channels for the airing of supposed grievances against the operation of the school system must remain open (*Martin v. Kearney,* 124 Cal.Rptr. 281, 1975). The same conclusion was reached by a judge in an earlier case where a teacher was not promoted on the basis of a letter the parent wrote through channels containing statements later proved to be false about the teacher (*Segall v. Piazza,* 260 N.Y.S.2d 543, 1965).

Q. ARE PARENTAL CRITICISMS OF THE TEACHER'S WORK "PRIVILEGED"?

A. Yes, so long as certain conditions are met, and the parent is not governed by malice in making the statements. In *Segall v. Piazza,* even though the statements were false, the court held that they were privileged, since the mother thought them to be true when she wrote them in a letter to the teacher's principal. Since the parent was not motivated by ill will or malice, but only by an interest in her son, the court did not find that she had stepped outside her normal right to criticize the teacher. She had gone through channels, had kept her son's interests central in her letter, and had acted in good faith. The fact that the teacher had been denied a promotion because of the letter, and had demonstrated a loss of income due to it, was not grounds for recovery of damages but only an unfortunate misunderstanding, said the court. And in *Martin v. Kearney,* the fact that the parent expressed the hope that the teacher would correct her personality defects was grounds for making the parental letter "privileged" and therefore not actionable.

Q. WHAT IS MEANT BY "PRIVILEGED COMMUNICATIONS"? ARE TEACHERS PROTECTED UNDER THIS DOCTRINE?

A. Teachers have what is called a "qualified" or "limited" — not absolute — privilege to handle information about their students, but they may lose this privilege if they act in a malicious way or without good faith in so doing. Even though the communication may be defamatory, it may be privileged "where made in the discharge of some public duty, where information is released to someone having the right to receive it, and without malice." Teachers can lose the privilege where they act "to get even" with a student. Where one teacher wrote that a student "was tricky and unreliable," she was held to have stepped outside the protection of privileged communications, and was held liable in damages for injury to the student's reputation (*Dixon v. Allen,* 11 Pac. 179, Calif., 1886). Similarly, where a teacher described a student as "ruined by tobacco and whiskey," the court held the teacher liable (*Dawkins v. Billingsley,* 172 P.2d 69, Okla., 1918).

Field Trips, Errands, and Similar Hazards

Q. DOES THE DUTY TO PROTECT THE CHILD APPLY TO FIELD TRIPS?

A. Yes. Teachers in charge of students on officially-sponsored trips owe the duty to protect the student the same as if they were in school. Ordinarily, claims for damages on field trips are not brought against teachers; rather, they are brought against owners of the visited site, but this is not always the case. In one instance, a younger child missed going to the zoo with his class, so he sought permission, which was granted, to go along with an older class. The teacher had already instructed the class, and time did not permit repeating same to the younger child. At the zoo, the child was injured when he stuck his arm into the lion's cage and was bitten. The teacher was held liable for failure to protect the younger child from harm.

Q. WHAT RULES OF LAW APPLY ON FIELD TRIPS WHICH ARE NOT PRESENT ON SCHOOL PROPERTY?

A. On other than school property, the legal status *(trespasser, licensee, invitee)* is the controlling factor to recovery of damages. One who goes on another's property without permission is a *trespasser,* and the owner owes no duty to that person except that he may not set a man-trap or use greater force in expelling him from the premises than is reasonably necessary. A *licensee* is on another's property at the sufferance of the owner, and he takes the risks which accompany such a legal status. Finally, an *invitee* has been invited (or implicitly invited) on the premises by the owner or occupant, and is owed a higher standard of care than would be accorded a trespasser or a licensee. So in field trip cases, the first step at trial is to determine the legal status (using these three classifications) to determine the standard of care which the law might expect from the owner or renter of the property where the accident occurred.

Q. WHAT CASES ILLUSTRATE THE LEGAL STANDING OF A TRESPASSER?

A. Trespassers are on someone's property without his knowledge or consent, but are owed at least the duty not to be exposed to more force than is absolutely necessary to expel the trespasser from the premises. Thus, when a farmer set a shotgun to go off, a trespasser who opened a door in an abandoned farmhouse and was shot in the leg was able to recover damages from the farmer because the force used was excessive. Another court held that an owner invited theft of his car by leaving the keys in the ignition; a child was hurt in a car struck by the stolen auto. In a case in which a student drowned while trespassing on a beach posted against swimming, the court held the teacher in charge blameless because the student was a senior and old enough to realize the risk he was taking. If the field trip is to take your students onto property on which there will be possible trespass, you may be held liable for negligence by not taking proper precautions in taking children into dangerous situations without the owner's knowledge or consent.

Q. WHAT CASE ILLUSTRATES THE LEGAL STANDING OF THE STUDENT AS LICENSEE?

A. A teacher called a power plant and obtained permission to bring a class of 30 boys to the plant for a field trip. Permission was granted. A guide from the company conducted the tour, but midway through it he excused himself because he had to return to work. He told the principal and class to continue to tour the facility. This the class did but without the services of a guide. Near the end of the visit, one of the boys fell into a vat of boiling water and was severely burned. Suit was brought by the injured boy's parents against the company for damages sustained in the fall. The court refused to hold the company liable. The boys were *licensees,* present on the grounds for their own benefit and at no benefit to the company. (One can only conjecture what would have been the outcome had the suit been against the principal and teacher.) (*Benson v. Baltimore Traction Company,* 26 Atl. 973, Md., 1893.) "If any negligence was apparent," said the court, "it was in taking 30 boys into a building filled with dangerous machinery."

Q. WHAT CASE ILLUSTRATES THE STANDARD OF CARE OWED AN INVITEE?

A. The sign in a combined bakery and creamery read "Inspection Invited." The company often acted as host to field trips. A girl was injured during one such trip through the plant when her hand was badly mangled in an ice crushing machine. Her suit against the company was successful. The court said that her status before the law was that of an *invitee,* rather than a licensee. The fact that the company "invited" people to come in and look around and that it secured advertising benefits from such tours caused it to have a higher standard of care towards those who accepted its invitation than if the visitors were mere *licensees* (*Gilliland v. Bondurant,* 59 S.W.2d 679, Mo., 1933). Of course, the teacher should exercise reasonable care even though the students will come onto the property as invitees. Instead of conducting the tour yourself, ask the host company to provide guides for the tour. Even though they may be invitees, the court might find that taking smaller children into a dangerous and unfamiliar place amounts to negligence on the part of the teacher.

Q. WHAT RULES SHOULD GOVERN FIELD TRIPS?

A. The younger the child, the more care you owe that child. Therefore, where you will be taking small children into dangerous places, you should use reasonable measures to see that adequate supervision of that age group is being supplied. Failure to have enough people around will result in negligence *per se.* You should have sufficient liability insurance to cover suits by class members. You should leave word with your principal that certain steps have been taken to assure the safety of the students. And prior planning with other teachers who have taken this field trip may cause you to take extra precautions while on the trip. Finally, be sure that the transportation (which causes many injuries on field trips) is adequate, that is, that it is fully insured and that a safe driver is available. While you are not supposed to have extraordinary clairvoyance, you are expected to foresee what a normal, prudent parent might consider a hazard and warn students about it before going on the trip.

Q. IS THE TEACHER WHO "TURNS THE PARENT IN" LIABLE IN DAMAGES?

A. No, even if the law is silent on the point. In Kentucky, which had a compulsory attendance law, a teacher told the board that a certain family was not in school, whereupon the board caused the parent to be arrested, convicted, and incarcerated for failure to enter children in school. The court held that the teacher and the board were immune from a damage suit by the parent (*Jones v. Bd. of Educ. of Daviss County,* 470 S.W.2d 829, Ky., 1971). Some states have legislation requiring the teacher to report any battered child signs; these same statutes usually "save harmless" the teacher who reports a case which he believes to be that of a battered child. Also, some states specifically exempt teachers from liability against parental damages in reporting incidents of venereal disease, abortions, use of contraceptives, or other problems with which the schools are currently dealing.

Q. DOES FURNISHING ALCOHOL TO A MINOR MAKE THE TEACHER LIABLE IN TORT?

A. Conceivably it could. A New Jersey court has held that a social host who furnished excessive amounts of intoxicants to a minor may be held liable for the minor's subsequent negligent acts which cause injury to an innocent third party (*Linn v. Rand,* 356 A.2d 15, N.J., 1976). But the adult must be proved to have known that the minor was under the influence and there must be of course a duty owed by that adult to the minor before liability will attach. It would all depend on the circumstances. If the students met at the teacher's house, and the teacher served intoxicating beverages, and if the minors were subsequently involved in an injury to third parties, it could reasonably be anticipated that the jury would find the teacher liable for negligence.

Q. SHOULD THE TEACHER REASONABLY KNOW THAT A STUDENT IS GOING TO COMMIT SUICIDE?

A. It all depends. In a case which arose in Wisconsin, a college student at one of the state colleges had been under the care of personnel in the counseling and testing center. She was told that she was in no more need of psychological assistance, and the sessions were discontinued. The girl committed suicide. The parents brought an action against the college. The court held that the college would be liable only if one of its employees, here the counselor, was negligent. To hold that a teacher who had no training, education, or experience in the medical field is required to recognize in a student a condition the diagnosis of which requires a specialized and technical medical knowledge would require a duty far beyond reason, said the court in exonerating the college of any liability (*Bogust v. Iverson,* 102 N.W.2d 228, Wisc., 1960).

Q. CAN THE DISTRICT BRING NEGLIGENCE ACTIONS AGAINST TEACHERS OR OTHER EMPLOYEES WHO FAIL TO DO WHAT THEY ARE SUPPOSED TO DO?

A. This is the age of educational malpractice suits, and districts may bring negligence actions against employees who do not perform, particularly if there is pecuniary loss. The city of Boston brought suit against seven principals for allegedly failing to keep accurate records for students who were being transported to school by taxi as a result of a desegregation court order. The city charged that because of faulty record keeping, the taxi company was charging for transporting students who were not even attending school. The city had earlier instituted a suit against the transportation company for $500,000. Accountability, minimal competency testing, and educational malpractice suits such as this may become more common should plaintiffs prove successful in winning certain negligence suits.

Q. IS THERE DANGER IN SPONSORING A SCHOOL SAFETY PATROL?

A. Yes. Some school districts are discontinuing placing children in dangerous situations and are disbanding their street safety patrols. It is well settled that students have no control over traffic in the streets, and that placing them in hazardous situations may expose the teacher to legal action for negligence. The district must determine for itself whether the possible educational values to be gained from patrol operation outweigh the risk of possible injury to patrol participants. A few states have "save-harmless" laws protecting school personnel from liability in patrol operation, but many do not. These statutes provide for 1) a short time to file claims for damages, usually ninety days or so; 2) holding the school district and not the principal or teacher liable if injury to students occurs; and 3) allowing the district to expend public moneys for purchase of liability insurance to cover possible injury in patrol operations.

Q. MAY THE TEACHER BE HELD LIABLE FOR INJURIES TO STUDENTS WHILE ON ERRANDS FOR THE TEACHER?

A. A teacher may be held liable if in sending a pupil on an errand the child is exposed to a danger which should have been apparent to the average parent of normal intelligence. In New York, a teacher sent a thirteen-year-old girl on an errand, and the girl was raped. The court required the plaintiff to show that other incidents had happened previously which would have led a reasonable teacher to foresee that such consequences would transpire (*Gallagher v. City of N.Y.*, 292 N.Y.S.2d 139, 1968). A weak, pale lad was dispatched on a working party moving cartons. He complained of a pain in his chest and was told to use "two boys to a carton." When a doctor examined the boy, he said the boy had sustained injury to his heart. The court rendered judgment in his behalf for $35,000 against the board of education. "Parents do not send their children to school to be returned to them maimed because of the absence of proper supervision," said the court (*Feuerstein v. Bd. of Educ. of City of N.Y.*, 202 N.Y.S.2d 524, 1960). A classroom teacher who also drove a school bus gave the key to a fifteen-year-old unlicensed student one cold morning, to warm up the bus. The student drove the bus around the block, striking a truck. The truckdriver brought an action for damages but was told the Industrial Commission lacked jurisdiction because the teacher was not operating the bus and the student had no authorization to do so (*Withers v. Charlotte-Mecklenburg Bd. of Educ.*, 231 S.E.2d 276, N.C., 1976). Finally, a New Mexico court ruled that the teacher may be held liable if a pupil, in performing an errand for the teacher, is injured even though the injury was the direct result of the student's inexperience and immaturity (*McMullen v. Ursuline Order of Sisters*, 246 P.2d 1052, N.Mex., 1952).

Q. MAY THE TEACHER BE LIABLE IF A STUDENT IS INJURED BY MISSING THE BUS?

A. This question was before a court in South Carolina. An eight-year-old girl was detained after school by her teacher and subsequently missed her bus. She was struck and killed by a truck as she walked home in a heavily congested area. But because the State of South Carolina was and still is an immunity state, the court refused to hold the district liable in damages (*Graham v. Charleston City School Bd.*, 204 S.E.2d 384, S.C., 1974). But the states still retaining the defense of governmental immunity to tort liability are few — about six or seven in number. In most states, the teacher would have had to face the suit, and even in South Carolina, and other states still retaining the governmental immunity defense, a teacher may not hide behind governmental immunity as a defense.

Constitutional Torts

Q. DO TEACHERS HAVE LIABILITY UNDER THE CIVIL RIGHTS ACTS — IN EFFECT, A CONSTITUTIONAL TORT LIABILITY?

A. A suit brought for damages under federal civil rights acts is really not a tort action, but, since the facts which induced the action are alleged injury to the person or reputation of another, it seems logical to treat them as tort liability actions. The question to be decided by the federal courts is whether a person has been deprived of a civil right, and most of the actions arise not so much under the Fourteenth Amendment as under the Civil Rights Act of 1871 (42 U.S.C. Sec. 1983). This section says that "any person who deprives another person of a civil right guaranteed under the Constitution or public laws is liable to that person in any action at law, suit in equity, or other proper proceeding for redress. . . ."

Q. WHAT ARE SOME EXAMPLES OF CONSTITUTIONAL TORTS?

A. In Tennessee, a student claimed the teacher jerked a chair from under him and caused him to fall to the floor of the study hall for a minor infraction, causing him injuries, embarrassment, and humiliation in the presence of his fellow students. He alleged violation of the Civil Rights Act of 1871, since the teacher was acting under color of state law as a representative of the state. The court said the county board of education was not a "person" under 42 U.S.C. Sec. 1983, but the teacher could be subject to Section 1983 if the proof established that he had been guilty of "the requisite degree of harm needed to constitute that denial of rights implicit in the concept of ordered liberty" (*Patton v. Bennett,* 304 F.Supp. 297, Tenn., 1970). Later, in 1975, the Supreme Court held that "school officials," which presumably includes teachers, are not immune from such liability "if they knew or reasonably should have known that the action they took would violate the constitutional rights of the student affected . . ." (*Wood v. Strickland,* 95 S.Ct. 992, Ark., 1975).

In 1978, after studying the intent of the Congress in enacting the CRA of 1871, the Supreme Court ruled that not only individual officials but also the governmental unit itself could be considered a "person" where state action triggered by policy, custom, or practice deprives someone of a civil right. (*Monell v. Dept. of Social Services,* 436 U.S. 658, 1978).

Q. IN WHAT WAY ARE EQUAL PROTECTION AND DUE PROCESS INVOLVED IN CONSTITUTIONAL TORTS?

A. The state, according to the Fourteenth Amendment, may not deny to any person equal protection of its laws, nor due process of the law, in depriving a person of life, liberty or property. The Supreme Court has held that the right to go to school is both a liberty and a property right guaranteed under the Fourteenth Amendment. Thus, school officials may not deprive a student of that right without first giving the student his or her day in court

(*Wood v. Strickland,* 95 S.Ct 992, Ark., 1975; *Goss v. Lopez,* 419 U.S. 565, Ohio, 1975). Earlier, the Court had held that "due process of law is not for adults alone," and districts may not maintain a double standard, one for students, the other for adults (*In re Gault,* 87 S. Ct. 1428, Ariz., 1967). Two years later, the Court further strengthened this doctrine in *Tinker v. Des Moines Sch.Bd.* (393 U.S. 502, Iowa, 1969), by ruling that the district had denied children who wore black armbands in school to protest the war in Vietnam the civil right of freedom of expression protected under the First Amendment.

Q. IN WHAT WAY DOES THE SUPREME COURT PROTECT THE CHILD'S RIGHT TO LEARN?

A. There is a long line of Supreme Court cases protecting the child's right to a free education. In 1943, the Court said that a state may not require the salute to the flag as a condition of attending a public school (*W.Va.St.Bd. of Educ. v. Barnette,* 319 U.S. 624, 1943). Earlier rulings protected the child's right to study a foreign language (*Meyer v. Nebraska,* 43 S.Ct. 625, 1923) and to go to private or parochial schools (*Pierce v. Society of Sisters,* 45 S.Ct. 571, Ore., 1925). In 1966, Justice Douglas wrote in *Haley v. Ohio* (331 U.S. 596), that "neither man nor child can be allowed to stand condemned by methods which flout constitutional requirements of due process of law." In *Brown v. Bd. of Educ.* (347 U.S. 483, Kans., 1954), the Court held that separate but equal facilities for the races "are inherently unequal." But the most influential case has been *Tinker v. Des Moines Sch.Bd.* (89 S.Ct. 733, Iowa, 1969), where the Court held that children are "persons" under our Constitution and do not shed their constitutional rights at the schoolhouse gate.

Q. IN ESSENCE, WHAT DOES THE *TINKER* DECISION GUARANTEE CHILDREN IN STATE SCHOOLS?

A. The question in this case was whether in the absence of disruption to the educational program children who go to public schools under compulsory attendance laws may express symbolic opposition to certain governmental activities. This "minority" ruling — rule of one against the many — holds that "in order for the State, in the person of school officials to justify prohibition of a particular expression of opinion, it must be able to show that its action was caused by something more than a mere desire to avoid the discomfort and unpleasantness that always accompany an unpopular viewpoint." In our system, "state-operated schools may not be enclaves of totalitarianism. School officials do not possess absolute authority over their students. Students in school as well as out are 'persons' under our Constitution. They are possessed of fundamental rights which the State must respect, just as they themselves must respect their obligation to the State. In our system, students may not be regarded as closed-circuit recipients of only that which the State chooses to communicate. They cannot be confined to the expression of those sentiments that are officially approved." The doctrine expressed here on free speech has been extended to other areas of constitutional rights in later decisions.

Q. ARE ALL ACTIONS SEEKING RELIEF UNDER CIVIL RIGHTS LAWS SUITS FOR DAMAGES?

A. No, quite the contrary. Most of the suits seek injunctive relief from what the State is doing to a student, such as failing to integrate the schools. Other suits are brought by teachers seeking reinstatement to a former position because what the board is doing to them allegedly amounts to a deprivation of their civil rights. Other teachers have brought Section 1983 actions against board members because they were fired for growing a beard, for being active in the teachers' union, or for some other official action of the board. Some plaintiffs seek relief charging denial of due process of law, and ask the court to grant them relief. Students have brought actions claiming that charging an annual fee violates the "free" education concept or for a clarification of their rights under the Constitution. Plaintiffs must decide for themselves whether they will seek damages or some other form of relief in filing their suits for equity.

Q. WHAT SUPREME COURT CASES ILLUSTRATE DUE PROCESS OF LAW?

A. A recent line of cases dealing with student punishment emphasizes that the board and school officials must render the student his day in court: *Goss v. Lopez* (419 U.S. 565, Ohio, 1975), pupils facing suspension are entitled to due process of law; *Wood v. Strickland* (95 S.Ct. 992, Ark., 1975), students facing expulsion are likewise so entitled; *Baker v. Owen* (395 F.Supp. 294, N.C., 1975, affirmed without comment U.S.S.Ct. Oct. 20, 1975), students are entitled to minimal due process before being subjected to corporal punishment; and *Ingraham v. Wright* (97 S.Ct. 1401, Fla., 1977), administering corporal punishment to a child in public school is not cruel and unusual punishment so long as the punishment is reasonable and certain due process safeguards outlined in *Baker v. Owen* are observed. One who exceeds "reasonable" punishment or who denies children their civil rights may be tried as tort-feasors. This includes teachers in the public schools. (See Chapter 3 for other cases on student discipline and control.)

Resolution of the Cases in Point

Case No. 1 — FIRST AID TURNS SOUR

Both teachers, as joint tort-feasors, were held liable. Although they stood *in loco parentis* to the child, the court held there was nothing in this relationship to justify their "exercise of lay judgment such as a parent may, in the matter of treatment of injury or disease suffered by a child." Joint tort-feasors are held to be equally at fault "if the parties act together in committing the wrong, or if their acts independent of each other unite in causing a single injury." The fact that one was principal and the other a teacher would be immaterial since the net result of their acts was to cause permanent injury to a child whom they were sworn to protect. The court held they were also not acting in an emergency. They were not school nurses and neither of them had any medical training or experience. Whether treatment of the infected finger was necessary was a question for the boy's parents to decide (*Guerrieri v. Tyson*, 24 A.2d 468, Pa., 1942).

Case No. 2 — TEACHER'S ABSENCE

The teacher was held liable for the injury. The court was convinced that had the teacher been on hand, the injury would not have occurred; therefore, her absence was the proximate cause of the injury. If she had been present, she would have noted the mounting tension in the room (the *time* element), and the six-inch knife in the hand of a boy (the *instrumentality*). Had the teacher been present she would have ordered quiet, and taken the knife from the hand of the boy. Therefore, she was liable because of the foreseeability of the impending injury. *The legal rule is that if a teacher's presence could reasonably be expected to have prevented an injury, then the teacher's absence is the proximate cause of the accident.* Having a flat tire would be immaterial; the fact remains that the teacher, as an adult, should have anticipated such an eventuality, and prepared for it. The principal would not be liable since he had fulfilled his duty to the injured party by assigning a teacher to cover the *in loco parentis* duty owed the child (*Christofides v. Hellenic E. Orthodox Christian Church,* 227 N.Y.S.2d 946, 1962).

Case No. 3 — LAYING ON OF HANDS

The coach was exonerated by the jury, which believed that if he had not taken immediate action, he would have had other students using unacceptable language on the playing field. Since no permanent injury resulted, there was really no loss to the boy, except, of course, to his pride. But the jury felt that the coach had acted as the average, normally prudent parent would have acted under the same circumstances. Coaches are expected to discipline their charges, as are all teachers, and the fact that there was "laying on of hands" does not *ipso facto* amount to corporal punishment or assault and battery in a legal sense. Coaches and teachers enjoy a limited immunity to tort liability where they can show that what they did was for the good of the youth. Nor would the court accept evidence from prior acts of the coach upon third parties under other circumstances as shedding any light on the present question of reasonableness of punishment (*La Frentz v. Gallagher,* 462 P.2d 804, Ariz., 1969).

Case No. 4 — SCHOOL DISTRICT LIABILITY

The doctrine of governmental immunity was abolished in this case by the Supreme Court of Pennsylvania (*Ayala v. Phila. Bd. of Pub. Educ.,* 305 A.2d 877, Pa., 1973). The court found that the doctrine was long since devoid of any valid justification, since cheap insurance was available to protect the district's finances. No longer can the state plead that "it is better that an individual should sustain an injury than that the public should suffer an inconvenience." Since the doctrine was judicially imposed in the first place, it could be judicially terminated. Pennsylvania thus joined forty-two other states in abolishing the doctrine of governmental immunity. There was evidence that the machine had been out of repair and that students had not been sufficiently warned of the known hazard. The teacher was not held liable since it is also well settled in the law that the master is responsible for the acts of his servants (doctrine of *respondeat superior*). Faulty equipment amounts in effect to the maintenance of a nuisance, which is in and of itself evidence of negligence on the part of the state.

Case No. 5 — WRONGFUL DEATH

The district was socked with a $42,000 judgment for wrongful death due to the negligence of its two employee coaches. During the trial, expert testimony by members of the medical profession was introduced which indicated that when a person sustains a heat stroke, every effort should be made to stop the accumulation of heat, not to conserve it. Once the process of stroke reaches a certain high level in the body, the damage becomes irreversible, like boiling an egg. The record supported the plaintiff's contention that the coaches were negligent in not seeking medical aid immediately. The court said that all that had to be done to establish negligence was to prove that it was more likely than not that the deceased would have survived with prompt and reasonable medical attention, which the court held had been done (*Mogabgab v. Orleans Parish Sch.Bd.*, 239 So.2d 456, La., 1970).

Chapter Five: You And Academic Freedom

American freedom in the classroom was influenced by *die akademische Freiheit* (academic freedom) which consisted of two parts: *Lernfreiheit* (freedom to learn) and *Lehrfreiheit* (freedom to teach). Although nineteenth century Germany was autocratic, the campus was free to both student and professor. The student was free to roam from place to place sampling academic wares, and was responsible to no one for regular attendance. The professor was free to experiment and try to convince his student that he was right.

When this system was transplanted here, two major changes took place. The student was required to attend classes and study certain specified curricula, and the professor was foreclosed from using his classroom as a forum to proselytize his students. Compulsory attendance took away, or at least limited, the student's freedom to choose what he would learn and what days he would attend.

The teacher in America stood *in loco parentis* and was therefore more authoritarian. Since he worked for the state, the professor (teacher) was expected to accept these specified curricula, and to present controversial issues in such a way that the student could make up his or her own mind concerning what conclusions were to be drawn from the facts. The teacher, furthermore, was limited to the area of his or her expertise, that is, he was not to stray into areas in which he had no preparation. On issues outside the teacher's competency, the teacher has no more expertise than the layman, and is supposed to remain silent. Thus. where a teacher taught sex education in a class in English, he was outside his area of specialization and was lawfully dismissed for his pains. Since the teacher is an employee of the state, he is expected to cover that content which is specified by the state, no more, no less.

Academic freedom in America, therefore, is much more limited: 1) the classroom may not be used as a forum for pet ideas; 2) certain materials must be covered as specified by the curriculum; and 3) the student's right to learn is far broader and deeper than the teacher's right to teach.

"To impose an intellectual straitjacket on our educational leaders," wrote Chief Justice Earl Warren, "would be to imperil the future of our nation." New and important scientific discoveries are being made all the time. It is important that teachers remain free to evaluate and criticize the values, styles, and truths of the past and the present. This is the purpose of academic freedom — to leave the door open to the new and the different. In 1969, the Supreme Court said that "in our system, students may not be regarded as closed-circuit recipients of only that which the State chooses to communicate. They may not be confined to those sentiments that are officially approved. In the absence of a specific showing of constitutionally valid reasons to regulate their speech, students are entitled to freedom of expression of their views" (*Tinker v. Des Moines School Board,* 393 U.S. 503, Iowa, 1969).

The same rule applies with teachers — being a teacher does not make you a second-class citizen. Like all other citizens, you have the right outside the classroom to take part in debate and discussion of issues which arise.

Within the classroom, you have certain rights to freedom of expression, too. May you assign books or articles that offend parents or school authorities? May you use teaching methods that are not approved by the majority of citizens in your community? Should you be permitted to express controversial personal views to students in your classroom? These are some of the major issues facing you as an employee of the board of education.

This chapter deals with such topics as academic freedom in the classroom, obscenity, vulgarity, four-letter words, assignments, loyalty oaths for teachers, symbolic speech, and your defenses against charges of having exceeded your sphere of academic freedom. Here are five cases to start on. Read the facts, discuss them with others, and speculate on how the cases turned out. Then leaf to the back of the chapter to find out how the courts resolved each of the five.

Cases in Point

Case No. 1 — THE HEMLOCK DRINK

His motto was "Know thyself." His students were Athenian youths of the fourth century B.C. Although not a religious man, Socrates frequently spoke of an "inner voice" that guided his course. The virtue that he sought among men through questioning them was the "good life" for everyone. But his questions cast doubt in the minds of his listeners. Anytus, a former pupil and a politician, secretly brought criminal charges under an Athenian law which prohibited "impiety." Although the evidence was weak, Anytus was depending on the jury of 600 to be swayed by his argument. "He is guilty of crime, first, for not worshiping the gods of the city, and for introducing new divinities of his own," he cried. "He has corrupted the youth of Athens." Socrates' *pro se* (in his own defense) speech was very moving. But Anytus was also convincing (he would be heavily penalized if one-fifth or more of the jury did not vote for conviction). What was the outcome of this first trial on academic freedom?

Case No. 2 — THE MONKEY TRIAL

It was steaming hot in Dayton, Tennessee, as some 900 people tried to jam into the small courtroom. On trial was one John Thomas Scopes, a first-year teacher who had violated Tennessee's statute making it a penal offense to expound the theory of evolution in the schools. Scopes, a science teacher, substituted for an ill biology teacher (it was never proved he actually taught that man descended from a strain of monkeys). On May 7, 1925 he was arrested and paid a $100 fine, never uttering a word in his own defense. The pyrotechnics of William Jennings Bryan, prosecuting attorney, and Clarence Darrow, who defended Scopes, far outshown his private life ("I really didn't know much about evolution, anyway"). Was Scopes guilty of violating the Tennessee law?

Case No. 3 — HOLY MONKEYS!

In November, 1968, the United States Supreme Court was asked to review a case originating in Little Rock, Arkansas, one of three remaining states having a law outlawing teaching of evolution. Mrs. Epperson, a biology teacher, had been cleared when the trial court held the statute unconstitutional, only to be reversed by the Arkansas Supreme Court, on the grounds that it was a valid exercise of the state's power to specify the curriculum in the public schools. There had been no record of any prosecutions under the statute in Arkansas, making it honored more in its breach than in its observance. If you were on the Supreme Court, how would you have decided the case?

Case No. 4 — LOYAL YOU MUST BE

Loyalty tests for government employment have been part of the job. A New York law made ineligible for governmental service any person who advocated the overthrow of the government by force or organized or helped organize or became a member of any society or group which taught such overthrow. The state made a listing of organizations membership in which would automatically lead to dismissal. One Adler, a teacher, was fired after a full hearing and he appealed to the U.S. Supreme Court for relief, claiming denial of his Fourteenth Amendment rights to due process. Did the New York law violate the due process clause of the Fourteenth Amendment?

Case No. 5 — I REFUSE TO ANSWER...

Paul M. Sweezy, a lecturer in sociology at the University of New Hampshire, refused to reveal the contents of a lecture to a legislative committee investigating subversive elements in the institution. He was held in contempt of court for refusal to answer. Sweezy had testified that he was not a member of the Communist Party or did not believe in overthrow of the government by force. Did the state's interest in catching Communists infringe on the professor's right to academic freedom in the classroom?

Academic Freedom in General

Q. WHERE IN THE CONSTITUTION IS ACADEMIC FREEDOM MENTIONED?

A. The First Amendment says that "Congress (and later on the states) shall make no law . . . abridging the freedom of speech or of the press. . . ." The meanings of this important constitutional right have been in continuous controversy ever since the birth of the Republic. In general, it says that "free speech is the rule, not the exception." Only where the state can show that free speech should be limited can this right be restricted in any way.

For example, one should not be allowed because of the dire consequences to shout "Fire!" in a crowded theatre. Like all our other constitutional rights, the right to freedom of expression is subject to limitation depending upon the time, place, and the conditions at the moment.

Q. WHAT HAS BEEN THE ATTITUDE OF THE U.S. SUPREME COURT OVER THE QUESTION OF ACADEMIC FREEDOM IN THE CLASSROOM?

A. The Court has chosen to take a case-by-case approach rather than to give final answers to the question of academic freedom in the public school classroom. In 1923, the Court overthrew a Nebraska statute which outlawed the teaching of German to any student under the eighth grade (*Meyer v. Nebraska,* 262 U.S. 390). Two years later, the Court unanimously held invalid an Oregon statute that required all children to attend the public schools only (*Pierce v. Society of Sisters,* 268 U.S. 510, 1925). "The child is not the mere creature of the state," said the Court. "Those who nurture him and direct his destiny have the right, coupled with the high duty, to recognize and prepare him for additional obligations." Thus, the Court has dealt with only a small fraction of the total area of academic freedom, and has never sought to establish academic freedom as an independent constitutional right, as it has, for example, the right to privacy.

Q. WHAT WAS THE REASONING OF THE COURT IN CONVICTING JOHN THOMAS SCOPES OF VIOLATING THE TENNESSEE LAW?

A. Scopes' lawyers contended that he had been deprived of his constitutional rights by action of the State. But the Supreme Court of Tennessee replied:

> We think there is little merit in this contention. Plaintiff in error was a teacher in the public schools of Rhea County. He was an employee of the state of Tennessee or of a municipal agency of the state. He was under contract with the state to work in an institution of the state. He had no right or privilege to serve the state except upon such terms as the state prescribed. His liberty, his privilege, his immunity to teach and to proclaim the theory of evolution, elsewhere than in the service of the state, was

> in no wise touched by this law....He was always at liberty to take his beliefs and go elsewhere.

Q. WHAT IS THE MOST COMMONLY APPLIED PENALTY AGAINST TEACHERS WHO VIOLATE THEIR RIGHT TO ACADEMIC FREEDOM?

A. Loss of position is most frequently invoked as a penalty for teachers who allegedly violate academic freedom in the classroom. But freedom of speech is a very prized possession of all Americans. Alexander Hamilton noted the potential for punishment of a constitutional right by writing, "A power over a man's subsistence amounts to a power over his will." Justice William O. Douglas wrote in support of freedom of speech in the schools: "To regard teachers as the priests of our democracy is therefore not to indulge in hyperbole" (*Wieman v. Updegraff*, 344 U.S. 183, Okla., 1952). It is the special task of teachers to foster those habits of open-mindedness and critical inquiry which alone make for responsible citizens, who, in turn, make possible an enlightened and effective public opinion. They must have the freedom of responsible inquiry. . . ." While one does not have the right to work for the state, one cannot be dismissed for exercising the right to freedom of expression, a constitutionally protected guarantee.

Q. WHAT TOPICS MAY BE PLACED "OFF LIMITS" BY THE BOARD FOR DISCUSSION IN THE CLASSROOM?

A. After a long and bitter teacher strike, the board finally got school open and running. The board enacted a resolution prohibiting teachers from mentioning or discussing the strike with their students in their classrooms. A teacher who felt that the time to discuss something is when students are ready disobeyed the prohibition, and discussed the strike with his students. For his pains, he was dismissed for insubordination. The court upheld his dismissal on the grounds that the board had a reasonable explanation — to prevent further hard feelings about the strike and to get on with the business of the schools which had been neglected. The court felt that it was a reasonable exercise of board policy to promote harmony and prevent further disharmony by enacting the rule in question (*Nigosian v. Weiss*, 343 F.Supp. 757, Mich., 1971).

Q. WHAT REASONABLE LIMITS CAN BE PLACED ON THE TEACHER'S ACADEMIC FREEDOM IN THE CLASSROOM?

A. These are all well-settled principles of law governing academic freedom: 1) teachers may not use their classrooms as forums for imposing their pet ideas on a captive audience, the students; 2) the age, size, and maturity of the students present some limits on what can or cannot be introduced; 3) the board may set reasonable limits on the bounds of the curriculum which control freedom to go outside those limits; 4) you are restricted to your own area of expertise; you should not stray outside; 5) the board may impose other prohibitions by resolution or prescribe in what ways controversial subjects are to be treated, if at all, in the classroom.

Q. WHAT IS THE *MOUNT HEALTHY RULE* CONCERNING A TEACHER'S EXERCISE OF THE PROTECTED RIGHT TO FREEDOM OF EXPRESSION?

A. A non-tenured teacher was involved in an altercation with another teacher, an argument with cafeteria workers, he swore at students, and made obscene gestures to girl students. He had also telephoned a radio station to complain about a principal's actions; the call was widely publicized in the media. The board fired him. The Supreme Court held that even though some of the teacher's actions were protected by the First Amendment, if the board could find enough grounds other than the protected actions, it might legally fire the teacher. *Mount Healthy City Sch. Dist. v. Doyle,* 97 S.Ct. 568, Ohio 1977.

Q. DOES THE IDEA OF ACADEMIC FREEDOM EXTEND TO STUDENTS AS WELL AS TO TEACHERS?

A. Yes. The right to learn *(Lernfreiheit)* is one side of the coin, the other being the teacher's right to teach *(Lehrfreiheit).* The American Civil Liberties Union and the American Association of University Professors both have published guidelines for student academic freedoms. The American Association of Colleges published a joint statement with other groups in 1967 in which it stated that "freedom to teach and freedom to learn are inseparable facets of academic freedom." The courts are also applying academic freedom to secondary schools, declaring that the rights to freedom of the press and of speech "are not for adults alone."

Q. WHAT IS THE DIFFERENCE, IF ANY, BETWEEN ACADEMIC FREEDOM IN THE PUBLIC SCHOOLS AND IN THE UNIVERSITY?

A. In the United States, the difference is in the way society views the function of the public schools in contrast with the university. The latter has the function of discovering truth wherever it may be found, and preparing people to transmit this information. The function of the elementary and secondary school, therefore, is to transmit such knowledge rather than to discover it.

Q. IS THE TEACHER'S RIGHT TO TEACH A DERIVATIVE OF THE STUDENT'S RIGHT TO KNOW?

A. Yes. There is a long line of Supreme Court cases stretching back to the 1920's which show that the student's right to learn, to be informed, and to know (his *Lernfreiheit*) far exceeds the teacher's right to teach. Teachers who maintain in court their right to freedom of speech in the classroom should approach such a right as a derivative of the student's (the teacher's *client's*) right to know. Thus, the teacher is arguing for greater freedom not for himself, but for his client. The teacher's role in this regard is that of the child advocate, the parent surrogate, and the *in loco parentis* status which has long been recognized and protected in the law. Students should not have to go outside the school to find materials they feel germane to their juvenile condition, as many do. They should not be placed in the position of Charlie Brown, who complained that going to school "interferes with my education."

Q. ARE THERE DIFFERENT LEVELS OF ACADEMIC FREEDOM FOR UNIVERSITIES AND COLLEGES THAN THOSE FOR SECONDARY AND ELEMENTARY STUDENTS?

A. Yes, the less mature the students, the greater the need for emphasis upon transmitting knowledge rather than discovering knowledge. What may be obscene or objectionable for an elementary child may be a protected right for a high school or college student. In *FCC v. Pacifica Foundation,* 98 S.Ct. 3026, N.Y. 1978, the Supreme Court ruled that the government can legally regulate "indecent" and "objectionable" as well as obscene broadcasts, especially during the daylight hours when children are most likely to be listening. The intent of the court was to protect "particularly susceptible individuals," against intrusions into their privacy in car or home. Teachers are expected to have professional judgment as to what is or is not objectionable based on the maturity of the students.

Q. HOW DOES MATURITY OF STUDENTS AFFECT WHAT IS INTRODUCED INTO THE CLASSROOM?

A. One teacher assigned his senior English class an article in the *Atlantic Monthly* which contained the word "motherfucker." He offered to let any student who objected to the article select another assignment. The article dealt with dissent, protest, radicalism, and revolt. The teacher was asked to appear before the school committee and was asked to discontinue the use of the word in class. He refused, and was fired. The court held for the teacher, saying in part: "The question is whether a teacher may, for demonstrated educational purposes, quote a 'dirty' word currently used in order to give special offense, or whether the shock is too great for high school seniors to stand. If the answer were that the students must be protected from such exposure, we would fear for their future" (*Keefe v. Geanakos,* 418 F.2d 361, Mass., 1969).

Q. HOW DO YOU KEEP FROM USING YOUR CLASSROOM AS A FORUM FOR YOUR PET IDEAS?

A. Easy. If you present one side of an issue, you are obligated to present the other side in such a way that your students can draw their own conclusions. Example: following WWII, there was a tendency to avoid any references to the Communist form of government found in Russia. That meant that students would have no access to information or only to that which was biased. So many state boards of education set up requirements that schools must teach the merits and disadvantages of the Communist form of government compared with that of the United States. Where teachers present objective, well-researched information on both economic systems, students will draw their own conclusions.

Q. WHAT LIMITS MAY A BOARD PLACE ON THE CURRICULUM?

A. Boards are expected to require that certain materials be covered each year by each grade. They can reasonably expect that these materials will be covered, and by limiting extraneous materials, zero in on completion of what is contained in the course of study. Such a limitation is not a denial of academic freedom such as would permit the teacher to challenge the board's policy in court.

Q. WHY IS THE TEACHER'S AREA OF EXPERTISE THE ONLY AREA IN WHICH HE OR SHE CAN SAFELY TEACH?

A. Outside your area of expertise, you are a mere layman in the eyes of the law, and your opinions are not protected nor respectable. Thus, a teacher who talked about sexual exploits when he was supposed to be teaching speech was legally dismissed for failure to teach what he was paid to teach (*State ex rel. Wasilewski v. Bd. of Educ., Milwaukee,* 111 N.W.2d 198, Wisc., 1961). If he had been teaching biology, said the court, his conduct might have been protected, but he exceeded the bounds of his teaching area. "We deem it would warrant his discharge even though there was no policy prohibiting such discussion and he had received no warning to desist therefrom. As an intelligent person taught to teach at the high school level, relator should have realized that such conduct was improper."

Symbolic Speech

Q. WHAT IS MEANT BY "SYMBOLIC SPEECH"? IS IT PROTECTED BY THE FIRST AMENDMENT?

A. Symbolic speech, which is protected by the First Amendment, is the conveying of any message without the use of words. In Des

Moines, students wore black armbands to school to protest the war in Vietnam. The principals, fearful that disruption would occur, told the students they had a choice: take off the armbands and stay in school, or go home. They chose instead to challenge the principal's warning. Since there was no disruption, the Supreme Court held that the students had been denied a civil right — namely, the right of freedom of expression. Unless the state can show a valid reason to regulate their speech (here symbolic speech), the board may not restrict their civil rights in the school. "Students are 'persons' under our Constitution," said the Court, "and they do not shed their constitutional rights at the schoolhouse gate" (*Tinker v. Des Moines School Board,* 393 U.S. 503, Iowa, 1969).

Q. WHY IS SYMBOLIC SPEECH A PROBLEM AT THIS TIME?

A. It's all part of the civil rights movement, which in essence is an attempt by the have-nots to clarify a status which was taken for granted. "Children are to be seen and not heard." "Teachers are second-class citizens." To move from one status to full constitutional rights, a group must raise the consciousness of the majority. Much of this can be done through the medium of symbolic speech, that is, through the wordless message. Therefore, you could say that symbolic speech is an attribute of the civil rights movement, coupled with the technology for instantaneous transmission of a message throughout the world.

Q. ARE THERE FORMS OF SYMBOLIC SPEECH OTHER THAN BLACK ARMBANDS?

A. Yes, many forms. In a way, the long hair of boys, sloppy appearance, and beards in school are a form of silent protest. There have been freedom buttons, armbands bearing the inscription "Strike," and many other "signs" that students are disenchanted with their educational opportunities. When students sit-in, or peaceably assemble in one area, or when they carry picket signs, or boycott the school, they are conveying a message to school officials and teachers. Black berets were a form of silent communication of Chicano power in one high school. Teachers who wore mini-skirts or refused to wear neckties were joining the silent protest movement. Burning draft cards, flags, refusing to salute the flag, or sing the national anthem are all forms of symbolic speech. And all these forms, so long as they are peaceable, are protected by the First Amendment.

Q. DOES FREEDOM OF EXPRESSION ALSO HAVE A COROLLARY: THE RIGHT *NOT* TO LISTEN?

A. Yes, particularly where the audience is "captive." In Florida, a teacher was offered another contract on the condition he would refrain from discussing his personal experiences with prostitutes, masturbation, and homosexuals. He refused and filed suit charging denial of First Amendment rights. The court said such a use of the classroom was not protected by the First Amendment (*Moore v. Sch. Bd. of Gulf Cty.*, 364 F.Supp. 355, Fla., 1973). And an instructor at a university challenged school officials who refused to allow him to display his art in a corridor where the public, including children, passed. The school officials were within their right, where there was, in effect, a captive audience, to afford protection against "assault upon individual privacy" (*Close v. Lederle*, 424 F.2d 988, Mass. 1CA, 1970).

Q. HOW DOES ONE AVOID RECEIVING THE MESSAGE INHERENT IN SYMBOLIC SPEECH?

A. The courts are saying that to avoid an invasion of your privacy, you should turn your eyes away from the message. In California, one Cohen was arrested for wearing a jacket which bore the inscription, "Fuck the Draft". The U.S. Supreme Court held that the inscription was constitutionally protected speech. Those who did not wish to read it could merely avert their eyes, and thus escape the message if they did not want to receive it (*Cohen v. California*, 403 U.S. 15, Calif., 1971). Government may not decide what people see, say, print, or read. One man's vulgarity is another's lyric. The government should not force all of society into the majority's view of what seems best. Criticisms of the government are protected even though people may find them vulgar and offensive.

Q. WHAT RIGHTS DO STUDENTS HAVE TO WEAR FREEDOM BUTTONS OR OTHER INSIGNIA IN SCHOOL?

A. So long as there is no substantial disruption, students are free to wear freedom buttons and other insignia constituting symbolic speech. In *Burnside v. Byars* (363 F.2d 744, Miss., 1966), the court held that in the absence of disruption,

> school officials cannot ignore expressions of feeling with which they do not wish to contend. They cannot infringe on their students' right to free and unrestricted expression as guaranteed to them under the First Amendment, where the exercise of such rights in the school buildings and classrooms do not materially and substantially interfere with the requirements of appropriate discipline in the operation of the school.

Utterances Outside the Classroom

Q. MAY THE BOARD CONTROL OR LIMIT FREEDOM OF EXPRESSION OUTSIDE THE CLASSROOM?

A. It all depends. A teacher cannot be compelled to give up his First Amendment right to comment on matters of public interest in connection with the operation of the schools, except where it might be demonstrated that such freedom violated confidentiality or seriously impaired the working relationship of the teacher to the administration of the school. Another exception might be where a teacher made statements knowing that they were baseless or intended to injure someone's reputation. The First Amendment also protects the teacher's right to circulate petitions on school premises during his free time unless such activity poses a serious and imminent threat to order and efficiency in the schools.

Q. MAY TEACHERS SPEAK UP AT MEETINGS OF THE BOARD OF EDUCATION?

A. Yes, so long as they ask for and are granted a place on the agenda of the meeting. Some boards, like the one in New York, encourage teachers to attend the meetings of the board (*Rocker v. Huntington,* 550 F.2d 803, N.Y. 1977). Such a stance on the part of the board would indeed mean that teachers would not be retaliated against because of remarks they made in open meeting, even though some of the remarks were critical of the board. In Wisconsin, the board was negotiating with the teachers' union, which wanted to bargain for an "agency" shop. A non-union teacher was permitted by the board to address the board in opposition to this union request. The union claimed an unfair labor practice, since it had exclusive bargaining rights with the board. The Supreme Court, however, held that a teacher may not be compelled to give up his right to speak out as a private citizen before the board of education (*Madison Bd. of Educ. v. WERC*, 429 U.S. 167, Wisc. 1976).

Q. MAY THE TEACHER ENGAGE IN CIVIL RIGHTS ACTIVITIES AND STILL KEEP A JOB AS TEACHER?

A. It all depends. So long as the outside activities do not interfere with the teacher's teaching competency in the classroom, or the teacher does not use his or her classroom as a forum, such activity outside the classroom is protected. In *Johnson v. Branch* (385 U.S. 1003, N.C., 1966) a black teacher was dismissed because of her civil rights activities. The board said that she was slighting her regular duties in supervising students, arriving late at an extracurricular activity at the school, and checking in late at school but before classes had begun. "In the emotional background of a small southern town fifty-one percent of which was black," said the court, "the board must give the teacher the benefit of the doubt." The grounds on which the board based its case were trivial after the teacher's twelve successful years in the same position and clearly showed the board was biased in its judgment.

Q. DOES A TEACHER WAIVE THE RIGHT TO DUE PROCESS WHEN HE REQUESTS A HEARING, THEN WALKS OUT DURING THE HEARING?

A. Yes. The United States Supreme Court in 1977 turned down an appeal by an Idaho teacher who asked for and received a hearing on his dismissal before the board of education. After asking one question, the teacher told the board it would be pointless to stay, because he believed that they had already decided to fire him. After he departed, the board decided not to continue with the full hearing, and after a brief discussion voted to dismiss the teacher on the basis of "known facts and circumstances." The court told him, "what the constitution does require is 'an opportunity' for a hearing. The teacher was granted such an opportunity, but he chose to walk out on it. He cannot now be heard to complain" (*Ferguson v. Board of Trustees of Bonner Co. Sch. Dist. No. 82*, 564 F.2d 971, Ida., 1977).

Assignments in the Classroom

Q. IN MAKING ASSIGNMENTS IN THE CLASSROOM, WHAT ARE THE RULE OF THUMB LIMITATIONS WHICH THE TEACHER MUST OBSERVE?

A. There are three defenses which the teacher may use to support any classroom assignment. First, does the assignment have a valid educational purpose; is it in the lesson plans; is it in the course of study? Second, is the objectionable material suited to the age, maturity, and general development of the students on whom it is being used? And, third, is the material in question barred by prior board action? Thus, in the absence of any prohibitory rules by a board, the teacher is virtually free to assign materials in the classroom so long as they meet the first and second requirements. It does not matter that the materials are experimental, or that some "expert" testifies that the materials are suitable or unsuitable for students of that age. What counts is that the teacher used the materials to teach a valuable lesson and that it was suited to the general maturation level of the children and was not prohibited by the board of education.

Q. WHAT IS MEANT BY "HAVING A VALID EDUCATIONAL OBJECTIVE" FOR MATERIALS INTRODUCED INTO THE CLASSROOM?

A. An Illinois case illustrates *not* having an educational objective, for which the teachers lost their jobs. Three non-tenured teachers were team-teaching. They attended a showing of the movie "Woodstock" and took to their classrooms and handed out without comment to their elementary school children some promotional materials on the movie they picked up in the lobby. The incident came to the attention of the board, which terminated them, claiming that the materials met no valid purpose, that they were obscene and induced students to kick off the traces and sample marijuana and LSD. The teachers tried to show connections between their work and the materials but were unsuccessful (*Brubacker v. Bd. of Educ., Dist. 149, Cook Co.*, 502 F.2d 973, Ill., 1974).

Q. IS ABORTION AN OBSCENE TOPIC OF DISCUSSION FOR A SEVENTH-GRADE CLASS?

A. A contract between the school district and the teachers' association provided that, whenever appropriate from the maturation level of the group, controversial issues could be studied in an unprejudiced and dispassionate manner, and delegated to the teacher and the union what subjects should be covered. A seventh-grade teacher was directed by the superintendent not to conduct a "debate" on the subject of abortion, so he filed a grievance. The court, however, said that the negotiated clause giving teachers the right to decide what topics to discuss in what class was *ultra vires* (outside the power of the board to grant) and therefore unenforceable as a grievance, since the agreement on its face was null and void (*Bd. of Educ. of Rockaway Twp. in Morris Co. v. Rockaway Twp. Educ. Assn.*, 295 A.2d 380, N.J., 1972).

Q. CAN TRANSCENDENTAL MEDITATION (TM) BE TAUGHT IN THE PUBLIC SCHOOLS?

A. A federal district court in New Jersey ruled that TM cannot be taught in the public schools because it violates the separation of church and state clause of the First Amendment. Defendants, said the judge, had failed to show that TM is not a form of Hinduism. Four high schools in New Jersey were offering TM on an experimental basis under a grant from HEW. Opponents claimed that TM was a religious exercise; proponents claimed it is designed to help students find self-awareness, define goals, and improve learning skills. However, the judge said that the school officials had failed to come up with sufficient proof to overcome the charge that TM is a religion (*Malnak V. Maharishi Mahesh Yogi*, 440 F.Supp. 1284, N.J. 1977, affirmed, 3CA Feb. 2, 1979).

Q. MAY YOU, THE TEACHER, BE REQUIRED TO LEAD THE CHILDREN IN THE PLEDGE OF ALLEGIANCE?

A. No. When a teacher in New York state was dismissed because she refused to carry out a school board regulation by leading her class in pledging allegiance to the flag, she won her job back in court. She objected on the grounds that Americans had not yet achieved "liberty and justice for all." Her attitude toward the flag was respectful and there was no indication that she tried to influence students to follow her example or that any classroom disruption resulted from her action. The courts recognized the importance of balancing state and personal interests, noted that the students were not children but young men and women who should be forming their own judgments about a wide range of conflicting values, and noted the absence of any proselytizing efforts on the part of the teacher in making its judgment (*Russo v. Central School Dist. No. 1,* 469 F.2d 623, N.Y., 1972).

Q. DO TEACHERS NEED TO SELECT MATERIALS CAREFULLY FOR THE CLASSROOM?

A. Yes. There must be a certain amount of self-censorship. A classroom is not a newsstand, an English textbook is not a girlie magazine, and the teenager is not the adult. There is a tendency to try to keep the attention of students by use of startling materials because this generation of youngsters is accustomed to being entertained by television and the other media. We make a grave mistake if we assume that today's bestseller is automatically a valid teaching tool in the classroom.

We have only so many hours of classroom time available to us. Gresham's law applies: bad literature will drive out the good. Every hour spent on *The Godfather* is one hour less to study the works of the world's greatest authors. Not that contemporary literature is of no use: it is simply that books that reek of violence, perversion, man's shadier side, and the put-down of ethnic groups need to be replaced by materials that have stood the test of time.

Q. WHAT PROBLEMS DO TEACHERS HAVE WITH DEFINING OBSCENITY IN THE CLASSROOM?

A. In *Miller v. California* (413 U.S. 15, 1973), the Supreme Court held that contemporary community standards in obscenity cases should be interpreted by *local* rather than national norms. One problem is defining what the "community" consists of — of a city, a county, or indeed a whole state. The second problem is to define "obscene." The Supreme Court used this definition: Obscene material is description or depiction of sexual conduct which. . .taken as a whole, by the average person, applying contemporary community standards. . .(a) appeals to prurient interest in sex; (b) portrays sex in a patently offensive way; and (c) does not have serious literary, artistic, political, or scientific value. No wonder there are so many court cases on the subject of obscenity: the definition is so vague that even the justices did not agree on what it meant. Third, it is not clear how teachers are supposed to learn what people in the "community" think is objectionable or obscene, since there is such a wide divergency from house to house and from region to region.

Q. DO COURTS ORDINARILY PASS UPON THE EFFICACY OF A CERTAIN TEACHING TECHNIQUE?

A. No. One court said that "it is not our function to pass upon the academic merits of the method being used by the teacher" (*Oakland School Dist. v. Olicker,* 102 Cal.Rptr. 429, Cal., 1972). Quoting with approval from an earlier case, the same court noted that "teachers are. . .protected by the fact that they cannot be disciplined merely because they made a reasonable, good faith, professional judgment in the course of their employment with which higher authorities later disagreed" (*Morrison v. State Bd. of Education,* 82 Cal.Rptr.175, Calif., 1970).

Q. HOW FREE IS THE TEACHER TO EXPERIMENT WITH HARD CASES?

A. Within reason, teachers have professional freedom to try to teach children with problems in learning according to their best judgment. A teacher in California, who had a class of non-readers, asked them to write about their own personal experiences in the hope they might develop an interest in better English. Because their writing was illegible, the teacher had the sentences typed and distributed them to the class. Some contained vulgar references to the male and female genitalia, and the sex act. She intended to collect all the papers at the end of the period. However, one copy turned up in the principal's box about two weeks later, and he called on the teacher to explain her methodology. After a hearing the teacher was dismissed.

She appealed to the courts, which said that under the circumstances the teacher had been within her rights in trying to teach the unteachable (*Oakland School Dist. v. Olicker,* 102 Cal.Rptr. 429, Calif., 1972).

Q. WHAT IS MEANT BY "FIGHTING WORDS"? ARE FIGHTING WORDS PROHIBITED IN THE CLASSROOM?

A. Fighting words, as used in the law, are those words which will elicit a belligerent attitude from hearers, much as a red flag will cause a bull to charge. A teacher, for example, who told his students they were "4,000 strong, and could drive out these warmongers" (meaning recruiters for the armed forces) was held to have exceeded his authority. He was a probationary teacher of algebra but he used his classes to suggest that students should bar R.O.T.C. officials from the campus. When the school board brought dismissal charges against him and provided for a hearing that he did not attend, he challenged the action in court. The court held that while a teacher has considerable freedom in talking about matters of public interest, he can still be dismissed for words that, under the guise of free speech, disrupt the school and wreck its learning climate (*Birdwell v. Hazelwood School Dist.,* 491 F.2d 490, Mo., 1974).

Q. HOW FAR MAY THE TEACHER GO IN URGING STUDENTS TO ACT?

A. There are three levels of freedom of expression: 1) the right to believe, which is practically unlimited; 2) the right of advocacy, which is likewise quite wide and deep; and 3) the right to urge action, which is limited where the action becomes non-peaceable, disruptive, or results in a riot. Teachers who, for example, have urged their students to resist the draft in time of war have been dismissed for their urging. The teacher who urged his students to drive out R.O.T.C. officials was likewise too free with his speech. The teacher can believe almost anything — that the world is flat, for example. He can also advocate that certain lines be taken in solving a problem. But when his words produce disruption, riot, destruction of property, or invade the rights of others, then he has overstepped the bounds of his First Amendment protections.

Q. MAY TEACHERS BARGAIN AWAY THEIR RIGHT TO ACADEMIC FREEDOM?

A. Apparently they can. A case in point arose in Aurora, Colorado (*Cary v. Bd. of Educ.*, 427 F.Supp. 945, Colo., 1977). There, the board approved a list of 1,275 textbooks for use in the high schools and disapproved a list of ten books which had been in use. Some English teachers brought a civil action claiming that the board had improperly restricted their right to teach. The district court, after saying that freedom of speech is the rule in the classroom, pointed out that there are also allowable exceptions, one of which was present here: it seems the teachers had bargained away their right to control curricular materials. "But for the bargained agreement," said the judge, "plaintiffs would prevail here," referring to Article V, "Board's Rights," which provided that the board "shall have the right to determine the processes, techniques, methods and means of teaching any and all subjects. . . . Thus, a teacher may bargain away the freedom to communicate. . . . One can, for consideration, agree to teach according to direction."

Q. MAY STUDENTS BE USED TO EMPHASIZE NEED FOR CHANGE IN THE SCHOOL?

A. Yes. This is not uncommon. In Arkansas, a teacher's water fountain broke. Some weeks later when it still had not been repaired the teacher during art class asked her pupils to draw pictures of other pupils to express how each one felt. Some of the pupils drew pictures of pupils lying down asking for water, and others drew wilted flowers. The teacher showed some of these to the principal but did not go further. Some of the pictures did come to the attention of the superintendent, however, and so did complaints about an incinerator outside the teacher's window which she said sent choking fumes into her classroom. Her contract was not renewed. The court barred her dismissal on the grounds that the teacher was being punished for something she had to do: namely, protect the health of her pupils (*Downs v. Conway School District*, 328 F.Supp. 338, Ark., 1971).

Q. MAY STUDENTS BE REQUIRED TO STUDY NOVELS OR OTHER MATERIALS WHICH THEY FIND OBJECTIONABLE?

A. Students are entitled to alternate assignments in case they object to readings or passages in books which to them or to their parents are indecent, irreligious, or embarrassing. Academic freedom does not mean the right of the teacher to force-feed students on the grounds that "it will be good for them." Our academic freedom is not so frail that it must rest upon one book or passage in a book. Academic freedom, on the other hand, is a two-way street — the teacher is entitled to make decisions as to what is best for students, allowing for their honest objections, while students are free to stand where they are in academic skills and expect that the teacher will reach out to them and pull them along toward mutually acceptable goals.

Q. DO STUDENTS HAVE THE RIGHT TO BE TAUGHT IN THEIR NATIVE TONGUE?

A. Yes. It appears that in order to bridge the native tongue and instruction in English, the student is entitled to some assistance from school officials. Just how much that should be is still undecided. In San Francisco, some 1,800 Chinese children brought an action against the board of education claiming denial of equal protection of the laws when they were refused bi-lingual assistance upon entering the local schools, where instruction was in English. The Supreme Court, however, did not go so far as to say that bi-lingual education is guaranteed under the Constitution; it merely held that any school district which receives federal funds would lose such funds if it practiced "discrimination" on the basis of race, color, or national origin (*Lau v. Nichols*, 94 S.Ct. 786, Calif., 1974).

Q. MAY THE STUDENT REFUSE TO SALUTE THE FLAG IN THE CLASSROOM?

A. Yes. The Supreme Court held in 1943 that saluting the flag cannot be used as a condition of attendance in any public school if the refusal is done on a religious basis. Nor may the student be required to stand at attention, or be banished from the room, during the pledge of allegiance (*W.Va. St. Bd. of Educ. v. Barnette,* 319 U.S. 624, 1943).

Q. ARE RELIGIOUS SUBJECTS AND SYMBOLS BARRED FROM THE PUBLIC SCHOOL CLASSROOM?

A. No, not directly. What is prohibited is the establishment of a religion by the state. Numerous challenges have been instituted against the use of Christmas carols, creches, displaying the Ten Commandments and religious symbols on the grounds that such practices amount in effect to establishment of a church in violation of the First Amendment. In *Stone v. Graham,* 449 U.S. 39, KY 1980, the Supreme Court held unconstitutional a statute requiring the posting of the Ten Commandments in every public school classroom, even though these were procured with private contributions and each plaque bore a sign that these Commandments form the "secular" basis of our system of laws. There is no prohibition against studying *all* religions on a comparative basis, nor the Bible as literature, or history. In matters of religion, the Supreme Court has directed that the state must remain "neutral." While it is important to teach students moral and spiritual values, this must be done so that no preference is shown for one religion over another, nor may any religion be hindered more than another. Neutral means even-handed, fair, with justice.

Q. MAY THE STATE COMPOSE A PRAYER AND REQUIRE THAT IT BE RECITED AT SPECIFIED TIMES IN THE CLASSROOM?

A. No. In *Engel v. Vitale* (82 S.Ct. 1261, N.Y., 1962), the Supreme Court held that a state board of regents' ruling to that effect violated the separation of church and state clause of the First Amendment, and was therefore unconstitutional. The next year, the high court also declared prayer and Bible reading resolutions in Baltimore and a state statute in Pennsylvania likewise offensive to the establishment clause (*Murray v. Curlett* [Md.] and *Abington Twp. v. Schempp,* [Pa.], 374 U.S. 203, 1963). But this does not prevent offering of a voluntary prayer; it is when the state or subdivision thereof designates or *requires* such religious observances that the establishment clause is offended.

Q. MAY STUDENTS BE RELEASED FROM REGULAR CLASSES TO ATTEND RELIGIOUS INSTRUCTION CLASSES?

A. Yes, so long as those classes are held off school property (*Zorach v. Clauson,* 343 U.S. 306, N.Y. 1952). An earlier plan which allowed students to miss classes to attend religious services and take instruction on school property was declared unconstitutional (*McCollum v. Bd. of Educ., Champaign, Ill.,* 333 U.S. 203, Ill., 1948). Even though the classes are held during the regular school hours, the board may arrange to have students instructed in religions of their choice off school grounds, if the time away from school is not unreasonably lengthy.

Q. DOES THE STUDENTS' RIGHT TO PRIVACY IN CONNECTION WITH BIRTH CONTROL EXTEND TO MINORS AS WELL AS TO ADULTS?

A. **Yes. The Supreme Court of the U.S. has so ruled (*Carey v. Population Services International*, 97 S.Ct. 2010, N.Y. 1977). The** State of New York had a statute which designated only certain centers for the distribution of contraceptives to minors under the age of 16. The Court held that a state cannot constitutionally stop the distribution of contraceptives to minors under sixteen even though the state has an interest in protecting the morality of young people. The state had not shown any connection between promiscuity, the evil it sought to control, and the availability of birth control devices. "The right to privacy in connection with decisions affecting procreation extends to minors as well as to adults," said the Court in striking down the statute.

Q. MAY A PARENT OR TEACHER CHALLENGE THE TEACHING OF THE THEORY OF EVOLUTION IN THE PUBLIC SCHOOLS?

A. No. One such suit in Houston sought to enjoin the teaching of evolution on the grounds that putting it into the curriculum constituted the establishment of a sectarian, atheistic religion and inhibited the free exercise of religion in violation of the First Amendment. The court held that it could not by judicial decree do that which the Supreme Court has declared the state legislatures are powerless to do, i.e., prevent teaching of the theory of evolution in public schools for religious reasons. To require the teaching of every theory of human origin as alternatively suggested by plaintiffs, said the court, would be an unwarranted intrusion into the authority of public school systems to control the academic curriculum (*Wright v. Houston Ind. Sch. Dist.*, 486 F.2d 137, Tex., 1973).

Q. COULD THE TEACHER GIVE HIS STUDENTS A HUMAN AWARENESS OF SEX TEST?

A. One teacher who administered the Human Sexual Awareness Inventory (HSAI) to his class was fired, and the court upheld his dismissal. He had returned to his teaching job after serving as an instructor in the army. Part IV of the test implicitly gave approval by the teacher and the school of the circled answers which represented the liberal view of sexual mores. Some parents objected, and the board acted by dismissing the teacher. Based on the "contemporary community standards" test handed down by the Supreme Court in *Miller v. California,* (413 U.S. 15, 1973), the use of a broad standard such as that in use on a national scale by the army was inimical to the best interests of the students. The teacher refused to accept the offer of the board to meet with it, and the court held he had waived his right to a due process hearing on the merits (*Fern v. Thorp Public Schools,* 532 F.2d 1120, Wisc., 1976).

Freedom of the Press

Q. IS THE BOARD OF EDUCATION REQUIRED TO HAVE STUDENT NEWSPAPERS?

A. No. Having student newspapers is a matter of discretion with boards of education. Once these have been established, however, they become public forums and are subject to the controls inherent in the First Amendment. This is true even though the board has a proprietary (ownership) interest in the student newspaper (*Gambino v. Fairfax Co. Sch. Bd.,* 429 F.Supp. 731, Va., 1977; affirmed, [2-1] 4CA, Oct. 17, 1977).

Q. WHAT LIMITATIONS MAY THE BOARD PLACE ON STUDENT NEWSPAPERS?

A. Freedom to print the truth is the rule, but there are exceptions. Boards may limit *after the fact but not before* under these conditions: 1) substantial disruption or material interference with the school program; 2) obscenity and pornographic publications; 3) vulgarity, four-letter words which lead to disruption; 4) defamation, such as libel; 5) malicious criticism of school officials; and 6) invasion of the privacy of others. Also, school officials may regulate student publications and establish rules on prior review procedures, as well as set standards regulating times, places and manner of distribution of student-produced newspapers, both official and underground.

Q. WHAT RULES GOVERN DISTRIBUTION OF AN UNDERGROUND NEWSPAPER WRITTEN AND EDITED BY STUDENTS?

A. The same rules apply as for officially sponsored newspapers. There must be no disruption due to its distribution, it must be free from libelous statements, and obscenity and vulgarity can be controlled. In *Shanley v. Northeast Ind. Sch. Dist.* (462 F.2d 960, 5thCA, 1972), the court held that the suspension of five high school seniors for the publication of an underground newspaper was unconstitutional. The paper, which was produced and distributed by the students outside school hours, advocated review of marijuana laws and contained information on birth control and abortion. The court ruled "expression by high school students cannot be prohibited because other students, teachers, and administrators may disagree with its content." In *Nitzberg v. Parks* (525 F.2d 378, 4th CA, 1975), the court held that high school officials may not preview non-school sponsored or underground publications prior to their distribution.

Q. WHAT IS LEGALLY WRONG WITH PRIOR CENSORSHIP OF THE STUDENT NEWSPAPER?

A. First, the student newspaper is a learning experience, and students should be allowed to make mistakes just as professional journalists do. Then there is the responsibility factor. Students need to learn that they are themselves responsible for what they print. Censorship is *a priori*, that is, in advance. But in advance of that must be certain clearly defined guidelines so that students may know what is permitted and what is prohibited by the board. Then if there is a question, they should have the right to argue that their writing is protected by the First Amendment. It is at this point that negotiations should take place, and final determinations made as to what will eventually be printed. Instead of prior censorship, this system then allows for negotiations and fair procedures in making the determination of what will be printed and what will not.

Q. WHAT PRIOR REVIEW PROCEDURES CAN BE ESTABLISHED RELATING TO STUDENT PUBLICATIONS?

A. The board may have rules specifying a person to whom the material is to be submitted, provide specific criteria and examples as to what will be considered out of bounds, obscene, or defamatory so that students will clearly understand what expression is prohibited, provide an opportunity for students to argue that their expression is protected by the First Amendment, set a limit on how long the board can tie up the questionable articles, and provide for speedy appeal to higher authority with a reasonable time specified during which the appeal must be decided. As to distribution, the rules must be reasonable and be related to the prevention of disruption, littering, traffic tie-ups, and the like. More specific instructions can be obtained from The Student Press Law Center, 1750 Pennsylvania Ave., N.W., Washington, D.C. 20006.

Q. WHAT IS A "PUBLICATION BOARD"?

A. It is a review board to assist principals in controlling the student press. In Los Angeles, for example, the board established "publication boards" to mediate any censorship disputes. Each board includes the principal, journalism advisor, and student editor, and representatives of student government, the community advisory council, and the PTA. Principals have the responsibility to review articles prior to publication, as long as they do so within twenty-four hours after receiving student copy. If the principal quashes an article, students may appeal his decision to their school's publication board, and from there, to the superintendent.

Q. CAN THE BOARD PREVENT STUDENTS FROM PUBLISHING THE RESULTS OF A SEX SURVEY TAKEN AMONG HIGH SCHOOL STUDENTS?

A. The courts are divided on this issue. In *Gambino v. Fairfax Co. Sch. Bd.* (429 F.Supp. 731, Va., 1977), a federal district judge upheld the students' right to publish such a news story and the Fourth Common Court of Appeals upheld the court below (2-1). The paper is not "a part of the regular school curriculum," said the judges, "so student editors are free to voice their opinions even if school officials object to the article." However, in New York City, the judge below held that such a sex survey might be acceptable for juniors and seniors, but not for younger students. Her decision was overridden (2-1) by the Second Common Court of Appeals, which ruled that school officials could prohibit student newspaper editors from conducting a confidential and voluntary survey of student sexual attitudes and experiences, on the grounds that the survey might cause psychological harm to some students. "A federal court ought not impose its views on schools where there is a rational basis for the actions of the school authorities," the court said (*Tractman v. Anker*, 426 F.Supp. 198, N.Y., 1976, affirmed [2-1] 2CA, Sept. 8, 1977). The U.S. Supreme Court let stand the decision of the Ciruit Court of Appeals (1978).

Q. WHAT IS "DEFAMATION OF CHARACTER"? ARE HIGH SCHOOL EDITORS RESPONSIBLE FOR LIBELOUS STATEMENTS PRINTED IN STUDENT NEWSPAPERS?

A. Defamation is generally defined as a false communication that injures an individual's reputation, or holds an individual up to hatred, contempt, or ridicule. Libel is written defamation, slander is oral. As a minimum, these things must be present for a publication to be considered libelous: 1) it must be communicated to a third party; 2) it must be false; 3) it must be specifically aimed at one individual or group of individuals; 4) it must injure the plaintiff's reputation; 5) it must be due to the defendant's negligence; and 6) it must be published with "actual malice," that is, with intent to harm someone. It is not clear yet whether student editors can be held liable in damages for printing defamatory statements in student newspapers, but it is conceivable that such might be found by a court of law. Since the burden of "actual malice" is on the plaintiff, it is unlikely that plaintiff would be able to prove such malice on the part of student editors.

Q. IS THERE NOT A RISK INVOLVED IN ALLOWING STUDENTS FREEDOM OF EXPRESSION IN PUBLIC SCHOOLS?

A. Yes, of course. But the risk of their not learning how important freedom of expression is to our way of life is even greater. In

Tinker v. Des Moines School Board (393 U.S. 503, Iowa, 1969), the Supreme Court said that, in our system, "undifferentiated fear or apprehension of disturbance is not enough to overcome the right to freedom of expression. . . .Our Constitution says we must take this risk. Our history says that it is this sort of hazardous freedom — this kind of openness — that is the basis of our national strength and of the independence and vigor of Americans who grow up and live in this relatively permissive, often disputatious society." When one risk is balanced against the other, there is only one answer — freedom of expression is the rule, governmental constraints the exception.

Q. MAY THE SCHOOL BOARD LEGALLY REMOVE BOOKS FROM THE SCHOOL LIBRARY ONCE THEY HAVE BEEN SELECTED?

A. The Supreme Court in *Board of Educ. v. Pico,* 102 S.Ct. 2799, N.Y. 1982 remanded (5-4) for further study this question with no less than seven diverse opinions being written. Since the federal courts below have been equally divided on this issue, it remains to be seen what a board's discretion may be in deselecting books for the school library. The plurality ruled that there are such limits but what these may be remains to be seen.

Q. WHAT DANGERS MIGHT ACCRUE WERE THE GOVERNMENT TO MUZZLE THE FREE PRESS?

A. Alan Barth, noted *Washington Post* columnist and commentator, called the free press the watchdog of our freedom against encroachment by government into our private lives. Wrote Barth:

> If you want a watchdog to warn you of intruders, you must put up with a certain amount of mistaken barking. Now and then he will sound off because a stray dog seems to be invading his territory. . . .And that kind of barking can, of course, be a nuisance. But if you muzzle him and leash him and teach him decorum, you will find that he doesn't do the job for which you got him in the first place. Some extraneous barking is the price you must pay for his services as a watchdog.
>
> A free press is the watchdog of a free society. And only a press free enough to be sometimes somewhat irresponsible — at least in the eyes of some of its critics — can possibly fulfill this vital function.

Loyalty Oaths

Q. WHAT IS THE PURPOSE OF HAVING TEACHERS TAKE A LOYALTY OATH AS A CONDITION OF WORKING IN THE CLASSROOM?

A. It goes without saying that anyone who could gain control of a nation's school system (as Hitler did in Germany) could wield a heavy club over its government. As early as 1925, the Supreme Court said that a state could require its teachers to "be of patriotic disposition" (*Pierce v. Society of Sisters,* 268 U.S. 510, Ore., 1925). During WWI and WWII, loyalty was important because "the slip of a lip can sink a ship." In the 1950's, the McCarthy era, citizens and government were suspicious of any teacher who might have been a Communist sympathizer. Part of the purpose is to see that no teacher uses the classroom as a forum to downgrade our system of government, since the schools exist in the law to provide continuity to the American way of life through preparing students to take their places as worthy, law-abiding citizens of the republic.

Q. WHY ARE TEACHERS SINGLED OUT FOR SPECIAL TREATMENT UNDER THE FREEDOM OF SPEECH GUARANTEE?

A. In *Adler v. Bd. of Educ.* (342 U.S. 485, N.Y., 1952), Adler, a teacher, was challenging his discharge for advocating, or belonging to an organization that advocated, unlawful overthrow of the government by force. This "guilt by association" principle was upheld by the Supreme Court on the grounds that "A teacher works in a sensitive area in a classroom. There he shapes the attitudes of young minds towards the society in which they live. In this the state has a vital concern. It must preserve the integrity of the schools." The Adler rule of guilt by association among governmental employees held up until 1967, when it was overthrown in *Keyeshian v. Bd. of Regents* (385 U.S. 589, N.Y., 1967).

Q. MAY A TEACHER REFUSE TO ANSWER QUESTIONS CONCERNING HIS LOYALTY?

A. It all depends on who is asking the questions. In 1956, a teacher was called before a Congressional committee investigating Communist activities in the schools. He pleaded the Fifth Amendment, and remained silent. A section of the city charter provided that if any teacher "took the Fifth" his employment would be terminated automatically. The Supreme Court held he had the right to remain silent and that the charter was unconstitutional (*Slochower v. Bd. of Higher Educ.,* 350 U.S. 551, N.Y., 1956). However, the opposite effect was obtained in Philadelphia, where the superintendent questioned a teacher concerning his loyalty. The teacher remained silent, and was fired by the board. The Supreme Court held he was legally fired for insubordination and lack of candor (*Beilan v. Bd. of Phila.*, 357 U.S. 399, Pa., 1958). The majority opinion stated that a teacher's classroom conduct is not the sole basis for determining his fitness to teach.

Q. WHAT IS MEANT BY A BALANCING OF THE INTERESTS IN FREEDOM OF SPEECH?

A. The courts must balance interests against each other to determine what is lawful and what is unlawful. On the individual's side, the interests are in a search for truth, in the right to know what government is up to, and to know how public officials are carrying out their duties. On the state's side is the interest in safety, public welfare, and security against enemies of the state, as in wartime. "Every reasonable attempt (to balance)," said Zechariah Chaffee, Jr., "should be made to maintain both interests unimpaired, and the great interest in free speech should be sacrificed only when the interest in public safety is really impaired, and not, as most men believe, when it is barely conceivable that it may be slightly affected."

Q. WHAT IS "MCCARTHYISM"? AND WHAT DOES IT HAVE TO DO WITH FREEDOM OF SPEECH?

A. McCarthyism is the label attached to our national search for "subversives" during the 1950's. It took its name from Sen. Joseph R. McCarthy, but is now applied to any investigation that flouts the rights of individuals in pursuit of its ends. Adlai Stevenson said of McCarthyism, which reached white-hot proportions, "We must take care not to burn down the barn to kill the rats." Much the same tactics are being used today in chastising those who are labeled as "secular humanists."

Q. WHAT ARE THE "FOUR ACADEMIC FREEDOMS"?

A. In a speech at the University of Rochester in 1966, Pres. Richard Nixon defined these as 1) to investigate any theory, to challenge any premise, to refuse to accept old shibboleths and myths; 2) to espouse any cause, to engage in the cut and thrust of partisan political or social debate, both on and off campus; 3) for the teacher — freedom from fear or reprisal while speaking or publishing the truth as he sees it; and 4) the freedom of the student from tyranny of the faculty, and conversely, freedom of the faculty from student tyranny. "A free society's greatest single advantage in its competition with totalitarian societies," said Nixon, "is its right to academic freedom."

Q. MAY YOU BE GUILTY OF PERJURY AND SUBJECT TO DISCHARGE IF YOU DENIED UNDER OATH THAT YOU WERE A MEMBER OF THE COMMUNIST PARTY?

A. No. Arizona had such a statute which was declared unconstitutional by the U. S. Supreme Court in 1966. The teacher who knowingly and wilfully became a member or remains a member of the Communist Party and who signed the loyalty oath having knowledge of its purpose to overthrow the government of the United States was subject to perjury and discharge. Barbara Elfbrandt, a Quaker teacher, challenged the law. Said the Court, in overthrowing the statute, "People often label as 'communist' ideas which they oppose. . . . Those who join an organization but do not share in its unlawful purposes surely pose no threat, either as citizens or as public employees. . . . it infringes on protected freedoms unnecessarily. It rests on the doctrine of 'guilt by association' which has no place here" (*Elfbrandt v. Russell*, 384 U.S. 11, Ariz., 1966).

Q. MAY YOU AS A TEACHER BE REQUIRED TO LIST ANNUALLY EVERY ORGANIZATION TO WHICH YOU HAVE BELONGED OR REGULARLY CONTRIBUTED DURING THE PAST FIVE YEARS?

A. No. In 1960, the Supreme Court overthrew such a law in *Shelton v. Tucker* (364 U.S. 479, Ark., 1960). Such loyalty oaths are "overly broad" and require employees of the state to be punished where they do not share the organizations' goals and objectives. Nor may teachers be required to swear that they are not "subversive persons" (*Baggett v. Bullitt*, 377 U.S. 360, Wash., 1964). One state's loyalty oath that was declared unconstitutional by the Supreme Court required all state employees to swear that they had never lent their "aid, support, advice, counsel or influence to the Communist Party" (*Cramp v. Bd. of Public Instruction*, 368 U.S. 278, Fla., 1961).

Q. MAY POLICE OFFICERS POSE AS STUDENTS TO GATHER INTELLIGENCE REPORTS ON SUSPECTED CRIMINAL ACTIVITIES?

A. Surveillance by police officers posing as university students to engage in covert practice of recording school class discussions, compiling police dossiers, and filing intelligence reports, so that police had records of both students and professors, amounted to a violation of freedom of speech and academic freedom in the classroom, and an invasion of privacy, according to the Supreme Court of California (*White v. Davis,* 533 P.2d 222, Cal., 1975).

Resolution of the Cases in Point

Case No. 1 — THE HEMLOCK DRINK

Socrates became the first of a long line of teachers who refused to compromise with Truth. The jury voted him guilty of corrupting the youth of Athens by a vote of 281 to 220, then voted the death penalty by eight more votes than had been cast for the verdict of guilty. Although he could easily have escaped, or have bought his freedom, Socrates chose death rather than dishonor. "The hour of departure has arrived," he said, "and we go our ways — I to die, and you to live. Which is better God only knows." For a political crime, Socrates was put to death on a religious charge — an indication that those who suffer rather than give up their principles are too often condemned on grounds other than the real charges that are made against them by their enemies.

Case No. 2 — THE MONKEY TRIAL

The Tennessee Supreme Court reversed his conviction on the ground that the jury, not the judge, should have set the fine. But Scopes, whose trial was funded by the newly formed American Civil Liberties Union (ACLU) studied geology at the University of Chicago, then got a job as a geologist in Venezuela. In 1960, he returned to Dayton to attend the premiere of *Inherit the Wind,* a new movie made about his trial. Later, he wrote his own account*, "At trial I never took the stand because they would question me and discover much to my embarrassment and that of my attorneys, that I really didn't know very much about evolution." (*State of Tennessee v. Scopes,* 289 S.W. 363, S.Ct.Tenn., Jan. 17, 1927.)

**Center of the Storm*

Case No. 3 — HOLY MONKEYS!

The U.S. Supreme Court reversed the Arkansas Supreme Court holding that the statute "is presently more of a curiosity than a vital fact of life." After some discussion of academic freedom and freedom of expression in the classroom, the Court finally based its decision on another First Amendment clause, that of establishment of religion. "Congress (and later, the states) shall make no law respecting an establishment of religion. . . ." It makes little difference whether the statute prohibits Darwin's theory as fact or fiction. "The overriding fact is that Arkansas' law selects from the body of knowledge a particular segment which it proscribes for the sole reason that it is deemed in conflict with a particular religious doctrine; that is, with a particular interpretation of the Book of Genesis by a particular religious group. The statute is unconstitutional because it establishes a religion — and because courts should not intervene in the resolution of conflicts which arise in the classrooms of the nation" (*Epperson v. Arkansas,* 393 U.S. 97, Ark. 1968).

Case No. 4 — LOYAL YOU MUST BE

In a 6-3 opinion, the Supreme Court said no, the law did not violate the due process clause of the Fourteenth Amendment. The state has the right to inquire of its employees relative to their fitness and suitability for public service, said the majority. If persons do not wish to work for the school system on the reasonable terms set down by the proper authorities, they are at liberty to retain their beliefs and associations and go elsewhere. "A teacher works in a sensitive area in the schoolroom. . . . One's associates, as well as one's conduct, may properly be considered in determining fitness to teach. Nor is there a problem of due process. The presumption is not conclusive but arises only in a hearing where the person against whom it may arise has full opportunity to rebut it" (*Adler v. Bd. of Educ., City of N.Y.,* 342 U.S. 485, NY, 1952).

Case No. 5 — I REFUSE TO ANSWER...

Sweezy won. The Court could find no compelling interest so substantial as to deny the professor his right to freedom of expression in the classroom of the university. Justice Frankfurter wrote, "When weighed against the grave harm resulting from governmental intrusion into the intellectual life of the university, such justification for compelling a witness to discuss the contents of his lecture appears grossly inadequate. . . . For a citizen to be made to forego even a part of so basic a liberty as his political autonomy, the subordinating interest of the state must be compelling" (*Sweezy v. New Hampshire,* 354 U.S. 234, 1957).

Chapter Six

The Teacher and Collective Bargaining

Collective bargaining came late to public employees. Private employees won the right to bargain in the Wagner Act of 1935, in which the Congress cut back employer power and legalized the strike. But it was not until 1961, when the United Federation of Teachers (UFT) won the right to represent teachers in New York City that collective bargaining came to teaching. The growth of union contracts for teachers during the 1960's and 1970's is testimony to the fact that there was a long way to go before government employees reached equity with workers in the private sector of the economy.

Blue collar jobs were on the decline, and it was not until the New York City victory that the AFL-CIO realized the potential for the survival of unionism via the avenue of organizing white collar workers. Before the sixties were over, all the major cities had fallen to the unions, and a fight to the death was on between the American Federation of Teachers (AFT) and the National Education Association (NEA). Although they both sought to represent teachers, the philosophies of these organizations were basically different. AFT was designed to represent *members,* while NEA sought to keep up its practice of representing *clients* (children). The battle turned out not to be conducive to the "either-or" framework — organizations for teachers are *both* membership *and* client oriented groups. Therefore, each group made adjustments to come near the center, and it was widely predicted that the two organizations would ultimately merge. While there is still that possibility, both the AFT and the

NEA won signal victories for teachers throughout the sixties and seventies, and both continue to thrive separately.

But it took hundreds of years for this to happen. From Revolutionary times the law protected property, not human rights. In 1890, the Congress enacted the Sherman Antitrust Act, under the provisions of which labor unions were sometimes found guilty of conspiracy to restrain trade. Violators were subject to fines and imprisonment, injunctive relief for owners, and firings. It was not until 1935 that the Congress, in response to bloody labor wars, finally declared it public policy for employers to sit down with employees and negotiate wages, hours, and other conditions of work. But the Act specifically *excluded* governmental employees from its coverage, a privilege they were to wait three decades to gain.

There are numerous instances of teachers being fired for union activity. In *People ex rel. Fursman v. City of Chicago* (116 N.E. 158, Ill., 1917), teachers who belonged to the Chicago Federation of Teachers were fired for mere membership. The Supreme Court of Illinois upheld the firings on the grounds that membership in the union was "inimical to proper discipline, prejudicial to the efficiency of the teaching force, and detrimental to the welfare of the public school system." A similar case in Seattle was to the same effect (*Seattle High School Chapter No. 200, AFT v. Sharples*, 293 Pac. 994, Wash., 1930).

It was not until 1951 that the courts began to feel that teachers had the right to bargain with employer school boards, but only if the board chose to bargain with them (*Norwalk Tea. Assoc. v. Bd. of Educ.*, 83 A.2d 482, Conn., 1951). But by 1968, the courts came around to the idea that teachers could not be discriminated against merely because they chose to join a union and be active in it (*McLaughlin v. Tilendis*, 398 F.2d 287, Ill., 1968). However, where teachers struck in violation of a state statute, the U.S. Supreme Court held they had been legally dismissed because they had not come into the court of equity with clean hands (*Hortonville Sch.Bd. v. Hortonville Tea. Ass'n.*, 426 U.S. 482, Wisc., 1976).

Much has been written on why teachers showed so much militancy during the 1960's. As Victor Hugo wrote in 1877, "Greater than the tread of mighty armies is an idea whose time has come." Seeing their counterparts in the private sector sit down with management and bargain on wages, hours and conditions of employment must have been partially responsible for the urge by teachers, at long last, to take their places at the table. After Sputnik, there was the implication that something was wrong with our American schools, and that it very well might be the teachers. To be responsible for something, yet have no control over the making of decisions which feed that responsibility, is not only inescapably illogical but truly un-American. On this basis, it seems inevitable that teachers would one day want to bargain as equals in the educational enterprise with their employers, the boards of education.

Here are five cases related to collective bargaining for teachers in the public schools. Read the situations given here, then discuss the case with your friends or class members. Finally, turn to the "Resolution of the Cases in Point" at the end of this chapter for the outcome of each case.

Cases in Point

Case No. 1 — OUT YOU GO!

The year was 1917. The Chicago Board of Education adopted a resolution prohibiting membership by any of its teachers in the Chicago Federation of Teachers, a teachers' union. Several teachers who violated this regulation of the board were dismissed from their jobs for mere membership, and without a hearing. The board, in making up its mind to enact the resolution, had decided that membership in the union was "inimical to proper discipline, prejudicial to the efficiency of the teaching force, and detrimental to the welfare of the public school system." Is this not a good example of "guilt by association," now outlawed in public employment? Could the board legally enact such a regulation, or was it unconstitutional on its face? Was this not a biased opinion by the board, rather than a proven fact?

Case No. 2 — GUIDELINES

The Norwalk Teachers' Association represented 298 of the 300 teachers employed in the City of Norwalk. In April, 1946, a dispute arose over salaries. Some teachers turned down their proffered contracts and refused to return to work. Some of them were thereupon dismissed. After negotiations, the teachers returned to work under contracts which were subject to the conditions to be set forth in the court's opinion. The questions related to teachers' rights to organize as a labor union, to use the strike or slowdown as a means of enforcing their demands, to enter into written contracts with their boards, and to mediate and arbitrate disputes. The guidelines set down in this case, *Norwalk Tea. Ass'n. v. Bd. of Educ. of City of Norwalk* (83

A.2d 482, Conn., 1951), were the rule in many states until the states got around to enacting legislation to control bargaining by governmental employees. What common points of law were laid down in the *Norwalk* case which still apply in the absence of legislation either permitting or requiring bargaining between teachers and their boards of education?

Case No. 3 — TO PEACEABLY ASSEMBLE

A damage suit was brought by two probationary teachers against the superintendent and the board of education because they were not re-employed. Reasons given were that the teachers were distributing union materials and soliciting union membership. Each sought $100,000 damages. The court below dismissed the suit because the teachers had no First Amendment right to form or join a labor union. The case was appealed to the Circuit Court of Appeals. Damages were sought under the Civil Rights Act of 1871 (42 U.S.C. Sec. 1983) for deprivation of a civil right, viz., "the right to peaceably assemble and to petition the government for a redress of grievances." Do teachers have such a right? Are board members immune from damages for "wrongful acts" which deprive teachers of their civil rights? Is firing teachers a violation of the right of free association?

Case No. 4 — RIGHT TO STRIKE

After negotiations for renewal of a collective bargaining agreement between the Hortonville teachers and the school board failed, the teachers went on strike in direct violation of state law. Letters were sent to striking teachers notifying them that they were violating state law and asking them to return to work. None returned. Some eighty-eight teachers were then systematically dismissed at twenty-minute intervals by the board in its judicial capacity. The teachers claimed that the board had denied them due process of law, and that it was not an impartial tribunal sitting as a quasi-judicial body. The case finally reached the Supreme Court of the United States. Did the teachers breach their contracts of employment by walking out? Did the board give them due process of law? Were other means of relief available to the board — injunction, mediation, or continued bargaining? Did the teachers come into court with clean hands? Should the courts keep hands off in deciding local matters such as these? Are teachers "hands" who work under the conditions laid down for them by the board of education?

Case No. 5 — RIGHT TO SPEAK OUT
The board and the union representing all teachers were deadlocked over the issue of "fair share" (agency shop). A small group of teachers who did not belong to the union asked to speak at a regular public board meeting and present the results of a petition relative to an attitude on the "fair share" clause. One of the members of this group was allowed to speak briefly in opposing passage of the clause. The teachers' union then charged that the board had committed a prohibited labor practice. The Wisconsin Employment Relations Commission, which administered the state's teacher negotiations law, held for the teachers, and the Wisconsin Supreme Court affirmed the decision. The board then appealed to the United States Supreme Court. Did the board commit an unfair labor practice in what it did? Does exclusive representation of all teachers by the union exclude minority opinions when expressed in a public meeting of the board of education?

Collective Bargaining as a Game

Q. WHAT IS "COLLECTIVE BARGAINING" AS APPLIED TO EMPLOYER-EMPLOYEE RELATIONSHIPS?

A. Collective bargaining has been described as "a knocking together of heads to get a meeting of the minds," but it is far more subtle than that. Collective bargaining is an orderly way of resolving conflicts of interest between employer and employee without resorting to outright physical assault, court action, or flipping a coin. It has other names: negotiations, collective negotiations, or management-labor negotiations. Collective bargaining in private industry has been the policy of this government since the passage by the Congress of the Wagner Act in 1935. It was not available, however, to workers in the public sector of the economy until the beginning of the 1960's. Now more than ninety percent of all teachers in the nation's public school systems are represented at the bargaining table by teachers' associations or unions.

Q. SHOULD LOCAL BOARDS OF EDUCATION COLLECTIVELY BARGAIN WITH TEACHERS OVER THE TERMS AND CONDITIONS OF THEIR EMPLOYMENT?

A. Yes, there is a great deal to be gained from a continuing dialogue between local boards and their teaching corps. Collective bargaining and court litigation are alternative ways of determining terms and conditions of employment. The latter method of settling labor disputes has its limitations — it is time consuming, the loser must pay the costs of litigation, and it tends to air labor-management problems outside the circle of those who are affected by the outcome. Collective bargaining, on the other hand, tends to keep labor problems "in-house," costs are divided among the parties, and bargaining tends to take less time to reach a conclusion than does litigation in a court of law.

Q. HOW DID THE WAGNER ACT FACILITATE COLLECTIVE BARGAINING BETWEEN LABOR AND MANAGEMENT?

A. No meaningful negotiations can take place if the parties are not approximately the same in their power to enforce demands. The Wagner Act, and later, the Taft-Hartley Act, tended to equalize latent power on each side of the table, the first in favor of labor (since management tended then to be stronger), the latter in the other direction where labor following WWII tended to dominate. Of course, each side may use its political clout to an advantage, and both sides appeal to public opinion in gaining their demands. The labor acts sought to make the parties somewhat equal so that negotiations would be nothing more than mere sham.

Q. WHAT PROVISIONS OF THE WAGNER AND TAFT-HARTLEY ACTS TENDED TO PROMOTE HARMONIOUS BARGAINING?

A. The Wagner Act enumerated certain practices which management could not utilize, such as refusal to bargain when a certain percentage of the workers had indicated a desire to bargain. Taft-Hartley, on the other hand, (Sec. 14-b) made it possible for state legislatures to outlaw the union shop in individual states. Approximately 20 state legislatures have done so by statute. This means that in approximately 30 states the union shop is legal. Not only is the union shop legal by states, but it also exists widely in many of our major industries, such as steel and the making of automobiles. One should study the various labor-management laws in the state in which you live in order to fully understand the extent of the legal framework for bargaining in the public sector of the economy.

Q. WHAT IS THE MODEL FOR COLLECTIVE BARGAINING IN PUBLIC EDUCATION?

A. The model for all collective bargaining is the bargaining table where equals face each other across the table. If the parties are not equal, the law makes them so. Hence, when the Wagner Act was first passed, management was stronger than labor, and the act cut management's power by requiring owners to bargain with laborers, and by defining certain "unfair labor practices" which were prohibited, such as firing workers for being active in unions. The first rule — that the parties must be equal in strength — is not always a fact in teacher-board bargaining. However, the fact that teachers can strike, even though illegally, works to make the parties equal despite the complete absence (as in Colorado) of any statute either requiring or permitting boards of education to bargain with teachers.

Q. WHAT ARE THE RULES BY WHICH COLLECTIVE BARGAINING IS CARRIED ON?

A. The postulates of collective bargaining are four in number: 1) the parties must agree in advance to bargain in good faith; any departure from good faith can be construed as an unfair labor practice; 2) the parties must give something in exchange for what they want (*quid pro quo*); 3) there must be some way *to resolve impasses* when they occur; and 4) the final agreed-upon details are reduced to writing and this *agreement* is binding on the parties during the life of the agreement. These four postulates will be discussed in the following four questions.

Q. WHAT DOES IT MEAN TO SAY THAT THE PARTIES AGREE TO BARGAIN IN GOOD FAITH?

A. It simply means that they both agree before bargaining begins to bring everything out in the open, to deal fairly and openly with the other party, and to honestly seek to reach a meeting of the minds on the points which separate them. Failure to act in this way can be construed (by fact-finders, for example) to be an unfair labor practice for which the perpetrating party may be censured. In those states having legislation on teacher-board bargaining, there may be listed certain "unfair labor practices," such as slowing down the process, or failure to honestly level with the opposite party. Those states with governing bodies may hold hearings to determine whether either of the parties is guilty of an unfair labor practice, and may issue a "cease and desist" order to the offending party. The agreement to bargain in good faith is a very important asset to successful bargaining; without it, nothing but collusion, confusion, stalemate, and misunderstanding will result. It is in the best interests of both parties to insist that each honestly seek resolution of their differences as rapidly as possible.

Q. WHAT IS MEANT BY THE TERM *QUID PRO QUO?*

A. This is a Latin term meaning "something for something." In theory, any offer must be honored by a counter-offer from the opposite side, so that negotiations will not come to impasse. But it indeed is not unusual for the union to seek many gains and for the employer to take a completely defensive position, not making any demands of its own. "I cannot meet your demands," management may say. "I cannot give any wage increase. I will, however, renew the expiring contract at the old wage rate but that is the best I can do." This is legal because his offer to renew without making an improvement in the wage rate is considered by the NLRB to be a counter-offer.

A well-worn story on the subject of *quid pro quo* has it that a federal mediator was trying to get a settlement of a coal strike many years ago. He said to the parties, "This question should be settled by give and take." To this, John L. Lewis, then head of the United Mine Workers, replied, "You are absolutely right; they give and we take." But like the game of tennis, the ball must pass from one side of the court to the other with some regularity if real progress toward solution is to be accomplished.

Q. WHAT ARE THE VARIOUS METHODS OF RESOLVING IMPASSES?

A. There are normally three: mediation, fact finding and arbitration. A mediator's job is to get the parties back to the table where impasse has occurred. He may suggest to the parties, "Why don't you consider the following as a way out of the impasse. I feel this would be a fair settlement for the following reasons," then help the parties get back to the table. Fact finding attempts to discover whether for example the board is acting from hard data when it says it does not have the money to meet wage demands made by the teachers. Arbitration may be interest arbitration (arbitration of disputes over what the terms of new or renewed contracts shall be) and grievance arbitration (disputes over whether the employer has violated some term of the agreement during the life of the agreement). The latter is widely written into the agreement by teachers and school boards as the last step in the grievance procedure. Arbitration may be either advisory (non-binding on the parties) or binding where the parties agree ahead of time that they will be bound by it (and there is no law to the contrary).

Q. WHAT IS INCLUDED IN THE SIGNED AGREEMENT?

A. All that the parties agree to during the negotiation process is, as the last step in the process, reduced to writing. Because it is outside the rights of the parties to determine it, the question of what is an appropriate bargaining unit is not normally included in an individual agreement. The agreement may contain a *zipper clause,* which has as its objective a) to discourage either of the parties from citing unwritten past practices to an arbitrator in support of that party's case, and b) it states that the agreement as here presented is the entire agreement between the parties.

Q. MUST THE PRINCIPALS (BOARD OF EDUCATION, UNION MEMBERSHIP) RATIFY THE AGREEMENT ARRIVED AT BY THEIR REPRESENTATIVES?

A. Ordinarily, yes. The representatives at the table deal with each other on the basis that what they agree to is subject to ratification by their principals (those whom they represent). But such a procedure slows bargaining, and defeats the spontaneity which the agents must have in order to know how far they can go. In the board's case, the agents know pretty well how far they can go. With teachers, the agents are likely to say "this is the best deal we can get under the circumstances." Also, there is less secrecy than formerly in bargaining, since many states now have "sunshine" laws requiring the parties to deal openly with each other (often in open meetings). Some agents for teachers even complain that if they recommend a proposal to the membership it may, in fact, mean its defeat because of the "activism" of union members. Or the membership may be at odds with what the union is implying it will settle for, and negotiations break down. (See *City of Madison v. Wisconsin Employment Relations Commission* [429 U.S. 167, Wisc. 1976], where a minority group approached the board to protest a "fair share" proposal then being bargained.)

Q. DO ALL THE STATES HAVE COLLECTIVE BARGAINING LAWS FOR TEACHERS?

A. No. Only about two out of three do. But bargaining between teachers and boards of education is taking place in those states which have no legislation on this point. These latter states are governed by the "common law" which is made up primarily of precedent set by the courts.

Q. DO TEACHERS HAVE THE CONSTITUTIONAL RIGHT TO BARGAIN WITH THEIR BOARDS OF EDUCATION?

A. No, not in so many words. But teachers do have the right, just as other citizens, to "peaceably assemble and petition the government for a redress of grievances" as outlined in the First Amendment. Teachers have the right as individuals to decide whether they will or will not join a teachers' organization. Teachers may not be punished for their failure to join, or for being active in a union of teachers. If an individual teacher works in a district where a teachers' union represents all the teachers, the teacher is bound by the conditions worked out by that organization with the board of education, and such an agreement does not deprive the teacher of a protected constitutional right.

Q. WHAT RIGHTS TO BARGAIN COLLECTIVELY DOES THE INDIVIDUAL TEACHER HAVE?

A. The teacher has the right to join, or not to join, organizations of his or her choosing, to peaceably assemble in such meetings, and to approach the board (government) for a redress of grievances. But the fact that the board will sit down with the representatives of the teachers does not mean that it must capitulate to all demands. The board has the right, even without an enabling law, to give certain groups exclusive representation, dues checkoff, to enter into a written agreement with the group, so long as it does not tie its hands unnecessarily, to discuss which items it will or will not negotiate, and to allow the use of school buildings for union activities. Since these so-called "union security clauses" are not immediately matters of right they must be negotiated with the board, since the board must protect its "management prerogatives."

Q. WHAT IS MEANT BY "MANAGEMENT PREROGATIVES"?

A. Management prerogatives is a term used to relate to the employer's right to govern the enterprise, it being understood that it cannot be required to bargain away that which will leave it without control over its own operations. In school affairs, the state legislature almost universally intends that the local board of education shall retain the right to have the final determination of what it will or will not do in dealing with its own employees. If there is a state statute governing bargaining, the statute ordinarily spells out the extent to which the local board can "give away the store." Where there is no statute, the matter is often open to arbitration. The courts do not favor intervention into a prerogatives dispute since courts tend to give state control of the educational enterprise wide discretion unless some obvious abuse of board power is implicated.

How the Rules are Enforced

Q. IS UNILATERAL (ONE-SIDED) ACTION BY EITHER ONE OF THE PARTIES CONSIDERED AN UNFAIR LABOR PRACTICE?

A. Yes, except that the board must be free to take such management prerogative action as it needs to to keep the enterprise running. Whether or not a new school building is to be constructed, for example, is usually considered a management prerogative and a school board making a unilateral decision to do so would not be considered acting in bad faith. Since the essence and spirit of collective bargaining is *bi-lateral* decision-making, the common law position is that any unilateral action other than the exception noted here is tantamount to an unfair labor practice, and arbitrators will not hold that party blameless which institutes unilateral action on a bargainable item.

Q. IS A UNILATERAL RULE BY THE BOARD REQUIRING TEACHERS TO WEAR "PROFESSIONAL ATTIRE" UNCONSTITUTIONAL?

A. Apparently not, if the board can show a valid reason for the rule. In *East Hartford Educ. Ass'n. v. Bd. of Educ.* (405 F.Supp. 94, Conn., 1975), the board had a rule that all teachers should be dressed in apparel "reflecting their professional role," and should set a good example for their students. The rule was challenged by the association, on the ground that it invaded personal privacy of teachers. Not so, said the court; the board had shown that good grooming "encourages respect for authority which acts as a positive factor in maintaining classroom discipline." Dress is different from beards and hair, said the court, because dress can be changed after working hours, while beards and hair styles are not so easily changed. "Those effects (beards) having once been made are continuous," said the court, "and may present a more significant invasion of personal choice and individual liberty."

Q. MAY THE BOARD ENTER INTO A FAIR-SHARE (AGENCY SHOP) AGREEMENT WITH THE TEACHERS' UNION?

A. At least one court has ruled that a fair-share statute is not unconstitutional. (*Robbinsdale Educ. Ass'n. v. Robbinsdale Federation of Teachers,* 239 N.W.2d 437, Minn. 1976). In those states which have outlawed the union shop under Section 14-b of the Taft-Hartley Law, it would be illegal to require the workers to join the union in order to work there. But there seems to be no bar to requiring the workers, if the legislature so stipulates, to pay a fair share of their wages for substantive representation at the bargaining table. The arrangement — which is also known as the "agency" shop, since the worker, while not a member of the union, is having the union act as his "agent" — requires payment to the union for services rendered. The U.S. Supreme Court (*Abood v. Detroit Board of Education,* 431 U.S. 209, 1977) upheld the agency shop but only insofar as the service fees collected were used to finance expenditures by the union for the purpose of collective bargaining, contract administration, and grievance adjustment (but not for influencing political outcomes). The Court remanded the case on the issue of what procedures meaningfully afforded employees an opportunity to obtain a refund of that portion of the dues spent on other purposes.

Q. HAVE THE COURTS OUTLAWED THE UNION SHOP IN EDUCATION?

A. No, but under Taft-Hartley some 20 states have chosen to do so. Thus, the board of education in Silver Bow County, Montana, was declared to be acting outside its power *(ultra vires)* when it enacted a resolution that all Silver Bow County teachers must join the union as a condition of working in the public schools of the county. (*Benson v. School District No. 1 of Silver Bow County,* 344 P.2d 117, Mont. 1959).

Q. MAY THE BOARD ENTER INTO AN AGREEMENT TO DO SOMETHING WHICH IS ILLEGAL?

A. No. State statute and constitution are the limits of the board's power. Where, for example, the state law limited teachers on sabbatical to one-half of their regular salary, and a board had agreed to pay full pay during a half-year sabbatical, the court said that the provision of the collective bargaining agreement was null and unenforceable (*Cumberland Valley Educ. Ass'n. v. Cumberland Valley School Dist.,* 354 A.2d 265, Pa., 1976).

Q. WHAT RIGHTS TO BULLETIN BOARD SPACE DOES THE EXCLUSIVE REPRESENTATIVE HAVE?

A. Normally, "to the victor belongs the spoils." The majority organization ordinarily wins the exclusive right to use school bulletin boards and mail boxes for its business while this privilege is closed to the minority group. It may depend on whether the court looks on the case as one of free speech or a case on labor relations. In Denver, the board allowed exclusive use of these facilities only to the majority group (except at election time) and was upheld on the grounds that this arrangement promoted labor peace in the public schools (*Local 858 of AFT v. Sch. Dist. No. 1*, 314 F.Supp. 1069, Colo., 1970). A New York court invalidated a similar arrangement stating that the teachers could not be required to pay for their First Amendment rights (*Friedman v. Union Free School Dist.*, 314 F.Supp. 223, N.Y., 1970).

Q. MAY LOCAL BOARDS AGREE TO BINDING ARBITRATION?

A. Yes, they may, but are not required to do so unless there is a state law requiring them to do so. But a prerogative given to teachers can be binding on the board only if the board had the power in the first place to give it. Courts have required boards to live up to the conditions of prior agreements which may have been improvidently entered into, not so much because it is the teachers' right, but that teachers have come to rely on the conditions of the agreement, and in effect, have a vested interest over time in anticipating that the board will live up to its part of the agreement (*Bd. of Educ. of Union Free Dist. v. Associated Teachers*, 282 N.E.2d 109, N.Y., 1972; *Dayton CR Teachers Ass'n. v. Dayton Bd. of Educ.*, 323 N.E.2d 714, Ohio, 1975).

Q. DO ORAL AGREEMENTS ON THE SIDE BECOME A PART OF THE WRITTEN AGREEMENT?

A. No. For example, an oral agreement between an education association and a superintendent providing that no deductions would be made for leaves of absence granted teachers attending a state teachers' conference and that the association would reimburse the district for the wages paid substitutes could not have become a part of the written agreement, said the court (*Matter of Arbitration between Ringgold Area School Dist. and Ringgold Educ. Ass'n.*, 356 A.2d 842, Pa., 1976). Hence, an arbitrator's award providing that the school district could not unilaterally return to its prior practice of granting such leaves of absence without salary was overthrown, since the oral arrangement was not valid in the first instance.

Q. IS AVOIDANCE OF BARGAINING WITH A CLASS OF WORKERS AN UNFAIR LABOR PRACTICE?

A. Yes, ordinarily. For example, a board revised its teachers' aide program to try to prevent the necessity of collective bargaining with that group. The court held that such a tactic was in effect an unfair labor practice (*School Comm. of Stoughton v. Labor Rel. Comm'n.*, 346 N.E.2d 129, Mass., 1976).

Q. WHAT ITEMS ARE NEGOTIABLE BETWEEN TEACHERS AND SCHOOL BOARDS?

A. The term, "wages, hours and conditions of employment," which supposedly includes the scope of bargaining, has been construed by the courts in a broad, rather than a narrow (money matters only) way. States with bargaining laws for teachers sometimes have spelled out the scope of bargaining, but the general trend is to include any item which conceivably could be considered under the broader term. Thus, class size is a condition of employment, as are transfers, materials used in classrooms, the length of vacations, and similar items. In practice, teachers and boards may legitimately negotiate on any item so long as it is not foreclosed to them by statute or constitution.

Q. MAY TEACHERS BARGAIN AWAY A RIGHT THEY FORMERLY HAD?

A. Yes. In Aurora, Colorado, English teachers objected when the board banned ten books formerly used by the teachers in district English classes. The teachers objected on the grounds that such action by the board violated their First Amendment rights to academic freedom. The board and teachers had in their agreement this clause: "The board shall have the right to determine the processes, techniques, methods and means of teaching any and all subjects." The court, in holding for the board, said that whatever the scope of the protection of the First and Fourteenth Amendments, such protection does not present a legal impediment to the freedom to contract. As teachers contract, so are they bound. "Thus, a teacher may bargain away the freedom to communicate in her official role in the same manner as an editorial writer who agrees to write the views of a publisher or an actor who contracts to speak the author's script. One can, for consideration, agree to teach according to direction" (*Carey v. Bd. of Educ.*, 427 F.Supp. 945, 956, Colo., 1977).

Q. SINCE TEACHER BARGAINING IS A CRAZY QUILT PATTERN IN THE U.S., WHY NOT ENACT A NATIONAL BARGAINING ACT?

A. For several years, teachers' groups backed the passage of a national public employees' bargaining act. In 1976, however, the U.S. Supreme Court cast doubt on the constitutionality of such an act. In *National League of Cities v. Usery* (426 U.S. 833, 1976), the Court ruled (5-4) that the Congress had overreached its authority under the commerce clause in making employees of state-owned governments subject to the federal minimum wage and hour requirements. Congressional power under the commerce clause, said the majority, is unconstitutional when it intrudes upon essential state functions. Under the Tenth Amendment, those powers not reserved to the federal government are by implication reserved to the states. Such a function is education. So the crazy quilt pattern of teacher bargaining from state to state cannot reasonably be expected to be solved through a uniform federal collective bargaining act covering state and local governmental employees.

Dealing With the Strike

Q. MAY TEACHERS RESIGN "EN MASSE" IN ORDER TO ENFORCE THEIR DEMANDS?

A. No, because such a mass resignation amounts to a strike even though it may not be called that in so many words. A New York court determined that the tactic of "mass resignations" was in essence a strike (*Bd. of Educ. v. Albert Shanker*, 283 N.Y.S.2d 432, 1967). When teachers in Florida refused to start work in the fall, but still laid claim to their jobs, the court held they could not retain their rights as teachers while on "strike" from their positions (*Pinellas Co. CR Teachers' Ass'n. v. Bd. of Pub. Instr.*, 214 So.2d 34, Fla., 1968).

Q. MAY THE BOARD PENALIZE TEACHERS FOR STRIKING?

A. Yes. The Supreme Court of Minnesota upheld an anti-strike statute that striking public employees could not later be reimbursed for pay lost while on strike and that they could not have their salaries raised for one year following the strike. Even though the board wanted to void the law, the law was the measure of the board's power (*Head v. Spec. Sch. Dist.*, 182 N.W.2d 887, Minn., 1970). In Florida, 425 teachers who resigned *en masse* in protest against board policy were required by the court to pay $100 to the board as mitigating damages to indemnify the board for extra costs of getting new teachers because of the illegal strike. The court said the teachers could decide whether to pay the fine or refuse to return to work; they could take either option. The situation would be quite different, said the court, if the teachers could show that they were by constitutional right entitled to reinstatement in tenure status without paying the $100 (*NEA v. Lee Co. Bd. of Pub. Instr.*, 467 F.2d 447, Fla., 1972).

Q. IS A STRIKE BY PUBLIC EMPLOYEES EVERYWHERE ILLEGAL?

A. In the absence of enabling legislation, a strike by governmental employees is considered to be illegal. Only a handful of states has legalized the strike for its public employees, and those limit it severely (cooling-off period is provided; union must file notice of impending plan to strike ninety days before strike is to occur). President Franklin D. Roosevelt said in 1937 that a strike by governmental employees is treasonable since it is in effect against the government which the employees have sworn to uphold. The Supreme Court has held that teachers who strike contrary to state law have abandoned their contracts, and are not entitled to due process hearings since they have already breached their contracts of employment (*Hortonville Sch. Bd. v. Hortonville Tea. Ass'n.*, 426 U.S. 482, Wis., 1976).

Q. WHAT RECOURSE DOES THE LOCAL BOARD HAVE WHEN TEACHERS STRIKE ILLEGALLY?

A. The board may fire those who strike illegally, as in *Hortonville*. Or the board may seek a court injunction against the illegal strike. Generally, upon a proper showing, an injunction will be granted. What constitutes a proper showing may vary, however, from one jurisdiction to another. Some courts have refused to issue injunctive relief believing that the board was not bargaining in good faith with teachers. Others may ask for a showing of irreparable injury or breach of the peace before an injunction will be issued. Where teachers ignore an injunction to halt a strike, the teachers or their organization's officials may be held in contempt of court, fined, and/or imprisoned. And it is not necessary to have jury trials for contempt proceedings growing out of public employees' strikes (*Rankin v. Shanker,* 242 N.E.2d 802, N.Y., 1968). In *Bd. of Ed. v. Newark Tea. Union* (114 N.J.Super. 306, 1971), union officials were sentenced to three months in jail with fines of $500 each and the union was fined $40,000 for contempt of court in defying a court order to go back to work.

Q. MAY A TEACHERS' GROUP INVOKE "SANCTIONS" AGAINST THE DISTRICT IN LIEU OF A STRIKE?

A. Where a board declined to re-employ three non-tenured teachers, one of whom happened to be the president of the local association, the local, state, and national organizations invoked "sanctions" against the district, which involved sending notices to teacher-preparing institutions asking candidates not to apply in the district. The state supreme court held that the purpose of the action was to support a refusal of others to continue to work, and thus to withhold services which the district needed in order to meet its obligation to children. In this light, the sanctions amounted to "the usual concerted refusal to work," that is, a strike. The association was ordered to undo what harm it had done by sending disclaimer letters to all those to whom it had mailed "sanction" letters earlier (*Bd. of Educ. Union Beach v. N.J. Educ. Ass'n.,* 247 A.2d 867, 1968).

Q. MAY PUBLIC EMPLOYEES PICKET THE SITE OF A STRIKE OR POSSIBLE STRIKE?

A. Picketing is equated by the courts to symbolic speech, hence has limited constitutional protection. But it does not enjoy the full set of rights accorded to pure speech and injunctive relief will issue where picketing, even though it be peaceable, tends to disrupt the normal operation of a governmental agency. In Illinois, custodial employees struck against a school board and proceeded to picket the area, causing some other union members (truck drivers, roofers) to stay away. The Supreme Court of Illinois held that the court could issue a temporary restraining order without notice of hearing (*Bd. of Educ. v. Redding,* 207 N.E.2d 427, Ill., 1965). Also, individual teachers may express an opinion or voice a point of view so long as such speech does not interfere with their duties. But where secondary teachers requested leave to go *en masse* to the state capitol and consult with legislators, the court held that such an absence would constitute a strike against the district (*Pruzan v. Bd. of Educ. of City of N.Y.,* 209 N.Y.S.2d 966, 1960).

Q. WHO IS AT FAULT WHEN STRIKES OCCUR, THE UNION OR THE TEACHERS?

A. The State of New York wrestled with that problem over many years. The Condon-Wadlin Act placed the blame on individual teachers, and loss of seniority, jobs, and pay were assessed but to no avail — the act did not stop strikes by teachers. A later law, the Taylor Law, placed the blame more squarely upon union officials who could be fined, imprisoned, and their union fined for each day the strike continued. Still, this did not end strikes by teachers, leading to the conclusion that punitive laws against the strike by public employees are ineffective in ending or eradicating strikes altogether. It is not an either-or proposition — individual teachers can still be fired if they strike illegally (*Hortonville*), and union officials who defy a court order may be imprisoned, fined, and their unions fined for contempt of court (*Newark*). Some states have spelled out what penalties for the strike can be assessed, and of course, these would be controlling in the event of a strike in your district. So the answer is that *both* teachers and their unions can be held responsible where an illegal (and most of them are illegal) teacher strike occurs.

Q. SINCE WORKERS IN THE PRIVATE SECTOR HAVE THE RIGHT TO STRIKE, IS IT NOT UNREALISTIC TO DENY THIS RIGHT TO WORKERS IN THE PUBLIC SECTOR?

A. There are valid arguments on both sides of this question. Those more familiar with collective bargaining think that the strike should be legalized, maintaining that there can be no real bargaining without it, only a paternalistic charade. Even without the strike, however, teachers tend to stand *in pari equalo* (as equals) since they can effectively close down the operation if they stick together. Even where the strike for teachers is allowed by law, there are certain restrictions which tend to force settlement prior to strike. The question is whether some agencies of government are so crucial (schools are not in the summertime) as to preclude strikes of any kind (as, for example, by police or firemen). It is admittedly difficult to apply the strike to public employment in the same philosophical framework as that which justified it in the private sector.

Other Considerations

Q. IS CLASS SIZE A VALID ITEM FOR NEGOTIATIONS?

A. There is disagreement on this point. Teachers claim that class size is definitely a "condition of employment" (under the general umbrella that bargaining may take place on "hours, wages, and other conditions of employment"). Boards have objected that this item is sometimes a false measure of teaching responsibility, since there are specialized teachers in some districts or parts of districts but not in others. The real problem seems to be by what measure class size shall be determined — numerical teacher adequacy, small classes for high school and special education classes, and other similar measures. Many courts have upheld class size as a negotiable item where the parties agree on what measure they will employ and where the board's hands are not tied (an elastic clause permits the board to enlarge class size where money is not available). This is a gray area of the law, and you should consult your state department of education to determine the current status of class-size negotiations in your state.

Q. MAY THE BOARD VOLUNTARILY NEGOTIATE ON ITEMS OF ITS CHOICE?

A. The courts have generally held that a board of education is free to voluntarily bargain on items of its choice unless the items are prohibited by statute or controlling decisional law (rulings of the governmental agency administering the act), or are contrary to public policy (*Bd. of Educ. v. Yonkers Fed'n. of Teachers,* 353 N.E.2d 569, N.Y. 1976).

Q. WHAT HAS BEEN THE EFFECT OF TEACHER NEGOTIATIONS ON PRINCIPALS AND OTHER SCHOOL ADMINISTRATORS?

A. In by-passing principals, and dealing directly with boards of education, teachers have weakened the principalship to some extent. Principals have needs other than those of teachers, and many are clamoring for the right to form their own bargaining units and approach the board to bargain for their management prerogatives. Obviously, a realignment of power is taking place between teachers and administrators. New ways must be found to work out mutually acceptable policy — which may not occur where principals are by-passed in the bargaining process. Many boards, who reacted initially to teacher demands "by giving away the store," must now find ways to gain back those prerogatives necessary to running the schools. The basic question involving the scope of bargaining is whether the interests of children are served by the active intervention of collective bargaining in the educational enterprise.

Q. MAY TEACHERS FORCE THE BOARD TO NEGOTIATE ON ITEMS WHICH IT INTRODUCES?

A. It all depends. If there is a state law governing board-teacher negotiations, the statute is usually the measure of the board's power. If the items on which parties may negotiate are not mentioned, they are usually open to third-party arbitration. In *Fargo Educ. Ass'n. v. Paulsen* (239 N.W.2d 842, N.Dak., 1976), the state supreme court affirmed the trial court's denial of a writ of *mandamus* (order to the board) requested by the association to force the board to negotiate on nine issues that were merely listed without elaboration. In the absence of a court order, an arbitrator or someone from the state's enforcement unit is usually empowered to say what is negotiable and what is not. In *Red Bank Bd. of Educ. v. Warrington* (351 A.2d 778, N.J., 1976), the assignment of teachers to an additional period of teaching where they previously had a free period was held to affect terms and conditions of employment and the matter in question was ruled an item for negotiations.

Q. IS THE DISTRICT'S PLAN FOR PROMOTION TO PRINCIPAL A BARGAINABLE ITEM?

A. No. The selection of candidates for promotion to an administrative position in a school system was held to be a managerial prerogative and not a term and condition of employment. Hence, the action of a board in making a promotion was not subject to arbitration. Procedures by which vacancies were to be filled were held to be negotiable, however. (*Bd. of Educ. of Twp. of N. Bergen v. N. Bergen Educ. Ass'n.*, 357 A.2d 302, N.J., 1976.)

Q. MAY TEACHERS "GRIEVE" WHERE THEIR PAY IS WITHHELD BECAUSE OF INCLEMENT WEATHER?

A. A grievance of teachers who reported to work on a day on which school had been cancelled because of inclement weather was held to be properly before an arbitrator under a contract which defined the term "grievance" as a complaint affecting wages, hours, or conditions of employment. An award of compensation for the day was affirmed. (*S. Allegheny School Dist. v. S. Allegheny Educ. Ass'n.*, 360 A.2d 829, Pa., 1976.)

Q. WHEN NECESSARY TO REDUCE ITS FORCE OF TEACHERS, MUST THE BOARD NEGOTIATE THE MEANS BY WHICH REDUCTION IN FORCE IS TO BE EFFECTED?

A. No. Where a local board decided it needed to reduce its teaching force, it was not obligated to negotiate with the teachers' association the criteria or guidelines to be used in selecting the specific individuals whose contracts were not to be renewed. Neither was it required to negotiate over the re-employment rights of those teachers selected for nonrenewal. (*Union City Reg. High School Bd. of Educ. v. Union City Reg. High School Teachers' Ass'n.*, 368 A.2d 364, N.J., 1976.)

Resolution of the Cases in Point

Case No. 1 — OUT YOU GO!

The resolution by the board to fire members of the CFT was upheld. Those who work for government must take conditions laid down for them by the board rather than the conditions they would choose to have (*People ex rel. Fursman v. City of Chicago,* 116 N.E. 158, Ill., 1917). "The board of education has the power to make and enforce any rules that it sees proper," said the court. "The board has the absolute right to decline to employ or re-employ any applicant for a position as teacher for any or no reason. No person has the right to demand that he or she shall be employed as a teacher. The board is the best judge of whether or not to employ or re-employ. It (the resolution) was an exercise of the discretionary power of the board which the courts will not overthrow." To the same effect was a Seattle case at a later date (*Seattle High School Chapter 200, AFT v. Sharples,* 292 Pac. 994, Wash., 1930).

Case No. 2 — GUIDELINES

The Norwalk guidelines are used as *stare decisis* (let the decision stand) to control bargaining in those states lacking legislation on this point even today. When some states, beginning with Wisconsin in 1959, enacted bargaining laws for teachers, their influence waned. These five points of law are still recognized in the common law: 1) public school teachers have the right to organize and be active in their unions; 2) a school board is permitted, but not legally required, to negotiate with a teachers' organization; 3) a school board may agree to arbitrate with teachers, but only on those issues that do not erode the sovereignty of the board; 4) a school board may not agree to a closed shop (where only members of the union may work); and 5) public school teachers may not strike to enforce their demands unless there is special permission given to do so by the legislature.

Case No. 3 — TO PEACEABLY ASSEMBLE

The superintendent and board members were held personally liable for deprivation of a civil right (*McLaughlin v. Tilendis,* 398 F.2d 287, Ill., 1968). "One should not be punished for exercising a right protected under the First Amendment (right of association)," said the court. The officials are not protected under the Illinois Tort Immunity Act; under the supremacy clause, this statute must give way to a federal statute. Even if the union was engaged in illegal activities, the two teachers, as members, could not be held accountable for their organization's misdeeds. The teachers were entitled to relief under Section 1983 which says that any person who deprives another of a civil right is answerable to that person in an action at law, suit in equity, or other proper proceeding for redress.

Case No. 4 — RIGHT TO STRIKE

The U.S. Supreme Court upheld the dismissals. In a 6-3 decision, the Court held that the due process clause did not guarantee the teachers that the decision to terminate them would be made or reviewed by a body other than the school board. The board was not a partial body, even though it had been engaged in bargaining with teachers. The teachers in effect had broken their contracts by walking out and did not come to court with clean hands. The Supreme Court held that the legislature had placed schools in good hands by giving power to local boards to decide matters of policy. Teachers were "hands" who must take conditions as they found them. In violating the state law against striking, the teachers had asked the law to protect them in their dismissals. A board is not biased because it has prior knowledge of the circumstances surrounding a certain given situation and does not have personal conflict of interest in deciding to fire the teachers. (*Hortonville Tea. Ass'n. v. Hortonville School Board,* 96 S.Ct. 2308, Wisc., 1976.)

Case No. 5 — RIGHT TO SPEAK OUT

The U.S. Supreme Court reversed the decision (*City of Madison v. Wisconsin Employment Relations Commission,* 97 S.Ct. 421, 1976). Holmquist, who spoke for the minority group, was speaking as a private citizen as well as a teacher who was interested in the outcome of contract negotiations. But he was not bargaining himself even though the board eventually signed a contract without fair share fees. Teachers cannot be compelled to give up valuable First Amendment rights they would otherwise enjoy as private citizens. Whatever its duty as an employer, when the board sits in public meetings to conduct public business and hear the views of citizens, it may not be required to discriminate between speakers on the basis of their employment, or the content of their speech. Teachers not only constitute the overwhelming bulk of employees but they are the very core of the system; restraining teachers' expressions to the board on matters involving the operation of the schools would seriously impair the board's ability to govern the district.

Chapter Seven

What To Do Till The Lawyer Comes

One of our most highly-prized rights as Americans is the right to be represented by legal counsel. In a very real sense, the civil rights movement has been an attempt to achieve that "fundamental" right for every individual.

Over the years, large groups of American citizens — the weak, the poor, the aging, children, to name a few — were deprived of the right to legal counsel. Frontier justice was often the law of the six-gun; property was protected by law, the rights of individuals were often ignored. Trials by jury were sometimes dispensed with in the interest of winning the west.

In more recent times, clogged court calendars have delayed justice, if not indeed denied it entirely. Suspects were often considered guilty until they could prove their innocence. Mental patients and the infirm were locked up for life with little attention to their therapeutic rights. Prisons held felons without thought to their rehabilitation.

The history of justice in America has too often been justice for those who could afford it, denial of justice for those who could not. Although every one is supposed to know the law, and cannot plead ignorance of the law as a defense, the intricate web of law crisscrossing our everyday lives makes such a simple standard unsupportable. We all need — and must provide for — our own legal defense or suffer the consequences. This is as it should be. Common sense tells us that we must get competent legal advice at the time we stand before the bar of justice.

In 1963, the Supreme Court overruled earlier decisions and declared that any individual faced with criminal charges is entitled to be represented by legal counsel, even though he has no money to hire an attorney (*Gideon v. Wainwright,* 372 U.S. 335, Fla., 1963). In this case of a man charged with misdemeanor theft, but denied counsel by Florida law, the Supreme Court held (9-0) that the right to counsel is "fundamental and essential to a fair trial" under the Fourteenth Amendment. "Any person who under our adversary system of justice is hauled into court and who is too poor to hire a lawyer, cannot be assured a fair trial unless counsel is provided for him. . . . The right of one charged with crime to counsel may not be deemed fundamental and essential to fair trials in some countries, but it is in ours." Thus was the guarantee of counsel in the Sixth Amendment (see Bill of Rights) applied to all cases in the state courts, both capital and noncapital (overthrowing *Betts v. Brady,* 316 U.S. 455, 1942).

Most litigation faced by teachers, however, is not criminal in nature, but consists of suits in equity, where the right to counsel is still not required unless the court feels that fundamental fairness cannot be obtained without counsel. Everyone has the right to plead his own case, but recent experience in which this was done tends to show that a layman is at a disadvantage against trained lawyers. The only avenue left is to arrange for legal counsel ahead of time, and thus reduce the odds against being overwhelmed by the complexity of the law while under pressure. Of course, if you are the plaintiff, your first act would be to employ counsel.

Due to the large number of class actions, you may already have won rights of which you are not aware. A class action is defined as litigation in which many persons having similar or identical claims sue in concert. The members of the class can range from a mere handful to more than two million. Those who favor class actions consider them "the greatest engines ever devised for protection of the powerless." Those who disapprove argue, with some justification, that class action suits are merely a device whereby the plaintiff's attorneys score high while the individual members recover a mere pittance. Each viewpoint is an extreme — the truth lies somewhere in between.

Whatever the arguments, the fact remains that blacks, women, children, illegitimates, fetuses, suspects, prisoners, juveniles, mental patients, the handicapped, individuals without native English, and students in colleges and universities have won considerable freedoms by means of class action suits in equity. Their claims were that they had been denied equal protection of state laws, and were therefore entitled to relief because of what the state was doing to them. The reading of these cases is like reading the pages of history — *Brown v. Board of Education* (1954), which outlawed segregation by race in public schools; *In re Gault* (1967), due process of law is not for adults alone; *Tinker v. Des Moines* (1969), children are persons under our Constitution; and *Wood v. Strickland* (1975), school officials may be held personally liable for deprivation of a civil right if they knew or reasonably should have known that what they were doing under color of state law would deprive a student of his or her civil rights. Millions have benefited from class action suits without even becoming aware that they were parties to an action. Yet their rights were protected and extended in such class action litigation just as if they had been plaintiffs of first impression.

If there is a moral to this, it must surely be that you, as a teacher, should first become aware of the rights which you have already won or which have been won for you *as a teacher.* There are vast areas of the law still unexplored, many unanswered questions which eventually must be resolved. You should bring yourself up to date on what your rights really are in order to avoid needless litigation.

Once having become knowledgeable of your rights (which can be accomplished in part by reading the earlier portions of this book), you must then attempt to keep up with future developments. Stories in the newspapers, professional journals, and attendance at conventions where school law is discussed can help keep you aware of changes in your legal status.

There is a third step which is equally important — availing yourself of legal counsel in case you must go into litigation. Your professional union or association may provide general advice, or you may contact your state department of public instruction (most have full-time legal advisers). And, or course, you should have in mind a competent lawyer *schooled in school law* who can come to your assistance when litigation looms. *Forewarned is forearmed* applies to educational law, and should be your first consideration even though you don't anticipate any lawsuits in the near future. Keep the phone number of your legal counsel handy and use it when legal action is forthcoming.

Ordinarily, you should not rely on legal counsel employed by the board of education, since the board may become the adversary in a court action. There has been some talk of providing legal insurance much like health, hospital, and dental insurance as one of the fringe benefits of your association membership, but this idea has not received widespread acceptance as yet. Your first task is to become legally literate and remain that way; your second, to know what to do till the lawyer comes. These following cases illustrate the need for close liaison with legal counsel.

Cases in Point

Case No. 1 — RETURN TO CLASSROOM

Plaintiff was employed by the district as an elementary principal. She had acquired tenure status as a classroom teacher in the district. The statute granting teachers tenure did not mention principals. She was advised by her superintendent that her services were no longer satisfactory as a principal, and that she would be transferred to a coordinator's job. Plaintiff replied that the transfer would be satisfactory, provided she continue to receive the salary commensurate with the position of principal. The superintendent refused to agree to this, and instead transferred her to the position of teacher at teacher's salary. She brought an action for reinstatement with appropriate pay, and compensatory and actual damages, maintaining that her transfer without a hearing on the merits amounted to a demotion. Should she be allowed to recover her position where the case is tried in a state court, and the court is being asked to interpret the intent of the legislature in enacting the tenure law?

Case No. 2 — TEACHER INCOMPETENCE

A black teacher in Louisiana charged racial prejudice when she was dismissed. In going from a dual to a unitary system, the district had to reduce the number of teachers. Plaintiff was dismissed when evidence was presented that the problems she had had in an all-black school were magnified after her transfer to an all-white school: she continued to use double-negatives, improper spellings, and showed other scholarship deficiencies in her teaching. She had twenty years experience in teaching. The board claimed it must let her go because she could not adapt "to current instructional procedures" where the district abandoned self-contained classrooms in a curriculum revision. Could the teacher be dismissed under these circumstances for incompetency?

Case No. 3 — EXTRA DUTIES

Various teachers were assigned by the board to ride a "pep" bus, supervise an afternoon football game, monitor an examination, and supervise a wrestling match all on Saturday. A state statute said: "A teacher shall not be required to teach on Saturdays or legal holidays. . . ." The teachers brought suit to bar the board from assigning them duties, whereas the board noted that the law said *"teaching"* and was not concerned about chaperoning or supervisory duties. Should the teachers be upheld or can a board unilaterally assign teachers non-teaching duties in the presence of such a state statute?

Case No. 4 — TEACHER'S POSSESSION OF DRUGS

The board of education sought dismissal of a teacher based on his possession of marijuana. In an earlier search of his automobile when stopped for a traffic violation, the teacher had inadvertently pulled out a clear plastic bag containing marijuana. After being placed on probation, the teacher was allowed to continue teaching. Subsequently he was arrested for possession and the board fired him. Was his dismissal proper under the circumstances of the case?

Case No. 5 — WHEN IN ROME...

An unmarried female teacher from New York obtained a teaching position in Union Center, South Dakota (pop. 100). Housing was scarce in the community, so the teacher lived in a trailer near the school. All went well until her boy friend moved in with her, causing the board to seek a conference with the teacher. It felt her lifestyle would have a detrimental effect on her pupils in the small community. (She was a popular teacher with her students, and a capable teacher.) The teacher replied that what she did with her time outside school was her own affair, and that to dismiss her would violate her constitutional rights to privacy and freedom of association. The board, however, produced a petition with 140 names of local citizens protesting the teacher's conduct. Should the teacher's right to privacy and association outweigh the parents' right to control the upbringing of their children?

Q. IS IT DESIRABLE THAT TEACHERS HANDLE THEIR OWN LEGAL PROBLEMS?

A. No, of course not. You are the expert in the field of education, the attorney in the field of law. The first question to be asked when a problem arises is whether this is an educational or a legal problem. Many problems judged to be legal in nature are simply educational or psychological problems, and should never be brought into the courtroom for adjudication. You should know enough law to know that you are not doing something which you should not do, nor neglecting to do something that you should do with respect to the education of those under your care and supervision. The formula outlined at the head of this chapter will assist you in placing yourself in such a favorable position — to be legally literate, and to keep up with the changes which the law has made and will continue to make in how we manage our schools. Your yardstick should be that of fundamental fairness in dealing with students and others. But you should remember that the courts will balance your right to run a peaceful school with the right of the individual to privacy, freedom of speech, and association, and other constitutional guarantees.

Q. WHAT SHOULD BE THE TEACHER'S RELATIONSHIP TO HIS OR HER ATTORNEY?

A. The attorney is your legal representative in matters having to do with the law. This might suggest a "team" relationship, since you are pooling your knowledge of education and psychology with his or her knowledge of the law. Your attorney will of course represent you if you feel you want to take a matter to court. But he or she can do you no service if you insist over his or her protestations that the odds against winning your case are too high. In either event, he or she will be paid — if you win, the opposite party will pay; if you lose, you will pay. The history of the law has not been as it *should be*; rather it is a balancing of the interests of the parties to take into account *what is.* The life of the law has not been logic, but expediency. Although teachers have won some victories, the legal trail is strewn with the fallen hopes and desires of those who have gambled on winning but have lost. Your relationship with your attorney should be close enough for mutual trust and respect, so that together, working as a team, you can see that your rights are vindicated before the law.

Q. SHOULD LAWYERS DEAL ONLY WITH LEGAL PROBLEMS?

A. Yes. That is the lawyer's stock in trade. Critics of the proliferation of educational litigation, however, say that we didn't have any legal problems until we got lawyers. You should recognize what is a purely educational problem, and learn to deal with it within the educational context. Even those problems which seem to hinge on your constitutional rights, as outlined in the earlier chapters of this book, might be mitigated had plaintiffs not decided that they would "sue the bastards," and thus end the whole problem. There are many more (and better) ways of resolving differences than to take them into court. Hasty or ill-advised litigation is costly, takes an inordinate amount of time, and forces the loser to pay. Such avenues as filing a grievance, seeking fact-finding or arbitration, or a hearing on the merits within the district are often much more productive than going to court. Court should be the last resort.

Q. HOW CAN A TEACHER FIND A LAWYER SKILLED IN SCHOOL LAW?

A. Lawyers in most states cannot advertise, but in those where they can, one way might be to look at these ads. Or you may wish to contact the local, county, or state bar associations. Your union or association can advise you on who is familiar with and up to date on cases dealing with school law.

In addition, you might want to ask other teachers who have had recent litigation. Not all attorneys are familiar with or wish to engage in cases along this line. Since the hunt may take some time, it is always important to do this search long before problems in which an attorney is needed come up. The information you accumulate often will be useful to you — and your colleagues later on.

Q. WHEN DID THE NEED FOR LEGAL COUNSEL FOR TEACHERS BECOME APPARENT?

A. The need for legal counsel available to every teacher first became apparent with the advent of the civil rights movement, in the early 1950's. What characterized this movement was its dependency on the class action suit for relief for a group who were allegedly denied their civil rights. In *Dixon v. Ala. St. Bd. of Educ.* (186 F.Supp. 945, Ala., 1960, reversed, 294 F.2d 150, 5CA, 1961), the need for university and college officials to obtain expert legal advice became apparent when students were expelled for sitting-in at Southern lunch counters. That movement later spread to the elementary and secondary areas of education. In all the cases, the issue was the same: *what should be the relationship of the state to its pupils and its employees?* Since the avenue in use is that of case law, and continues to be case law, it is apparent that every individual, including the teacher, needs to have his own legal advocate always at hand.

Q. HOW CAN AN ATTORNEY HELP THE EDUCATOR?

A. The lawyer is primarily a legal advisor or advocate for the teacher. He or she is skilled in decision making and conflict resolution. While he or she is not an educator trained in the niceties of how children learn, an attorney can provide a valuable service to educators that will allow them to get on with their principal occupation.

Q. WHAT SERVICES CAN AN ATTORNEY PROVIDE THE TEACHER?

A. First, an attorney can provide you with some *predictability* in your search for equity for yourself and for your peers. This means that an attorney can give you the probable odds that a particular course of action will be successful. Second, an attorney will help you *in making policy,* and in formulating rules which can be followed safely in your work. An attorney who is familiar with the case law in your jurisdiction can help in making policy related to a particular problem with the assurance that it is the safest alternative in a situation. Third, the attorney can provide you with *crisis counseling.* But if you wait until a crisis arises to consult an attorney, you may have waited too long.

Q. INTO WHAT CATEGORIES DO LEGAL PROBLEMS FALL WHICH CONFRONT THE TEACHER?

A. The chapters of this book might be of assistance in looking at your own legal rights and liabilities. You will note that these relate to your relationship with students (Chapter 3, Pupil Discipline and Control; Chapter 4, Teacher Liability for Pupil Injury); to your rights as a teacher (Chapter 5, Academic Freedom; Chapter 2, Employment Security); and to your rights in relation to your peers (Chapter 6, Collective Bargaining and the Teacher). Most problems fall into these categories. All of them concern the civil rights of yourself, your peers, and your students and your relationship with your employer, the board of education.

Q. IN SUMMARY, WHAT PRECAUTIONS SHOULD BE TAKEN BY THE TEACHER TO AVOID NEEDLESS LITIGATION AND STILL ENJOY CONSTITUTIONAL RIGHTS?

A. Be prepared. You spent considerable time, money and effort to prepare yourself for teaching. Yet you may not be prepared for an event that could becloud your entire career. A good procedure is to assess your position from time to time using these questions:

1. Am I *firm,* do I have reasonable limits in my teaching, and do the students know what those limits are?
2. Am I *friendly,* do I look out for the interests of the children as if I were their surrogate parent?
3. Finally, am I *fair,* do I realize that children will make mistakes, and that one of the functions of the school is to provide life-like experiences where children can learn that democracy works?

These are good operational questions. The last is perhaps the most important: Do I have the name and address and the telephone number of a good school lawyer?

If you can answer all these questions in the affirmative, you have nothing to fear from the law.

Resolution of the Cases in Point

Case No. 1 — RETURN TO CLASSROOM

Although she was advised by her attorney not to go forward with the suit, plaintiff continued the litigation through the court system until it reached the state supreme court. Her suit was lost on the grounds that the tenure statute mentioned only *teachers,* not principals. "In our view," said the court, "the legislative intent clearly was to make such a return from administration to teaching a matter of subjective determination of the board as to whether the teacher in question was performing satisfactorily in the administrative job. . . . Teachers who acquire tenure are guaranteed by law that they cannot be dismissed from their position as *teachers* except for certain reasons and in accordance with a statutory provision for notice and hearings. The power of school boards to control the hiring and firing and transfers of teachers in their districts is limited only by the express terms of the statutes with respect to these aspects of the operation of the district" (*Draper v. School District No. 1, City and County of Denver,* 486 P.2d 1048, Colo., 1971).

Case No. 2 — TEACHER INCOMPETENCE

The board was successful in dismissing the teacher for incompetency. There was nothing to indicate anything racial in the appearance of parents at hearings as they had children being taught by other black teachers without complaints. The burden of proof was on the teacher to back up her claim of racial prejudice. Her suit brought into the open her deficiencies in classroom scholarship which might not have occurred had she not challenged the board's action (*Jennings v. Caddo Parish School Board,* 276 So. 2d 386, La., 1973; see also *George v. Davis,* 365 F.Supp. 446, La., 1973).

Case No. 3 — EXTRA DUTIES

Courts have come full circle since the 1950's in requiring teachers to accept non-teaching duties, so long as these duties reasonably relate to their overall jobs as teachers. Thus, the teacher who was assigned to "baby-sit" a bowling club was upheld in his challenge to such an assignment (*Pease v. Millcreek Twp. Sch.Dist.,* 195 A.2d 104, Pa., 1963). But in *District 300 Educ. Ass'n. v. Bd. of Education* (334 N.E.2d 165, Ill., 1975), the teachers were *unsuccessful* in challenging unilateral assignment by the board to Saturday duties even in the presence of a state law that teachers should not be required "to teach" on Saturdays or legal school holidays. "The broad grant of authority to fix duties of teachers is not restricted to classroom instruction," said the court. But the court pointed out that supervisory work with students is not to be equated with janitor or police service where extra-curricular activities are concerned. The duties assigned were not too time-consuming or demeaning to the professional stature of the teacher and there was no sign of discrimination against any one teacher. They were necessary adjuncts to normal school activities and were well within the power of the board to require.

Case No. 4 — TEACHER'S POSSESSION OF DRUGS

Mere possession of a controlled substance such as marijuana does not in itself constitute immorality, said the court. Normally the board must show that possession destroyed the teacher's credibility as a teacher, or affected his teaching ability. Since the teacher's conduct was remediable his conduct in being arrested a second time destroyed his effectiveness as a teacher and the court upheld his dismissal for that cause. (*Chicago Bd. of Educ. v. Payne,* 430 N.E. 2d 310, Ill. 1981).

Case No. 5 — WHEN IN ROME...

An attorney might have advised the teacher that constitutional rights are never absolute — only circumstantial and conditional always on the facts in each case at bar. When she lost at the district court level, the teacher appealed. The Eighth Circuit Court of Appeals upheld the lower court, declaring that "the state is entitled to require teachers to maintain a properly moral (sic) scholastic environment" in view of the independent "interest in the well-being of youth" as well as its interest "in preserving the right of parents to control the upbringing of their children." These rights (of the state) are to be weighed against the teacher's right to privacy. In denying her damages and attorney's fees, the court noted that it is not yet clear that the Constitution "affords the teacher's lifestyle some protection" (*Sullivan v. Meade County Indep. Sch. Dist.,* 530 F.2d 799, S.Dak., 1976).

Amendments to the United States Constitution

(The first 10 Amendments were ratified December 15, 1791, and form what is known as the "Bill of Rights")

AMENDMENT I

Congress shall make no law respecting an establishment of religion, or prohibiting the free exercise thereof; or abridging the freedom of speech, or of the press; or the right of the people peaceably to assemble, and to petition the Government for a redress of grievances.

AMENDMENT II

A well regulated Militia, being necessary to the security of a free State, the right of the people to keep and bear Arms, shall not be infringed.

AMENDMENT III

No Soldier shall, in time of peace be quartered in any house, without the consent of the Owner, nor in time of war, but in a manner to be prescribed by law.

---

*Amendment XXI was not ratified by state legislatures, but by state conventions summoned by Congress.

AMENDMENT IV

The right of the people to be secure in their persons, houses, papers, and effects, against unreasonable searches and seizures, shall not be violated, and no Warrants shall issue, but upon probable cause, supported by Oath or affirmation, and particularly describing the place to be searched, and the persons or things to be seized.

AMENDMENT V

No person shall be held to answer for a capital, or otherwise infamous crime, unless on a presentment or indictment of a Grand Jury, except in cases arising in the land or naval forces, or in the Militia, when in actual service in time of War or public danger; nor shall any person be subject for the same offence to be twice put in jeopardy of life or limb; nor shall be compelled in any criminal case to be a witness against himself, nor be deprived of life, liberty, or property, without due process of law; nor shall private property be taken for public use, without just compensation.

AMENDMENT VI

In all criminal prosecutions, the accused shall enjoy the right to a speedy and public trial, by an impartial jury of the State and district wherein the crime shall have been committed, which district shall have been previously ascertained by law, and to be informed of the nature and cause of the accusation; to be confronted with the witnesses against him; to have compulsory process for obtaining witnesses in his favor, and to have the Assistance of Counsel for his defence.

AMENDMENT VII

In suits at common law, where the value in controversy shall exceed twenty dollars, the right of trial by jury shall be preserved, and no fact tried by a jury, shall be otherwise reexamined in any Court of the United States, than according to the rules of the common law.

AMENDMENT VIII

Excessive bail shall not be required, nor excessive fines imposed, nor cruel and unusual punishments inflicted.

AMENDMENT IX

The enumeration in the Constitution, of certain rights, shall not be construed to deny or disparage others retained by the people.

AMENDMENT X

The powers not delegated to the United States by the Constitution, nor prohibited by it to the States, are reserved to the States respectively, or to the people.

AMENDMENT XI

(Ratified February 7, 1795)

The Judicial power of the United States shall not be construed to extend to any suit in law or equity, commenced or prosecuted against one of the United States by Citizens of another State, or by Citizens or Subjects of any Foreign State.

AMENDMENT XII

(Ratified July 27, 1804)

The Electors shall meet in their respective states and vote by ballot for President and Vice-President, one of whom, at least, shall not be an inhabitant of the same state with themselves; they shall name in their ballots the person voted for as President, and in distinct ballots the person voted for as Vice-President, and they shall make distinct lists of all persons voted for as President, and of all persons voted for as Vice-President, and of the number of votes for each, which lists they shall sign and certify, and transmit sealed to the seat of the government of the United States, directed to the President of the Senate;—The President of the Senate shall, in presence of the Senate and House of Representatives, open all the certificates and the votes shall then be counted;—The person having the greatest number of votes for President, shall be the President, if such number be a majority of the whole number of Electors appointed; and if no person have such majority, then from the persons having the highest numbers not exceeding three on the list of those voted for as President, the House of Representatives shall choose immediately, by ballot, the President. But in choosing the President, the votes shall be taken by states, the representation from each state having one vote; a quorum for this purpose shall consist of a member or members from two-thirds of the states, and a majority of all the states shall be necessary to a choice. [And if the House of Representatives shall not choose a President whenever the right of choice shall devolve upon them, before the fourth day of March next following, then the Vice-President shall act as President, as in the case of the death or other constitutional disability of the President.—]* The person having the greatest number of votes as Vice-President, shall be the Vice-President, if such number be a majority of the whole number of Electors appointed, and if no person have a majority, then from the two highest numbers on the list, the Senate shall choose the Vice-President; a quorum for the purpose shall consist of two-thirds of the whole number of Senators, and a majority of the whole number shall be necessary to a choice. But no person constitutionally ineligible to the office of President shall be eligible to that of Vice-President of the United States.

---

*Superseded by section 3 of the twentieth amendment.

AMENDMENT XIII

(Ratified December 6, 1865)

SECTION 1. Neither slavery nor involuntary servitude, except as a punishment for crime whereof the party shall have been duly convicted, shall exist within the United States, or any place subject to their jurisdiction.

SECTION 2. Congress shall have power to enforce this article by appropriate legislation.

AMENDMENT XIV

(Ratified July 9, 1868)

SECTION 1. All persons born or naturalized in the United States, and subject to the jurisdiction thereof, are citizens of the United States and of the State wherein they reside. No State shall make or enforce any law which shall abridge the privileges or immunities of citizens of the United States; nor shall any State deprive any person of life, liberty, or property, without due process of law; nor deny to any person within its jurisdiction the equal protection of the laws.

SECTION 2. Representatives shall be apportioned among the several States according to their respective numbers, counting the whole number of persons in each State, excluding Indians not taxed. But when the right to vote at any election for the choice of electors for President and Vice-President of the United States, Representatives in Congress, the Executive and Judicial officers of a State, or the members of the Legislature thereof, is denied to any of the male inhabitants of such State, being twenty-one years of age,* and citizens of the United States, or in any way abridged, except for participation in rebellion, or other crime, the basis of representation therein shall be reduced in the proportion which the number of such male citizens shall bear to the whole number of male citizens twenty-one years of age in such State.

SECTION 3. No person shall be a Senator or Representative in Congress, or elector of President and Vice-President, or hold any office, civil or military, under the United States, or under any State, who, having previously taken an oath, as a member of Congress, or as an officer of the United States, or as a member of any State legislature, or as an executive or judicial officer of any State, to support the Constitution of the United States, shall have engaged in insurrection or rebellion against the same, or given aid or comfort to the enemies thereof. But Congress may by a vote of two-thirds of each House, remove such disability.

SECTION 4. The validity of the public debt of the United States, authorized by law, including debts incurred for payment of pensions and bounties for services in suppressing insurrection or rebellion, shall not be questioned. But neither the United States nor any State shall assume or pay any debt or obligation incurred in aid of insurrection or rebellion against the United States, or any claim for the loss or emancipation of any slave; but all such debts, obligations and claims shall be held illegal and void.

---

*Changed by section 1 of the twenty-sixth amendment.

SECTION 5. The Congress shall have power to enforce, by appropriate legislation, the provisions of this article.

AMENDMENT XV

(Ratified February 3, 1870)

SECTION 1. The right of citizens of the United States to vote shall not be denied or abridged by the United States or by any State on account of race, color, or previous condition of servitude—

SECTION 2. The Congress shall have power to enforce this article by appropriate legislation.

AMENDMENT XVI

(Ratified February 3, 1913)

The Congress shall have power to lay and collect taxes on incomes, from whatever source derived, without apportionment among the several States, and without regard to any census or enumeration.

AMENDMENT XVII

(Ratified April 8, 1913)

The Senate of the United States shall be composed of two Senators from each State, elected by the people thereof, for six years; and each Senator shall have one vote. The electors in each State shall have the qualifications requisite for electors of the most numerous branch of the State legislatures.

When vacancies happen in the representation of any State in the Senate, the executive authority of such State shall issue writs of election to fill such vacancies: *Provided,* That the legislature of any State may empower the executive thereof to make temporary appointments until the people fill the vacancies by election as the legislature may direct.

This amendment shall not be so construed as to affect the election or term of any Senator chosen before it becomes valid as part of the Constitution.

AMENDMENT XVIII

(Ratified January 16, 1919)

[SECTION 1. After one year from the ratification of this article the manufacture, sale, or transportation of intoxicating liquors within, the importation thereof into, or the exportation thereof from the United States and all territory subject to the jurisdiction thereof for beverage purposes is hereby prohibited.

[SECTION 2. The Congress and the several States shall have concurrent power to enforce this article by appropriate legislation.

[SECTION 3. This article shall be inoperative unless it shall have been ratified as an amendment to the Constitution by the legislatures of the several States as provided in the Constitution, within seven years from the date of the submission hereof to the States by the Congress.]*

AMENDMENT XIX

(Ratified August 18, 1920)

The right of citizens of the United States to vote shall not be denied or abridged by the United States or by any State on account of sex.

Congress shall have power to enforce this article by appropriate legislation.

AMENDMENT XX

(Ratified January 23, 1933)

SECTION 1. The terms of the President and Vice President shall end at noon on the 20th day of January, and the terms of Senators and Representatives at noon on the 3d day of January, of the years in which such terms would have ended if this article had not been ratified; and the terms of their successors shall then begin.

SECTION 2. The Congress shall assemble at least once in every year, and such meeting shall begin at noon on the 3d day of January, unless they shall by law appoint a different day.

SECTION 3. If, at the time fixed for the beginning of the term of the President, the President elect shall have died, the Vice President elect shall become President. If a President shall not have been chosen before the time fixed for the beginning of his term, or if the President elect shall have failed to qualify, then the Vice President elect shall act as President until a President shall have qualified; and the Congress may by law provide for the case

*Repealed by section 1 of the twenty-first amendment.

wherein neither a President elect nor a Vice President elect shall have qualified, declaring who shall then act as President, or the manner in which one who is to act shall be selected, and such person shall act accordingly until a President or Vice President shall have qualified.

SECTION 4. The Congress may by law provide for the case of the death of any of the persons from whom the House of Representatives may choose a President whenever the right of choice shall have devolved upon them, and for the case of the death of any of the persons from whom the Senate may choose a Vice President whenever the right of choice shall have devolved upon them.

SECTION 5. Sections 1 and 2 shall take effect on the 15th day of October following the ratification of this article.

SECTION 6. This article shall be inoperative unless it shall have been ratified as an amendment to the Constitution by the legislatures of three-fourths of the several States within seven years from the date of its submission.

AMENDMENT XXI

(Ratified December 5, 1933)

SECTION 1. The eighteenth article of amendment to the Constitution of the United States is hereby repealed.

SECTION 2. The transportation or importation into any State, Territory, or possession of the United States for delivery or use therein of intoxicating liquors, in violation of the laws thereof, is hereby prohibited.

SECTION 3. This article shall be inoperative unless it shall have been ratified as an amendment to the Constitution by conventions in the several States, as provided in the Constitution, within seven years from the date of the submission hereof to the States by the Congress.

AMENDMENT XXII

(Ratified February 27, 1951)

SECTION 1. No person shall be elected to the office of the President more than twice, and no person who has held the office of

President, or acted as President, for more than two years of a term to which some other person was elected President shall be elected to the office of the President more than once. But this Article shall not apply to any person holding the office of President when this Article was proposed by the Congress, and shall not prevent any person who may be holding the office of President, or acting as President, during the term within which this Article becomes operative from holding the office of President or acting as President during the remainder of such term.

SECTION 2. This article shall be inoperative unless it shall have been ratified as an amendment to the Constitution by the legislatures of three-fourths of the several States within seven years from the date of its submission to the States by the Congress.

AMENDMENT XXIII

(Ratified March 29, 1961)

SECTION 1. The District constituting the seat of Government of the United States shall appoint in such manner as the Congress may direct:

A number of electors of President and Vice President equal to the whole number of Senators and Representatives in Congress to which the District would be entitled if it were a State, but in no event more than the least populous State; they shall be in addition to those appointed by the States, but they shall be considered, for the purposes of the election of President and Vice President, to be electors appointed by a State; and they shall meet in the District and perform such duties as provided by the twelfth article of amendment.

SECTION 2. The Congress shall have power to enforce this article by appropriate legislation.

AMENDMENT XXIV

(Ratified January 23, 1964)

SECTION 1. The right of citizens of the United States to vote in any primary or other election for President or Vice President, for electors for President or Vice President, or for Senator or Representative in Congress, shall not be denied or abridged by the

United States or any State by reason of failure to pay any poll tax or other tax.

SECTION 2. The Congress shall have power to enforce this article by appropriate legislation.

AMENDMENT XXV

(Ratified February 10, 1967)

SECTION 1. In case of the removal of the President from office or of his death or resignation, the Vice President shall become President.

SECTION 2. Whenever there is a vacancy in the office of the Vice President, the President shall nominate a Vice President who shall take office upon confirmation by a majority vote of both Houses of Congress.

SECTION 3. Whenever the President transmits to the President pro tempore of the Senate and the Speaker of the House of Representatives his written declaration that he is unable to discharge the powers and duties of his office, and until he transmits to them a written declaration to the contrary, such powers and duties shall be discharged by the Vice President as Acting President.

SECTION 4. Whenever the Vice President and a majority of either the principal officers of the executive departments or of such other body as Congress may by law provide, transmit to the President pro tempore of the Senate and the Speaker of the House of Representatives their written declaration that the President is unable to discharge the powers and duties of his office, the Vice President shall immediately assume the powers and duties of the office as Acting President.

Thereafter, when the President transmits to the President pro tempore of the Senate and the Speaker of the House of Representatives his written declaration that no inability exists, he shall resume the powers and duties of his office unless the Vice President and a majority of either the principal officers of the executive department or of such other body as Congress may by law provide, transmit within four days to the President pro tempore of the Senate and the Speaker of the House of Representatives their written declaration that the President is unable to discharge the powers and duties of his office. Thereupon Congress shall decide the issue, assembling within forty-eight hours for that purpose if not in session. If the Congress, within twenty-one days after receipt of the latter written declaration, or, if Congress is not in session, within twenty-one days after Congress is required to assemble, determines by two-thirds vote of both Houses that the President is unable to discharge the powers and duties of his office, the Vice President shall continue to discharge the same as Acting President; otherwise, the President shall resume the powers and duties of his office.

AMENDMENT XXVI

(Ratified July 1, 1971)

SECTION 1. The right of citizens of the United States, who are eighteen years of age or older, to vote shall not be denied or abridged by the United States or by any State on account of age.

SECTION 2. The Congress shall have power to enforce this article by appropriate legislation.

Table of Cases

Abington Twp. School Dist. v. Schempp (Pa.) **59, 154**
Abood v. Detroit Bd. of Educ., (Mich.) **178, 223**
Acanfora v. Bd. of Educ. of Montgomery County (Md.) **33**
Adler v. Bd. of Educ., City of N.Y. (N.Y.) **136, 161, 165**
Anderson v. Banks (Ga.) **67**
Anderson v. San Francisco Unified School Dist. (Cal.) **42**
Andrews v. Drew Sep. School District (Miss.) **47**
Arnold v. Hafling (Colo.) **107**
Augustus v. School Bd. of Escambia County (Fla.) **83**
Ayala v. Phila. Bd. of Public Education (Pa.) **96, 131-2**
Baggett v. Bullitt (Wash.) **163**
Baird v. Hosmer (Ohio) **111**
Baker v. Owen (N.C.) **55, 72, 91, 115, 129-30**
Beck v. San Francisco Unified School District (Cal.) **107**
Beilan v. Board of Phila. (Pa.) **161-2**
Benson v. Baltimore Traction Co. (Md.) **121-2**
Benson v. School Dist. No. 1 of Silver Bow County (Mont.) **178**
Bertot v. School Dist. No. 1 (Wyo.) **45**
Betts v. Brady (Md.) **191**
Birdwell v. Hazelwood School District (Mo.) **151**
Black Coalition v. Portland School Dist. No. 1 (Ore.) **83**
Blackwell v. Issaquena Co. Bd. of Educ. (Miss.) **75-6**
Board of Education v. Albert Shanker (N.Y.) **181**
Board of Education v. Ambach (N.Y.) **67**
Board of Education v. Yonkers Fed. of Teachers (N.Y.) **185-6**
Board of Education of Union Free Dist. v. Assoc. Teachers of Huntington (N.Y.) **179**
Board of Education, Newark v. Newark Tea. Union (N.J.) **183-4**
Board of Education v. Pico (N.Y.) **160**
Board of Education v. Redding (Ill.) **183-4**
Board of Education, Rockaway Twp. v. Rockaway Twp. Educ. Assn. (N.J.) **148**
Board of Education, North Bergen v. N. Bergen Educ. Assn. (N.J.) **187**
Board of Education, Union Beach v. N.J. Educ. Assn. (N.J.) **183**
Board of Regents v. Roth (Wisc.) **40, 223**

Bogust v. Iverson (Wisc.) **124**
Brenden v. Ind. Sch. Dist. 742 (Minn.) **76, 78**
Brown v. Board of Educ., City of Topeka (Kans.) **9, 22, 53, 128, 192, 223**
Brubaker v. Bd. of Educ., Dist. 149, Cook County (Ill.) **147-8**
Bruenn v. N. Yakima School Dist. No. 7 (Wash.) **100**
Bunger v. Iowa H.S. Ath. Assn. (Iowa) **71**
Burnside v. Byars (Miss.) **75-6, 144-5**
Burton v. Cascade School Dist. No. 5 (Ore.) **5**
Butcher v. Santa Rosa H.S. District (Cal.) **104**
Buzzard v. East Lake School District (Cal.) **109**
Calway v. Williamson (Conn.) **116-7**
Canfield v. School Dist. No. 8, El Paso County (Colo.) **84**
Carey v. Piphus (Ill.) **75**
Carey v. Population Services Int. (N.Y.) **90, 155**
Carroll v. Fitzsimmons (Colo.) **99, 103**
Cary v. Bd. of Educ. of Aurora (Colo.) **7, 23-4, 152, 180-1**
Celestine v. Lafayette Parish School Board (La.) **44, 79**
Chappel v. Franklin Pierce School District (Wash.) **101**
Chicago Bd. of Educ. v. Payne (Ill.) **194, 200**
Christofides v. Hellenic E. Orthodox Christian Church (N.Y.) **95-6, 97, 103, 130-1**
Clemmer v. Unified School Dist. No. 501 (Kans.) **86**
Cleveland Board of Education v. LaFleur (Ohio) **27, 51-2, 223**
Close v. Lederle (Mass.) **144**
Cochran v. Odell (Tex.) **48**
Coe v. Gerstein (Fla.) **90-1**
Cohen v. California (Cal.) **144**
Cohen v. Chesterfield County School Board (Va.) **27, 51-2**
Connell v. Higginbotham (Fla.) **223**
Cordova v. Chonko (Ohio) **76**
Corne v. Bausch and Lomb (Ariz.) **48**
Cornwell v. State Board of Education (Md.) **86-7**
Cox v. Barnes (Ky.) **107**
Cramp v. Bd. of Public Instruction (Fla.) **163**
Crews v. Cloncs (Cal.) **76**
Crossen v. Bd. of Educ., City of N.Y. (N.Y.) **109-10**
Cumberland Valley Educ. Assn. v. Cumberland Valley Sch. Dist. (Pa.) **178**
Dailey v. Los Angeles Unified School District (Cal.) **101**
Damgaard v. Oakland H.S. District (Cal.) **104**
Davis v. Meek (Ohio) **92**
Dawkins v. Billingsley (Okla.) **120**
Dawson v. Tulare Union School District (Cal.) **105**
Dayton Classroom Teachers Assn. v. Dayton Bd. of Educ. (Ohio) **179**
Debra P. v. Turlington (Fla.) **67**
Decker v. Dundee Central School District (N.Y.) **110-11**

De Gooyer v. Harkness (S. Dak.) **97-8**
Dist. 300 Educ. Assn. v. Board of Education (Ill.) **194, 199**
Dixon v. Alabama State Board of Education (Ala.) **196-7**
Dixon v. Allen (Cal.) **120**
Dixon v. Beresh (Mich.) **85**
Doe, Peter W., v. San Francisco Unified School District (Cal.) **74, 98**
Doherty v. Wilson (Ga.) **28, 52**
Donaldson, In re (Cal.) **68-9**
Donohue v. Copiague (N.Y.) **74**
Downs v. Conway School District (Ark.) **152**
Draper v. School Dist. No. 1, City and Co. of Denver (Colo.) **193, 198-9**
Dunn v. Tyler Ind. School District (Tex.) **84**
Dunham v. Pulsifer (Vt.) **76**
East Hardford Educ. Assn. v. Bd. of Education (Conn.) **177**
Edwards v. Jersey Shore Area School District (Pa.) **83**
Elfbrandt v. Russell (Ariz.) **163**
Engel v. Vitale (N.Y.) **59, 154**
Epperson v. Arkansas (Ark.) **60, 135-6, 165**
Fargo Educ. Assn. v. Paulsen (N. Dak.) **186**
Farley v. M.M. Cattle Co. (Tex.) **112**
FCC v. Pacifica Foundation (N.Y.) **140**
Ferguson v. Bd. of Trustees of Bonner Co. S.D. No. 82 (Ida.) **146-7**
Fern v. Thorp Public Schools (Wisc.) **155-6**
Ferraro Bd. of Educ., City of N.Y. (N.Y.) **98**
Ferreira v. Sanchez (N. Mex.) **101**
Feuerstein v. Bd. of Educ., City of N.Y. (N.Y.) **98**
Fielder v. Bd. of Education (Nebr.) **67**
Foe v. Vanderhoof (Colo.) **90-1**
Friedman v. Union Free School District (N.Y.) **179**
Gaincott v. Davis (Mich.) **102**
Gallagher v. City of New York (N.Y.) **125**
Gambino v. Fairfax County School Board (Va.) **156, 158-9**
Garber v. Central H.S. District (N.Y.) **100**
Gault, In re (Ariz.) **84, 127-8, 192**
Gay Students' Organization, U of N.H. v. Bonner (N.H.) **85**
George v. Davis (La.) **193, 199**
Gideon v. Wainwright (Fla.) **191**
Gilliland v. Bondurant (Mo.) **122**
...onsol. Sch. Dist. (Miss.) **42**
...l District (Ill.) **114, 117**
...**, 77, 91-2, 128, 129, 223**
...)
...School Board (S.C.) **126**

Gray v. Union County Intermediate Educ. Dist. (Ore.) **45**
Grayned v. Rockford (Ill.) **223**
Greene v. Moore (Tex.) **83**
Griffin v. DeFelice (La.) **80**
Griggs v. Duke Power Company (N.C.) **63**
Guerreri v. Tyson (Pa.) **95, 130**
Haley v. Ohio (Ohio) **128**
Hanson v. Reedley Joint School District (Cal.) **113**
Harrah Ind. Sch. Dist. v. Martin (Okla.) **35**
Hazelwood Sch. Dist. v. U.S. (Mo.) **49**
Head v. Special School District (Minn.) **182**
Healy v. James (Conn.) **85**
Hernandez v. School Dist. No. 1, City and Co. of Denver (Colo.) **81**
Hillman v. Elliott (Va.) **77**
Hobson v. Hansen (D.C.) **62**
Hoover v. Meiklejohn (Colo.) **78**
Hortonville School Board v. Hortonville Tea. Assn. (Wisc.) **8, 24, 36, 167, 169, 182, 184, 189**
Ingraham v. Wright (Fla.) **72, 115-6, 130, 223**
Jacobs v. Benedict (Ohio) **80**
Jacobson v. Massachusetts (Mass.) **60**
James v. Board of Education (N.Y.) **43**
Jennings v. Caddo Parish School Board (La.) **193, 199**
Johnson v. Branch (N.C.) **146**
Johnson v. Joint School District (Ida.) **80-1**
Johnson v. Sampson (Minn.) **116**
Jones v. Hallahan (Ky.) **50**
Jones v. Kansas City (Kans.) **105**
Karp v. Becken (Ariz.) **85**
Keefe v. Geanakos (Mass.) **141**
Keyes v. Sch. Dist. No. 1 (Colo.) **223**
Keyeshian v. Board of Regents (N.Y.) **161, 223**
Kramer v. Union Free Sch. Dist. (N.Y.) **223**
Ladson v. Board of Education (N.Y.) **79-80**
LaFrentz v. Gallagher (Ariz.) **96, 131**
Larry P. v. Riles (Cal.) **62**
Lau v. Nichols (Cal.) **153, 223**
Leonard v. School Committee of Attleboro (Mass.) **64**
Lilienthal v. San Leandro Unified School District (Cal.) **100**
Linn v. Rand (N.J.) **123-4**
Local 858, AFT v. School Dist. No. 1 (Colo.) **178-9**
Long v. Zopp (W. Va.) **81-2**
Lovitt v. Concord School District (Mich.) **8, 24**
McCarthy v. Phila. Civil Service Comm. (Pa.) **35**
McCollum v. Board of Education, Champaign (Ill.) **154, 223**

McConnell v. Anderson (Cal.) **50**
McCullough v. Bd. of Trustees, Panola (Miss.) **28, 52**
McLaughlin v. Tilendis (Ill.) **167, 169, 188-9**
McMullen v. Ursuline Order of Sisters (N. Mex.) **126**
Madison Jt. Sch. Dist. No. 8 v. Wisc. E.R.C. (Wisc.) **145-6, 170, 175, 189, 223**
Malnak v. Maharishi Mahesh Yogi (N.J.) **148**
Marlar v. Bill (Tenn.) **67-8**
Marshall v. Marshalltown Sch. Dist. (Iowa) **48**
Martin v. Kearney (Cal.) **119**
Matter of Arbitration Between Ringgold Area Sch. Dist and the Ringgold Education Association (Pa.) **179**
Maxwell v. Santa Fe Public Schools (N. Mex.) **104**
Medeiros v. Kiyosaki (Hawaii) **87**
Melton v. Young (Tenn.) **83**
Mercer v. State (Tex.) **70-1**
Merriken v. Cressman (Pa.) **79**
Meyer v. Nebraska (Nebr.) **128, 137**
Miller v. California (Cal.) **149-50, 156**
Mills v. Board of Education (D.C.) **71**
Minorics v. Board of Education (N.J.) **71**
Mitchell v. La. H.S. Ath. Assn. (La.) **78**
Mogabgab v. Orleans Parish School Board (La.) **96-7, 132**
Monell v. Dept. of Social Services (N.Y.) **127**
Moore v. School Board of Gulf City (Fla.) **144**
Moran v. School Dist. of West Yellowstone County (Mont.) **56-7, 92**
Morris v. Douglas County School District (Ore.) **101, 109**
Morrison v. State Board of Education (Cal.) **14, 150**
Mount Healthy City School Dist. v. Doyle (Ohio) **139**
Mower v. Leicester (Mass.) **94**
Murray v. Curlett (Md.) **59, 154**
Murray v. West Baton Rouge Parish School Board (La.) **82-3**
National Educ. Assn. v. Lee County Bd. of Educ. (Fla.) **182**
NEA v. South Carolina (S.C.) **31**
National League of Cities v. Usury (Cal.) **181, 223**
Negrich v. Dade County Bd. of Instruction (Fla.) **33**
Nga Li v. Yellow Cab Co. of Calif. (Cal.) **112**
Niles v. City of San Rafael (Cal.) **108**
Nigosian v. Weiss (Mich.) **138**
Nitzberg v. Parks (Md.) **157**
Norwalk Teachers Assn. v. Bd. of Educ. (Conn.) **167, 168-9, 188**
Oakland School District v. Olicker (Cal.) **150-1**
O'Connor v. Board of Education (N.Y.) **79**
Ohman v. Bd. of Educ., City of N.Y. (N.Y.) **102**
Ordway v. Hargraves (Mass.) **77**
Owens v. Commonwealth of Kentucky (Ky.) **8, 24-5, 114-5**
Patton v. Bennett (Tenn.) **127**

Pa. Assn. for Retarded Children v. Commonwealth (Pa.) **62**
Pease v. Millcreek Twp. Sch. District (Pa.) **194, 199-200**
People v. Barksdale (Cal.) **82**
People v. Bowers (N.Y.) **70-1**
People v. D (N.Y.) **70**
People ex rel Fursman v. City of Chicago (Ill.) **167, 188**
People v. Smith (Ill.) **117**
Perry v. Sindermann (Tex.) **40, 223**
Phillips v. Martin-Marietta Corp. (Fla.) **45**
Pickering v. Board of Education (Ill.) **27, 42, 51, 223**
Pierce v. Society of Sisters, See *Society of Sisters v. Pierce* (Ore.)
Pinellas County Classroom Tea. Assn. v. Bd. of Pub. Instr. (Fla.) **181**
Potts v. Wright (Pa.) **67-8, 69-70**
Pruzan v. Bd. of Educ., City of N.Y. (N.Y.) **184**
Rankin v. Shanker (N.Y.) **183**
Red Bank Bd. of Educ. v. Warrington (N.J.) **186-7**
Reid v. Nyquist (N.Y.) **82**
Robbinsdale Educ. Assn. v. Robbinsdale Federation (Minn.) **177-8**
Rocker v. Huntington (N.Y.) **145**
Rodriguez v. Seattle (Wash.) **106-7**
Rolando v. School Directors (Ill.) **58**
Russell v. Men of Devon (Eng.) **94**
Russo v. Central School Dist. No. 1 (N.Y.) **148-9**
St. Ann v. Palisi (La.) **65-6**
San Antonio Ind. Sch. Dist. v. Rodriguez (Tex.) **21, 73, 74, 223**
Sarac v. State Board of Education (Cal.) **14**
Scheelhaase v. Woodbury Community School Dist. (Iowa) **66**
School Community of Stoughton v. Labor Re. Comm. (Mass.) **180**
Scoma v. Chicago Board of Education (Ill.) **61**
Seal v. Mertz (Pa.) **85**
Sears v. City of Springfield (La.) **108**
Seattle High School Ch. 200, AFT v. Sharples (Wash.) **167-8, 188**
Segall v. Piazza (N.Y.) **119**
Shanley v. Northeast Ind. Sch. Dist. (Tex.) **157**
Shelton v. Tucker (Ark.) **163**
Shenefield v. Sheridan County Sch. Dist. No. 1 (Wyo.) **47**
Simms v. School Dist. No. 1, Multnomah County (Ore.) **117**
Singleton v. Jackson Mun. Sep. School Dist. (Miss.) **49**
Slochower v. Bd. of Higher Education (N.Y.) **161**
Sly v. Bd. of Education, Kansas City, Ks. (Kans.) **106**
Smith v. Miller (Kans.) **81**
Smith v. Uffelman (Tenn.) **111**
Society of Sisters v. Pierce (Ore.) **59, 128, 137, 160-1**
Socrates, Trial of (Greece) **135, 164**
So. Allegheny Sch. Dist. v. So. Allegheny Educ. Assn. (Pa.) **187**

Spanel v. Mounds View School District (Minn.) **94**
Speake v. Grantham (Miss.) **68**
State v. McKinnon (Wash.) **68**
State v. Scopes (Tenn.) **135, 137-8, 164**
State v. Stein (Kans.) **69**
State v. Vaughn (Colo.) **83-4**
State v. Young (Ga.) **68**
Station v. Travelers Insurance Co. (La.) **98-9**
Stoddard v. School Dist. No. 1 (Wyo.) **7, 23**
Stone v. Graham (Ky.) **154**
Stroman v. Bd. of Education (Pa.) **44**
Sullivan v. Meade Co. Ind. Sch. District (S. Dak.) **194, 200**
Summers v. Milwaukie Union High School (Ore.) **107**
Suits v. Glover (Ala.) **116**
Sweezy v. New Hampshire (N.H.) **136, 165**
T. H. v. Jones (Utah) **90**
Tinker v. Des Moines School Board (Iowa) **54, 57, 64, 72, 84, 128, 134, 142-3, 159-60, 192, 223**
Tractman v. Anker (N.Y.) **159**
Unified Sch. Dist. No. 480 v. Epperson (Kans.) **27-8, 52**
Union City Reg. H.S. Bd. v. U.C. Reg. H.S. Teachers' Assn. (N.J.) **187**
U.S. v. Coffeeville Consol. School District (Miss.) **78-9**
U.S. v. Price (Miss.) **69-70**
U.S. v. South Carolina (S.C.) **31, 41**
Vail v. Board of Education (N.H.) **82**
Vendrell v. School Dist. No. 26C (Ore.) **110**
Walsh v. La H.S. Ath. Assn. (La.) **78**
Walston v. Bd. of Education (Va.) **41**
Wardell v. Bd. of Educ. of Cincinnati (Ohio) **35**
Ware v. Estes (Tex.) **72, 115**
Wasilewski v. Bd. of Educ. Milwaukee (Wisc.) **142**
Weems v. Robinson (Ala.) **110**
West Va. State Bd. of Educ. v. Barnette (W. Va.) **59, 83, 128, 153**
Wheeler v. Barrera (Mo.) **223**
White v. Davis (Cal.) **164**
Wieman v. Updegraff (Okla.) **138, 223**
Wiener v. Bd. of Educ., City of N.Y. (N.Y.) **104-5**
Wisconsin v. Constantineau (Wisc.) **61**
Wisconsin v. Yoder (Wisc.) **56, 92, 223**
Withers v. Charlotte-Mecklenburg Bd. of Educ. (N.C.) **125-6**
Wood v. Strickland (Ark.) **55, 64, 91, 128, 129, 192**
Woodsmall v. Mt. Diablo Unified School Dist. (Cal.) **110**
Wright v. Dewitt (Ark.) **60**
Wright v. Houston Ind. School District (Tex.) **155**
Zorach v. Clauson (N.Y.) **59, 154**
Zucht v. King (Tex.) **60, 223**

How Much Do You Know About The Gay Rights Issue?

Directions: Indicate either T or F whether the statement is true or false. Answers on next page.

1. Most major cities already have laws on the books prohibiting discrimination against gay men and women. The trouble is, they are not enforced.
2. Gay people who feel they've been discriminated against in jobs, housing, or public accommodations have no federal agency to turn to — not even the Civil Rights Commission.
3. Even if gay people do face discrimination, there aren't enough of them to worry about, or pass laws to protect.
4. Because Congress has failed to enact gay rights legislation, major corporations refuse to put in writing their employment policies toward gay people.
5. Homosexuals who have served in combat and have unblemished service records can be denied veterans benefits.
6. The Internal Revenue Service denies gay rights groups the same tax privileges it grants to other non-profit minority rights groups.
7. In many ways, Anita Bryant's anti-gay rights campaign reflects the attitude of the church toward homosexuals.
8. The American Psychiatric Association no longer considers homosexuality a mental disorder.
9. Support for gay rights is pretty much limited to gay rights organizations.
10. Respect for gay rights has grown to the point where false and malicious statements about homosexuality are rarely made public.

1. *F* 90% of our major cities, including Denver, have absolutely no laws protecting gays.

2. *T* The U.S. Civil Rights Commission acknowledges jurisdiction to attack discrimination on unequal application of the law, but it does not cover jobs, housing, etc.

3. *F* Between 10-20 million Americans are homosexual. Actual numbers are difficult to obtain because gay people are forced to join a conspiracy to protect their jobs.

4. *F* A number of major corporations have voluntarily adopted policies of non-discrimination against gays: AT&T, Bank of Am., Citicorp, Honeywell, McDonalds, etc.

5. *T* Since WWII, 75,000 Americans have been denied veterans benefits for being gay. Most received less than honorable discharges, making it difficult to obtain work.

6. *F* Until recently the answer was True. The IRS has reversed its policy recently.

7. *F* The Nat'l. Council of Churches and many churches have gone on record as protecting the legal rights of gays.

8. *T* "Homosexuality per se does not constitute any form of mental disorder." — APA

9. *F* Many civil rights groups now support gay rights: ACLU, NOW, AMA, NEA, YWCA, et al.

10. *F* Every newspaper has some crack about gays. "Some homosexuals who want to become teachers even want to wear dresses to work," says Anita Bryant.

For copies of the most recent brochures on the legal rights of gays, write to National Gay Task Force (NGTF), 80 Fifth Avenue, N.Y., N.Y. 10011. The organization has the purpose of protecting the civil rights of gays and educating the public to the problems associated with homosexuality.

A TEST ON SUPREME COURT DECISIONS AFFECTING EDUCATION

Perry A. Zirkel

Please place an X in one of the first three boxes at the right of each item to indicate whether the U.S. Supreme Court has held the practice or procedure described to be mandatory ("must"), permissive ("may"), or prohibited ("must not"). Use the fourth box if you don't know what the Court has ruled. Answers at end.

	Must	May	Must Not	Don't Know
1. The school district ___ have a statutory funding system that relies largely on the local property tax and that offers at least a minimum education to all pupils without discriminating against any recognized disadvantaged group of them.	☐	☐	☐	☐
2. The school district ___ limit, pursuant to a state statute, the right to vote in school board elections to residents who either own taxable real property or have children who are students in the school district.	☐	☐	☐	☐
3. The school district ___ provide for comparable services to parochial school pupils in its plan for spending federal Title I funds.	☐	☐	☐	☐
4. The school district ___ have a program permitting religious instruction during "released time" within public school facilities.	☐	☐	☐	☐
5. The school district ___ have mandatory maternity leave rules for teachers that have a cutoff date several months before the expected date of birth.	☐	☐	☐	☐
6. The school district ___ provide for a hearing prior to nonretention of a nontenured teacher if a) under state law his/her contract created a reasonable expectation of reemployment or b) if he/she can show that nonretention damages his/her reputation in the community or forecloses employment elsewhere.	☐	☐	☐	☐
7. The school district ___ dismiss a teacher for openly criticizing the school board or administration's policies on issues of public importance where the board cannot prove knowing or reckless falsity of his/her statements.	☐	☐	☐	☐
8. The school district ___ require, pursuant to state statute(s), teachers or other school employees to take a broad or vague loyalty oath as a requisite of employment.	☐	☐	☐	☐
9. The school district ___ have contractual arrangements for nonprofessional staff that are *not* in conformity with the minimum-salary maximum-hour provisions of the Federal Fair Labor Standards Act.	☐	☐	☐	☐

	Must	May	Must Not	Don't Know
10. The school district ___ dismiss teachers who are engaged in an illegal strike where the teachers do not show that the board's decision was based on personal, pecuniary, or antiunion bias.	☐	☐	☐	☐
11. The school district ___ allow teachers who are not members of the teachers organization that is the exclusive bargaining agent to speak at a public board meeting about matters subject to collective bargaining.	☐	☐	☐	☐
12. The school district ___ enter into a collective bargaining agreement that has an "agency shop" provision (i.e., a requirement that nonunion employees pay a service fee for expenses relating to the union's collective bargaining function).	☐	☐	☐	☐
13. The school district ___ provide special language-based instruction for limited English-speaking pupils, at least where there are substantial numbers of such pupils enrolled in the district.	☐	☐	☐	☐
14. The school district ___ allow an exemption from compulsory high school education for students affiliated with religious sects that have a long history of informal vocational training during the adolescent ages.	☐	☐	☐	☐
15. The school district ___ allow pupils to wear armbands, picket peacefully, distribute publications, or otherwise express their beliefs where such means of expression are not shown to materially disrupt or substantially interfere with school activities.	☐	☐	☐	☐
16. The school district ___ have regulations to prohibit deliberately making disturbing noise outside school buildings while school is in session.	☐	☐	☐	☐
17. The school district ___ provide oral or written notice and an informal hearing prior to suspensions for periods up to 10 days for students whose presence does not pose an immediate threat to persons, property, or the academic process.	☐	☐	☐	☐
18. The school district ___ permit reasonable corporal punishment of students under the authorization or in the absence of a state statute.	☐	☐	☐	☐
19. The school district ___ require, under authorization of a state statute or under compulsion of a local ordinance, vaccination as a condition of school attendance for all pupils except those with medical excuses.	☐	☐	☐	☐
20. The school district ___ intentionally provide for segregation of pupils solely on the basis of race in the whole or in a substantial part of the district.	☐	☐	☐	☐

ANSWERS TO SUPREME COURT TEST

1. May	**5. Must not**	**9. May**	**13. Must**	**17. Must**
2. Must not	**6. Must**	**10. May**	**14. Must**	**18. May**
3. Must	**7. Must not**	**11. May**	**15. Must**	**19. May**
4. Must not	**8. Must not**	**12. May**	**16. May**	**20. Must not**

DECISIONAL AUTHORITY

1. *San Antonio Independent School Dist.* v. *Rodriguez,* 411 U.S. 1 (1973).
2. *Kramer* v. *Union Free School Dist. No. 15,* 395 U.S. 621 (1969).
3. *Wheeler* v. *Barrera,* 417 U.S. 402 (1974).
4. *Illinois* ex rel. *McCollum* v. *Board of Education,* 333 U.S. 203 (1948).
5. *Cleveland Board of Education* v. *LaFleur,* 414 U.S. 632 (1974).
6. *Board of Regents* v. *Roth,* 408 U.S. 564 (1972); *Perry* v. *Sindermann,* 408 U.S. 593 (1972).
7. *Pickering* v. *Board of Education,* 391 U.S. 563 (1968).
8. *Wieman* v. *Updegraff,* 344 U.S. 183 (1952); *Keyishian* v. *Board of Regents,* 385 U.S. 589 (1967); *Connell* v. *Higginbotham,* 403 U.S. 207 (1971).
9. *National League of Cities* v. *Usery,* 426 U.S. 833 (1976).
10. *Hortonville Joint School Dist. No. 1* v. *Hortonville Education Association,* 426 U.S. 482 (1976).
11. *City of Madison* v. *Wisconsin Employment Relations Commission,* 429 U.S. 167 (1976).
12. *Abood* v. *Detroit Board of Education,* 431 U.S. 209, Mich. (1977).
13. *Lau* v. *Nichols,* 414 U.S. 563 (1974).
14. *Wisconsin* v. *Yoder,* 406 U.S. 205 (1972).
15. *Tinker* v. *Des Moines Independent Community School Dist.,* 393 U.S. 503 (1969).
16. *Grayned* v. *Rockford,* 408 U.S. 104 (1972).
17. *Goss* v. *Lopez,* 419 U.S. 565 (1975).
18. *Ingraham* v. *Wright,* 97 S. Ct. 1401 (1977).
19. *Zucht* v. *King,* 260 U.S. 174 (1922).
20. *Brown* v. *Board of Education,* 347 U.S. 483 (1954); *Keyes* v. *School Dist. No. 1,* 413 U.S. 189 (1973).

Index

ABANDONMENT OF CONTRACT, **24**
ACADEMIC FREEDOM
  and student maturity, **141, 148**
  as bargainable item, **152**
  classroom as a forum, **141-2**
  four freedoms in, **162-3**
  influenced by, **133**
  outside the classroom, **145-7**
  penalty for violation of, **138**
  purpose of, **134**
  restrictions on, **24, 43, 133-65, 180**
  right to, **6-7, 133-65, 180-1**
  vulgar words, and, **44, 134, 148**
  where located, **136-7**
ACCIDENTS See Liability, Tort
ACTIONS AND DEFENSES, **6**
  by students, **154**
  ignorance as defense in, **10-11, 190**
  in collective bargaining, **166-8**
  on academic freedom, **133-65**
  pro se defenses, **12, 135, 164, 191, 194-5**
  tort, **93-132**
ACCOUNTABILITY, **9-10**
  and National Teachers Exam, **31, 41**
  in malpractice cases, **66-7, 124-5**
  in tort actions, **24**
  of citizen, **11**
  of parents, **65-6**
  of teachers, **66, 74**
AGENCY SHOP, **170, 175, 177, 189**
ARBITRATION OF GRIEVANCES, **12-3, 148, 173, 187**
  binding, **13, 179**
ARMBANDS, **43, 128, 143**
  Freedom buttons, **75-6**
  See Also First Amendment, Symbolic Speech
ASSAULT AND BATTERY
  actions in, **8, 25**
  by board members, **116**
  by parents, **65-6**
  by students, **83, 98, 106**
  by teacher, **67-8, 96, 116-7, 131**
  defined, **114-5**
  necessary force in, **117**
  self-defense and, **117**
  test for, by courts, **115-6**
ASSUMPTION OF RISK
  by students, **8**
  in athletics, **109-10**
ATHLETICS
  and civil rights, **49**
  and eligibility, **71**
  bowling, **36**
  due process in, **78**
  football, **8, 96-7, 132**
  letter for, **79**
ATTORNEY(S) See Lawyers
AUTOMOBILES
  injuries caused by, **113**
  riding in, **71**
  search of, **69**

BOARD(S) of EDUCATION
 and academic freedom, 133-65
 and collective bargaining, 166-89
 and the Constitution, 37-8
 and sponsorships, 36
 appeals from decisions of, 38
 arbitrary actions by, 36, 168, 194, 199-200
 as employer, 14, 26, 33, 166-89
 as judicial body, 34, 36, 39, 75
 bias in, 8, 24, 80, 169, 189
 capricious acts by, 36, 37, 178
 conflicts in, 27, 51, 170
 conspiracy by, 37
 contracting by, 32, 35, 36, 37
 drug control, 79, 194, 200
 incompetency of teachers, See Burden of Proof
 judicial decisions by, 21, 36, 38, 178
 liability of, as body, 29, 30, 93-4, 96, 127, 131-2
 liability of, as individuals, 99, 127, 169, 188-9, 192
 malicious acts by, 23, 35, 116
 management prerogatives of, 176
 notification of non-renewal, 38-9
 policies of, as law, 9, 35, 39-40, 41, 77, 186
 powers of, 16-7, 57, 79, 138, 142, 182
 resolutions of, 3, 32
 sex education, 86-8
 students and, 54-7, 72-3, 77
 students newspapers and, 156
 teacher dismissal by, 24, 34-5, 36, 38
 teacher lifestyles and, 28, 52, 177, 194, 200
 teacher selection by, 46-7
BURDEN OF PROOF
 in home instruction, 61
 in incompetency matters, 14, 44
 in injury cases, 99
 in malpractice suits, 10, 98
 in teacher dismissal, 34, 42, 44
BURGER COURT, 9, 20
BUSING, 17

CASES See Litigation
CENSORSHIP
 by the state, 134, 156-60
 controls on, 158-9
 of student newspapers, 157
 of textbooks, 7, 23-4, 180-1
CERTIFICATE, CERTIFICATION
 as evidence of competency, 14
 as prerequisite to employment, 28-32
 by examination, 31
 defined, 30
 lack of a, 30, 32
 laws on, 28
 life certificate, 31
 legal status of, 29
 purpose of, 29
 qualifying for, 31
 reciprocity in, 31-2
 renewal of, 29, 31
 revocation of, 13, 29, 31, 34
 standards for, 29
 suspensions of, 37
CHILDREN
 and freedom, 53-5
 and stigma, 53, 61-2
 and vandalism, 66
 appearance of, 64, 76
 as chattels, 53-57
 as persons, 23, 53, 54, 61, 72, 89, 192
 child abuse, 63-4, 123
 civil rights of, 61, 76, 190
 guilt by association, 71
 handicapped, 62-3, 190-1
 legality of punishment of, 78-9
 right to
  due process of law, 72-85
  a free education, 17, 21-2, 128-9
  schooling, 74

sue, **111**
treatment as equals, **22-3**
53-5
theories about, **54**
CHURCH-STATE RELATIONS
and evolution, **59-60, 135-6,** 155, 164-5
and religious subjects, **153-4**
and sex education, **86-8**
and TM, **148**
as an issue, **19, 20**
Bible reading, **59-60**
establishment of religion, **128**
freedom of religion, **37-8, 50, 59-60, 128**
non-public schools, **59-60, 128**
prayers in school, **59-60, 154**
released time, **59, 154**
CITATIONS (how to read) **5**
CIVIL RIGHTS ACTS
and torts, **126-30**
CRA of 1871, **37, 55, 64, 80, 91, 127, 169, 188-9**
CRA of 1964, **26, 48, 88**
CIVIL RIGHTS MOVEMENT, **9, 37, 53, 143, 190**
CLASS ACTIONS, **11, 42**
by children, **53-5, 89**
by minorities, **41-2, 62, 190-3**
categories of teachers, **43**
"suspect" classifications, **42, 46**
COLLECTIVE BARGAINING
agreement, master **174-6**
and loss of rights, **7, 23**
and mediation, **51, 173-4**
and reduction in force, **41, 187**
and shared costs, **13**
and strikes by teachers, **24, 172, 181-5**
arbitration in, **12, 173-4**
as alternative to litigation, **12, 170-1**
as constitutional right, **175**
fact-finding in, **173-4**
good faith in, **172-3**
history of, in America, **167-8**
impasse resolution in, **173-4**
model for, **170, 172-4**
negotiable items in, **180, 185-7**
oral agreements, status of, **179**
quid pro quo, **172-3**
rules for the game, **172, 176-84**
sanctions under, **183**
seniority, **41**
Taft-Hartley Act, **171, 177-8**
teacher activity in, **27-8, 52**
textbook selection and, **7, 23, 24, 180-1**
unfair labor practices in, **172, 176-7, 180**
union membership, **168-9, 170, 175, 188-9**
union shop in, **178**
Wagner Act, **166**
white collar workers and, **166**
COMMON LAW, **9, 72, 97, 168**
COMPULSORY ATTENDANCE, 59, 60-1, 92, 123
CONSTITUTION
Bill of Rights, **20, 38, 67, 70, 71 75, 128-9, 136-7, 191**
Federal, **15-6, 17, 21, 23, 33, 37-8, 39, 44-5, 57, 73, 78, 143, 181, 192**
State, **14, 16, 17, 33, 73**
CONTRACT(S)
act of drawing, **26, 32-8**
breach of, **24, 35, 36, 37**
dismissal under, **34**
duties under, **35**
elements of a valid, **32**
illegal, **32**
law violations and, **37**
non-renewal of, **7, 28, 34, 52**
offer and acceptance, **32**
probationary teacher's, **39**
spring-notification type, **28, 38**
when binding, **32, 35**
CORPORAL PUNISHMENT (see also Assault and Battery)
by teacher, **8, 115**
cases on, **53-5, 91**
cruel and unusual punishment, **58, 115**

in violation of policy, **44**
stages in, **72**
COURTS
arbiters of the law, **9, 16**
clean hands doctrine, **8, 24, 167, 169, 182, 184, 189**
costs of the, **4, 12, 13, 170-1, 195**
role of the, **19-20, 36, 190**
stare decisis, **188**
CURRICULUM, **133-4, 139, 153-4**

DAMAGES
compensatory, **23, 108**
for excessive acts, **54, 95, 130**
for injuries, **8, 24**
mitigation of, **35, 182**
nominal, **34, 108**
punitive, **7, 23, 35, 37, 108**
DESEGREGATION, **12, 19, 20, 192**
of faculty, **49-50**
DISCRIMINATION
affirmative action, **41-2, 46-48 49**
constitutional protection against, **26-7, 39, 40-1**
double jeopardy, **37**
employment, **30, 39, 46**
grouping patterns, **61**
quotas, goals, **46, 49**
racial, **31, 42, 46, 49**
sex, **33, 45-51, 52**
DUE PROCESS OF LAW
boards and, **37-8, 55, 91**
collective bargaining and, **8, 24, 27-8, 52, 166-89**
defined, **75**
procedural, **38, 45, 75-85, 129-30, 164**
stigma, **40-1, 60-3**
students and, **55, 57, 63-5, 77, 92, 129**
substantive, **66, 75-6**
waiver of, **28, 48, 52, 111, 146-7, 180-1, 194, 200**
DUTIES OF TEACHERS, **10-11, 190, 194, 199-200**

EIGHTH AMENDMENT, **72, 116**
EMPLOYMENT
EEOC, **47-8, 88-91**
pregnancy leaves during, **27, 39, 45, 51-2**
remediable defects in, **43-5**
right to employment, **19, 28, 29-30, 39, 41, 135**
right to succeed in, **43-4**
security in, **6-7, 17, 26-7, 38, 41-3, 135, 166-89**
EQUAL PROTECTION, **15, 16, 22, 37-8, 47-8, 72-85, 127-30, 192**
EVOLUTION, See Church-State
EXCLUSION, **56-7, 92**
EXTRA-CURRICULAR ACTIVITIES, **36**

FACT-FINDING See Collective Bargaining
FIELD TRIPS, **111, 120-23**
duty owed during, **122-3**
errands, **125-6**
invitees, **120-2**
licensees, **120-2**
trespassers, **120-1**
FIFTH AMENDMENT, **136, 161-2, 165**
FIRST AMENDMENT, **13, 19 23-4, 37-8, 45, 50, 64, 75-6, 85, 92, 128, 136, 144-5, 148, 156, 169, 175, 188-9**
FLAG SALUTE, **59, 83, 128, 143, 153**
flag desecration, **84**
pledge of allegiance, **148-9**
FOURTEENTH AMENDMENT, **10, 22, 27-8, 40, 41, 52, 76-7, 88, 191**
FOURTH AMENDMENT, **69**

GRIEVANCES, See Collective Bargaining

HAIR STYLES, **64, 76, 81-2, 85, 143**
HANDICAPPED, See Children, Handicapped
HEARING
legality of, **4, 27, 51, 76-7**
power to hold, **51**
teacher's right to, **28, 34, 38, 52**
waiver of right to, **28, 48, 52, 180-1, 194, 200**
HOME INSTRUCTION See Parental Rights
HOMOSEXUALS, **3, 13-4, 27, 33, 50, 144, 219-220**
HIGHER EDUCATION, **17, 30, 45-6, 85, 136, 140-1, 144, 165, 197**

IMMORALITY, **3-4, 10, 27, 34, 44**
INCOMPETENCY, **14, 29, 31, 41-5, 66, 74, 194, 200**
IN LOCO PARENTIS DOCTRINE, **57-64**
liability under, **93-132**
search and seizure and, **67-70**
standard of care in, **58-9, 93-130, 98-9, 104**
INSURANCE, **94, 112-14, 193**
IMMUNIZATION, See Vaccination

JUDICIAL ACTIVISM, **19-20**
JUSTICE, **190-1**

LAW
awareness of, **10-12, 19, 30, 32, 39-40, 190, 192**
complexity of, **12, 190-1**
defined, **9**
LAWYERS
choosing a, **192, 196**
fees, **7, 12, 23, 35, 37**
need for personal, **5-6, 11-12, 164, 196-7**
right to counsel, **22, 190-3**
school's and the teacher, **112, 192-3**
teacher as a, **11-12, 191, 195**
till the l. comes, **6, 190-200**
LEGISLATURE(S), **3, 6, 9, 15-6 19, 33, 46-7, 67, 73, 88-91, 94, 135-6, 164-5, 182**
LIABILITY
civil rights, **63-4, 126-30**
for wrongful death, **96-7, 132**
governmental immunity from, **94, 96, 111, 131-2**
immunity from, **8, 93-4**
in giving first aid, **60, 95-6, 130, 132**
LIBEL, **27, 40, 51, 118-9, 156-60**
LITIGATION
alternatives to, **170-1, 196**
avoiding needless, **2, 5, 11-2, 192, 195, 198**
awareness of, **190, 192**
odds in, **11, 191, 197**
volume of, **5, 9, 13, 26, 35, 37, 190-1**
LOYALTY OATHS, **19-20, 28, 32-3, 35, 134, 136, 160-4, 165**

MALPRACTICE, **9-10**

NATIONAL TEACHERS EXAMINATION See Tests
NEGLIGENCE, **24, 93-130**
NUISANCE, **99, 104-6**

OBSCENITY, **134, 144, 148**
defined, **149-50, 156**
ORGANIZATIONS
right to be active in, **39, 161-3**
right to belong to, **39, 161-3, 168-176**
subversive, **32-3, 161**

PARENTAL RIGHTS, **57, 59-61, 63, 64, 65-6, 72, 79, 86-88, 90-92, 93-130**

PHYSICAL EDUCATION, **107-8, 110-11**
PICKETING, **85, 183-4**
PREGNANCY
  leaves for teachers, **27, 51-2**
  school girls, **77**
  unwed mothers, **47**
PRIVACY, **19, 23, 37-8, 90-2, 144, 156**
PUBLIC RECORDS, **20-1, 62, 124**
PUBLIC SCHOOLS, **15-17, 21, 73-4**
RELEASED TIME See Church-State
RELIGION See Church-State
SAFE PLACE CONCEPT, **58-9, 94**
SCHOOL BOARDS See Boards of Education
SEARCH AND SEIZURE, **22, 67-70, 71**
SECTION 1983 See Civil Rights Acts
SECULAR HUMANISM, **162**
SEX DISCRIMINATION, **27, 45-51, 52, 88-91**
SEX EDUCATION, **133, 155-6**
SIXTH AMENDMENT, **191**
STATE BOARDS OF EDUCATION, **13, 14, 31-2, 86**
STRIKES See Collective Bargaining
STUDENTS
  civil rights of, **20, 127**
  discipline and control, **7, 53-92**
  dress codes for, **80-1, 177**
  family planning and the, **155**
  freedom of expression, **134, 142-5, 156-60**
  grouping of, **85, 88-91**
  minimum competencies for, **67**
  native tongues, **153**
  rights of, **71, 79-80, 86-88, 134, 139-40, 144**
  to schooling, **21**
SUBVERSIVE ACTIVITIES, **32-3, 162**
SUPREME COURT, **5, 6, 8, 15-16, 18, 20, 21, 26-7, 49, 57, 61-2, 72, 91, 135-6, 169-70, 188-9, 221-23;** See also Due Process of Law
TEACHERS
  absence of, **95-6, 102, 130-1**
  and fighting words, **151**
  as first class citizens, **20, 27, 51, 134, 143**
  as mere volunteer, **30**
  certification of, **28-32**
  civil rights of, **35, 37, 43, 50-1, 180-1**
  contracts, See Contracts
  discrimination among, **45-51**
  dismissal
    for cause, **34, 39, 41, 48, 134**
    for decreasing enrollments, **41, 187**
    for grounds, **34, 50, 134, 194, 200**
    for homosexuality, **3-4, 50**
    for illegal reasons, **3, 38, 178**
  efficiency of, **26-7, 37, 41, 43-4, 50, 66, 74, 98, 150, 193-4, 199**
  exemplary role of, **37, 64, 149, 177**
  faculty racial balance among, **49**
  fitness of, **27, 51-2, 133, 193, 199**
  freedoms
    of speech, **39, 137, 145-7**
    to experiment, **150-1**
    to go elsewhere, **10**
    to lifestyle, **26-7, 28, 44, 52, 177, 194, 200**
    to press, **27, 42, 51, 156-60**
    to work, **40, 44-5**
  in loco parentis, **57-64**
  legal status of, **94, 133**
  libel by, **118-20**
  malpractice, **9-10, 74, 98**
  maternity leaves for, **39**

non-tenured, **4, 7, 34, 39, 43-4, 45**
paternity leaves, **40**
performance, **29, 146, 149**
physical dangers to, **4**
physical exams, **33**
right to academic freedom, **133-65, 180-1**
to assemble, **169, 188-9**
to association, **23, 39, 136, 165, 176**
to bargain collectively, **6, 166-89**
to continuing employment, **37-41, 52, 171**
to group students, **61**
to make assignments, **147-50, 180-1**
to privacy, **13**
to reinstatement, **27, 39, 51, 52**
to supervise, **97, 99-100, 105-6**
to strike, **8, 24, 169, 188**
vested property right, **40-1**
TENTH AMENDMENT, **15, 86**
TENURE, **4, 34, 35, 38, 40-1, 139, 198-9**
TESTS, **31, 41, 44, 60, 63, 66-7, 89-90, 155-6**
TORT LIABILITY
constitutional torts, **126-30**
defined, **93**
risks of, **58-9, 123-4**
teacher immunity from, **93, 111-12**

VACCINATION, **60**

WARREN COURT, **9, 19, 20**
WEAPONS
cattle prod, **58**
sneeze gun, **8, 25**
WRONGFUL DEATH, **8, 96, 124, 132**